BECOMING ELIJAH

Becoming Elijah

Prophet of Transformation

DANIEL C. MATT

Jewish Lives

Yale
UNIVERSITY
PRESS
New Haven and London

Yale University Press books may be purchased in quantity for educational, business, or promotional use. For information, please e-mail sales.press@yale.edu (U.S. office) or sales@yaleup.co.uk (U.K. office).

Frontispiece: Bernardo Strozzi, *Prophet Elijah and the Widow of Sarepta*, 1640–1644, oil on canvas, 106 × 138 cm, Kunsthistorisches Museum, Vienna
(See text discussion on pp. 14–17)

Set in Janson Oldstyle type by Integrated Publishing Solutions.
Printed in the United States of America.

Library of Congress Control Number: 2021942371
ISBN 978-0-300-24270-6 (hardcover : alk. paper)

A catalogue record for this book is available from the British Library.

This paper meets the requirements of ANSI/NISO Z39.48-1992 (Permanence of Paper).

10 9 8 7 6 5 4 3 2 1

To the memory of my mother, Gustine Kanarek Matt,
who passed away at the age of ninety-five
as this book took final shape,
and to my grandchildren, taking shape now:
Sara, Rebecca, Asher, and Raphael

His mystery is really the mystery of divinity spreading. Divine energy clothes itself in him, extending to the world . . . Elijah never appears in the world without the mystery of divinity revealing itself through him. The mystery of God on earth is the mystery of Elijah . . . The closest that divinity can possibly come to humanity is the mystery of Elijah.

—Moses Cordovero, *Or Yaqar*

CONTENTS

ACKNOWLEDGMENTS

I WANT TO thank Steven Zipperstein for inviting me to contribute a volume to *Jewish Lives*, for stimulating my thinking about Elijah, and for offering valuable suggestions as I revised the book.

I have discussed Elijah with numerous people, some of whom I wish to thank here: Alan Block, Alan Godlas, Arthur Green, Melila Hellner-Eshed, Menachem Kallus, Ruth Kara-Ivanov Kaniel, Yehuda Liebes, Shlomo Naeh, Yehiel Poupko, Biti Ro'i, and George Savran.

Translations of biblical passages are shown in italics and are heavily indebted to Robert Alter's *The Hebrew Bible*. Translations from other Hebrew (and Aramaic) writings are my own.

I want to thank the Stanhill Foundation for supporting my work.

Hana, my wife, has accompanied me throughout this journey, deepening my understanding and guiding me. My gratitude to her is overflowing; my love for her, boundless.

Introduction

His electrifying name—*Eliyyahu*—means "YHVH is my God." Many Hebrew names include a divine element, but Elijah has two, an excess of divinity. In the biblical book of Kings, he lives his intense name. A zealous devotee, he is enraged by the idolatrous worship of Baal and Asherah spreading through Israel, promoted by King Ahab and especially by Queen Jezebel and her cohort of prophets. He seeks to purge the Israelites of this taint and restore their faith in the one true God, bringing them back "beneath the wings of *Shekhinah* (the Divine Presence)."[1]

Empowered by his intimacy with YHVH, Elijah confronts Ahab and declares a devastating drought. After several years, by silent prayer, Elijah finally brings rain, but only after he champions YHVH by vanquishing the prophets of Baal on Mount Carmel, rousing throngs of Israelites to exclaim, *YHVH, He is God; YHVH, He is God!* (1 Kings 18:39).

The biblical Elijah is a miracle worker, promising a starving widow that her jar of flour and jug of oil will be wondrously replenished for as long as she needs. Soon afterward, he revives the woman's lifeless child with divine help, after accusing God of having killed the boy. Twice he calls down fire from heaven: once to consume his sacrifice during the contest with the prophets of Baal, and later when he incinerates a hundred soldiers sent to apprehend him.

Immediately after defeating the false prophets on Mount Carmel, Elijah's zeal to extirpate idolatry impels him to slaughter them. Yet he can be zealous for human justice too, as when he condemns King Ahab to death for murdering an innocent man to expropriate his vineyard.

Elijah is fearless, fierce, and untamed—*a hairy man, with a leather loincloth bound round his waist* (2 Kings 1:8). The world, it seems, cannot bear him; finally, he is taken up to heaven in a chariot of fire.

His ascent may have been a spectacular, supernatural death; but the scriptural account is ambiguous, leaving open the possibility that Elijah endures, living forever. If so, couldn't he return to earth? He frequently does so in rabbinic literature, Jewish folklore, and popular imagination. In this scenario, Elijah's disappearance from the world marks the beginning of a new career, in which he is transformed. His outstanding quality is no longer zealotry but compassion. He helps the poor, rescues those in danger, defends Israel from its enemies, and will one day redeem the whole world by heralding the Messiah.

Because of Elijah's messianic role, Jews open the door for him at each Passover seder—the ceremonial meal that commemorates the liberation from Egyptian slavery and includes the hope for ultimate redemption. Similarly, every Saturday night around the world, as the Sabbath departs, traditional Jews chant: "*Eliyyahu ha-Navi* (Elijah the prophet)! . . . May he come to us speedily with the Messiah, son of David!"

Elijah follows the path of the archetypal hero: uncertain origins, trials and adventures, transformation, and return into the world.[2] In his case, the fierce biblical zealot turns into the most beloved, cherished figure in Judaism. In the Israel Folktale Archives (fittingly located in Haifa on Mount Carmel, site of the prophet's triumph), there are more stories about Elijah than Moses, King Solomon, or anyone else. Over the centuries, the belief in his powers sustained the masses, while his inspiration enthused the mystics.

Whereas the biblical Elijah is a chastiser of Israel, the postbiblical Elijah is a benevolent savior. Undeniably, there are compassionate elements in his biblical personality and harsh elements in his later one, but it often seems there are two different Elijahs. What links them? Why does Elijah return to earth? How does the original figure become full-fledged?

To explore him we must begin, of course, with the biblical account. But how reliable is it? Some scholars contend that if he ever existed, Elijah was a charismatic holy man, purportedly able to bring rain, who lived in the time of King Ahab in the ninth century BCE. Gradually, legends were woven around him and then given literary form in the scriptural saga.

According to one view, the biblical tale of Elijah was composed to justify a coup against Ahab's son, King Jehoram, led by an army commander named Jehu. As the book of Kings records, Jehu assassinated Jehoram, had Jezebel thrown down from a window of her palace, and killed Ahab's descendants and then the prophets and followers of Baal. To legitimate this extermination, court scribes may have produced accounts of Elijah condemning Ahab and predicting Jehu's rise to power and his slaughter of the idolaters.[3]

Whether or not such speculation is correct, there are certainly legendary elements in the biblical cycle of Elijah stories. Over the following two millennia, Jewish folklore (in the Talmud, Midrash, and countless later tales) expanded his role and his powers. He became the protean prophet, capable of assuming numerous forms—often that of an old man, but also a young man, an Arab, a Roman official, a slave, and once (for a noble purpose) even a prostitute.

Who is Elijah? His flexible identity keeps us wondering. In his fervor, he recalls the earlier biblical zealot Phinehas, grandson of Aaron the priest, who stopped a divinely sent plague by killing two flagrant sinners. But according to a persistent tradition, Elijah did not just resemble Phinehas; he was Phinehas! Despite the chronological impossibility of this identification, it is psychologically revealing and accords with Elijah's timeless, elastic nature.

Elijah is not limited to the confines of a single personality. Since he is destined to return and announce the Messiah, followers of Jesus could believe that John the Baptist was none other than Elijah, proclaiming Jesus as the Christ, the anointed one. According to the New Testament, Jesus accepted this identification of John with Elijah, while some of Jesus's followers thought that Jesus himself was Elijah.

Elijah is elusive, like the *ruaḥ* (wind, spirit) with which he is associated. King Ahab's God-fearing steward knows how hard it is to locate Elijah and tells the prophet worriedly, *The spirit of YHVH will carry you off to I know not where* (1 Kings 18:12). This is how Elijah's contemporaries conceived of him: appearing and disappearing unexpectedly, as if blown by the wind, conveyed by the divine *ruaḥ*. When he leaves earth—vanishing in a whirlwind, aboard the fiery chariot—his disciple's followers wonder if *the spirit of YHVH has carried him off and flung him down on some hill or into some valley* (2 Kings 2:16).

Elijah's disciple, Elisha, yearns to inherit his master's *ruaḥ*. As Elijah ascends heavenward, Elisha lifts up the master's fallen mantle and receives the spirit. Empowered, Elisha proceeds to strike the Jordan River with the mantle, splitting the waters in two. Elisha's followers declare, *The spirit of Elijah has settled upon Elisha!* (2 Kings 2:15).

As Elijah evolves in rabbinic literature, he learns how to convey *ruaḥ ha-qodesh* (the Holy Spirit). To worthy sages, he transmits teachings from the Academy of Heaven, which he regularly attends; occasionally he reveals what God is saying or feeling. He personifies the Holy Spirit.

In the Kabbalah, Elijah expands his inspirational role. According to various sources, several founders of Kabbalah experienced *gillui Eliyyahu* (a revelation of Elijah), channeling mystical insights. If some of those insights seemed radically new or unorthodox, their authenticity was guaranteed by the noble figure of Elijah, whose felt presence validated the mystics' creativity. With some exaggeration, it has been claimed that "what Moses was to the Torah, Elijah was to the Kabbalah."[4]

Elijah is filled with *ruaḥ*, at times obsessed by it. The spirit makes him zealous and stormy, unpredictable, restless. He is always on the move, his biblical roaming spanning the entire land of Israel: from Zarephath in Phoenicia (north of the Israelite border) to Beersheba in the south and on to Mount Horeb in the Sinai Desert; from the wadi of Cherith (east of the Jordan River) to Mount Carmel on the Mediterranean coast. Fittingly, in the Talmud, he is credited with originating *tefillat ha-derekh* (the Prayer for the Way). By then, he has become Master of Wings, riding the *ruaḥ*, and his range has increased immensely. With four strokes of his angelic pinions, he can traverse the entire world.[5]

In roaming the world, Elijah enacts a narrative that parallels the theme of the Wandering Jew; but he is the antitype of that dark, derogatory image. In medieval Christian folklore, this mythical Jew is seen as cursed for rejecting the Messiah, doomed to wander aimlessly until Christ returns at the end of days. Elijah, too, is destined to rove the world until the Messiah arrives, but always for a purpose or on a mission: helping those in need, spreading the awareness of God, and ultimately making the world fit for redemption.[6]

Elijah refuses to be pinned down. We should refine the question "Who is Elijah?," reframing it: "How is Elijah imagined and reimagined? Who does Elijah become?" Each generation pours their yearnings into him and draws comfort from him. Consequently, the various portrayals of the immortal prophet reveal at least as much about the mind of the people of Israel—their needs and ideals—as about the character of Elijah.[7]

The chapters that follow explore the major stages so far in Elijah's endless career. Chapter 1 traces the prophet's biblical life in the book of Kings. Chapter 2, focusing on rabbinic literature, shows Elijah evolving from a zealot into a compassionate hero and an angelic colleague of the sages. Chapter 3 discusses Elijah's formative influence on Kabbalah, his role and personality in the *Zohar*, and his relationship with the messianic pretender Shabbetai Tsevi.

In Chapter 4, I turn to the figure of Elijah in Christianity and Islam—the daughter religions of Judaism. As mentioned above, the New Testament links Elijah with both John the Baptist and Jesus. In medieval times, Elijah inspired the formation of the Carmelites, who became one of the main mendicant orders of the church. The original Carmelites were crusader pilgrims who forged a monastic life on Mount Carmel and who believed they were following in the footsteps of Elijah, who long ago had supposedly established a contemplative group there.

In Islam, the mysterious figure of al-Khiḍr (the Green One) is associated, and sometimes identified, with Elijah. Al-Khiḍr shares many characteristics of Elijah, including immortality. Often appearing as an old man, he is capable of numerous other guises. He saves those in trouble, spreads kindness, and enlightens spiritual seekers, before suddenly vanishing.

Chapter 5 discusses Elijah's extensive role in Jewish ritual, especially at the Passover seder, circumcision, and Havdalah (concluding the Sabbath). Every year, every week—even several times a day in the grace after meals—Jews around the world mention Elijah or chant his name, many anticipating his arrival. Most Jews who know anything about Elijah remember opening the door for him during the seder or seeing his goblet of wine on the seder table. These enduring ritual moments demonstrate that whoever he was twenty-nine hundred years ago, Elijah is still active.

In the concluding chapter I delve further into Elijah's transformation and reflect on *beḥinat Eliyyahu* (an aspect of Elijah) within each of us, which expands the meaning of this book's title.

1

I Have Been So Zealous for YHVH: *Elijah in the Hebrew Bible*

In his first biblical appearance, Elijah springs out of nowhere, fully formed—with no mention of his parents or birth or his prophetic call, without any introduction or narrative setting. Thrust upon the reader, he thrusts himself upon King Ahab of Israel, delivering an ominous threat: *Elijah the Tishbite, of the inhabitants of Gilead, said to Ahab, "By the life of YHVH God of Israel, whom I have served, there shall be no rain or dew these years except by my word"* (1 Kings 17:1). This opening verse of the Elijah saga seems like the middle of a story, which is appropriate for the legendary figure who often appears suddenly and then vanishes.[1]

Of his many titles throughout Jewish literature, this initial one—*Eliyyahu ha-Tishbi*, Elijah the Tishbite—is fittingly unclear. The supposed place Tishbe may be identical with the ancient town el-Istib, located in Gilead, east of the Jordan River. Nearby el-Istib stands a shrine dedicated to Elijah, named Mar Elias (St. Elijah). In the late fourth century CE, a Christian pilgrim named Egeria wrote in her diary: "Thus, going on for a while through the valley of the Jordan along the bank of that river . . . we suddenly saw the city of the holy prophet Elijah, that is, Tishbe, from which he had the name of Elijah the Tishbite."[2]

It seems, at least, that Elijah lived in Gilead around the middle of the ninth century BCE, but he was not necessarily born or raised there by whoever his parents were.

Elijah's biblical career extended over approximately twelve to fifteen years, during the reigns of King Ahab and his son, Ahaziah, of the Northern Kingdom of Israel. That kingdom had been volatile ever since its ten tribes split off from the united monarchy after the death of King Solomon. (By contrast, the Southern Kingdom of Judah was essentially a single tribe centered in Jerusalem, maintaining stability for more than 350 years.) Ahab's father, Omri, was an army commander who was acclaimed king in a military coup, following the assassination of the previous ruler—another army commander, Baasha, who had himself murdered the previous ruler and exterminated the entire royal family. During his brief reign, Omri established the first stable dynasty of the Northern Kingdom.

The reign of Omri and his son Ahab opened a new epoch in the history of the Northern Kingdom. Omri built the new capital city of Samaria, strategically located on a hill near the crossroads of major highways. Following in the footsteps of Solomon (who had close relations with Hiram, king of Tyre, on the Phoenician coast), he forged an alliance with King Ethbaal of Tyre. In accordance with ancient Near Eastern practice, their treaty was confirmed by a royal marriage between Omri's son Ahab and Ethbaal's daughter Jezebel (just as Solomon had made numerous political marriages, including one with the daughter of Pharaoh, king of Egypt).

Ahab apparently served as coregent with his father during the last years of Omri's reign. During Ahab's reign (871–852 BCE), the kingdom of Israel became one of the major states in the region, enjoying prosperity through the development of industry and commerce, along with territorial expansion and increased urbanization.

During the ninth century, the empire of Assyria asserted its military power, which motivated numerous rulers, including Ahab and the king of Aram (based in Damascus), to form a defensive alliance. The major confrontation between the Assyrians (led by Shalmaneser III) and the "Damascus coalition" took place at Qarqar (in modern northwestern Syria) in 853 BCE. Ahab's military might is demonstrated by the fact that according to an Assyrian royal inscription, "Ahab of Israel" deployed ten thousand foot soldiers and two thousand chariots—more chariots than all of his allies combined. Shalmaneser boasted of victory, but more likely, the battle ended in a deadlock.[3]

Successfully holding the Assyrian threat at bay, Ahab's Northern Kingdom of Israel experienced an economic prosperity unprecedented since the golden age of Solomon. Israel now controlled the Transjordan (including Moab) and enjoyed secure military and trade alliances not only with Phoenicia, but with Aram and with its own southern sister, Judah.[4]

The power and prestige Israel achieved under the rule of Ahab is reflected by the fanciful talmudic exaggeration that Ahab was one of three kings who "ruled over the realm of the whole world."[5]

Ahab's political marriage to the Phoenician princess Jezebel had profound consequences, which set the stage for Elijah's confrontation with the king of Israel. She came not as an ordinary wife, but in an official capacity—representing not only her father, the king of Tyre, but the entire Phoenician populace. She arrived with a purpose: to cement cooperative relations between the two peoples.

Jezebel would have brought along a retinue of servants and attendants. Proper provisions had to be made for the princess and her entourage, including the opportunity to worship their native, national deity. Therefore, a shrine to the Phoenician storm and fertility god, Baal, was erected in Samaria, and priests of Baal had to be brought from Phoenicia.

Jezebel was adept and ambitious. From the vantage point of her superior Phoenician culture, she must have looked out upon the Israelite scene with condescension, sensing that one of her tasks was to improve her surroundings and raise them to the Phoenician level. Above all else, she sought to spread in her adopted land the cult of her own native Phoenician Baal.[6]

The very names of Jezebel and of her father, King Ethbaal, indicate their intimate connection with Baal. The name Ethbaal probably means "Baal exists" or "with Baal," or "Baal is with him," and according to the historian Josephus, before becoming king Ethbaal was a priest of Astarte (a consort of Baal).[7] As for Jezebel, her biblical name *Izevel* is probably a double parody on her original Phoenician name *Izevul*, meaning "Where is the Prince [a title of Baal]?" This was a cultic chant, mourning the annual disappearance of Prince Baal when vegetation dies in the summer before its resuscitation (and Baal's resurrection) in the autumn. Her name may have first been transformed into *I-zevul* (No nobility) before it was distorted further into *I-zevel* (Where is the dung?).[8] This crude parody on the name of the Phoenician princess sets the tone for her thoroughly negative depiction throughout the saga. The biblical author (committed to YHVH alone) portrays Jezebel as the arch-villainess, the embodiment of evil. Her promotion of Baal worship is characterized as *zenunim*, "whoring, fornication": *the whoring of Jezebel . . . and her abundant witchcraft* (2 Kings 9:22).

Right before Elijah bursts on the scene, the book of Kings condemns Ahab for marrying Jezebel and for not only tolerating the worship of Baal but participating flagrantly:

> *Ahab son of Omri did evil in the eyes of YHVH, more than all who preceded him. As though it were a light thing for him to follow in*

> *the sins of Jeroboam son of Nebat* [who had set up golden calves], *he took as his wife Jezebel, daughter of Ethbaal king of the Sidonians,*[9] *and he went and served Baal and bowed down to him. And he set up an altar to Baal in the house of Baal that he built in Samaria. And Ahab made an* asherah [a cultic pole or stylized tree symbolizing the goddess Asherah, a consort of Baal]. *Ahab did more to vex YHVH, God of Israel, than all the kings of Israel who preceded him.* (1 Kings 16:30–33)

Similarly, the book of Kings describes how Solomon had first allowed his foreign wives to worship their gods and was then drawn to their pagan ways:

> *King Solomon loved many foreign women—Pharaoh's daughter and Moabites, Ammonites, Edomites, Sidonians, Hittites, from the nations of which YHVH had said to the Israelites, "You shall not come among them and they shall not come among you, for they will surely lead your heart astray after their gods." To these did Solomon cling in love. He had seven hundred princess wives and three hundred concubines, and his wives led his heart astray. . . . Solomon went after Ashtoreth, goddess of the Sidonians, and after Milcom, abomination of the Ammonites. . . . Then Solomon built a high place for Chemosh, the abomination of Moab, on the mountain facing Jerusalem and for Molech, the abomination of the Ammonites. Thus he did for all his foreign wives who would burn incense and would sacrifice to their gods.* (1 Kings 11:1–3, 5, 7–8)

Unlike Solomon, as far as we know, Ahab married only one foreign princess: Jezebel. But she was eager to disseminate the worship of Baal as widely as possible. Her immense cultic staff included *four hundred fifty prophets of Baal and four hundred prophets of Asherah, who eat at Jezebel's table* (1 Kings 18:19). As for Ahab himself, he seems (like many of his Israelite subjects) to have wavered between worshiping Baal and YHVH—or rather, to have practiced syncretism, worshiping one along with the other. As we have just seen, the biblical text records that *he went and served Baal and bowed down to him.* In a later confrontation, Elijah accuses Ahab of *forsaking YHVH's commands and going after the Baalim* (1 Kings 18:18). And yet Ahab gave three of his children names that include variations of the divine element *yhv: Atalyah* (Athaliah), *Yehoram* (Jehoram), and *Aḥazyah* (Ahaziah). Still, because of the king's role in spreading idolatry, the biblical author reckons him as the worst ruler of Israel: *Surely there was no one like Ahab, who gave himself over to doing evil in the eyes of YHVH, enticed by Jezebel his wife* (1 Kings 21:25).[10]

A few verses after the description of Ahab's idolatry, Elijah makes his first appearance, exclaiming to the king, *There shall be no rain or dew these years except by my word* (1 Kings 17:1). The implication is that the impending drought is a punishment for Ahab's idolatry—a fitting retribution for the king's defection to the cult of Baal, the Canaanite god of rain.[11] Although Elijah does not explicitly link the drought with Ahab's idolatrous worship, a midrashic work attributed to Elijah (*Seder Eliyyahu*) does so:

> Ahab challenged Elijah the Tishbite, saying to him, "It is written in the Torah: *Take care, lest your heart be seduced, [so that you turn aside and serve other gods and bow down to them.] Then the anger of YHVH will flare up against you, and He will shut the heavens [so that there will be no rain]* (Deuteronomy 11:16–17). Yet as for me, who worships all the idols in the world, come and see how many blessings have come in my days!" . . .
>
> Immediately, Elijah was filled with great wrath at [Ahab], and said to him, "You good-for-nothing! You spurned the One who created the entire world for His glory—the One who gave words of Torah for His glory. By your life! I will punish you according to your very own words." As is said, *Elijah the Tishbite, of the inhabitants of Gilead, said to Ahab, "By the life of YHVH God of Israel, there shall be no rain or dew these years except by my word"* (1 Kings 17:1).[12]

In this opening verse of Elijah's biblical tale, the prophet fittingly invokes God's name, yet he claims the power to bring or end the drought by his own human word. Fully convinced that he is fighting for the one true God, he feels no constraint in asserting his own will. He is the passionate champion of YHVH—as evidenced by his very name: *Eliyyahu*, "My God is *Yahu*."[13] He is permeated by divine fervor.

For Elijah, the battle lines are clearly drawn: YHVH versus Baal. Any syncretistic blending is tantamount to a rejection of the one true God, who is *El qanna*, "a jealous God" (Exodus 20:5), demanding absolute, exclusive loyalty.[14] As a true prophet of *El qanna*, Elijah is suffused with *qin'ah*, "zealousness, jealousness." He is jealous on God's behalf, jealous for God. Later he declares: Qanno qinneiti, *I have been so zealous, for YHVH, God of Hosts, for the Israelites have forsaken Your covenant—Your altars they have destroyed, Your prophets they have killed by the sword, and I alone remain, and they have sought to take my life* (1 Kings 19:10).

MIRACLES IN THE WADI AND FOR A WIDOW

Elijah's threat to King Ahab would have aroused royal wrath, so God directed His prophet to flee to the wilderness: *Go from here and turn eastward and hide in the wadi of Cherith, which is by the Jordan. And it shall be, that from the wadi you shall drink, and the ravens I have commanded to sustain you there* (1 Kings 17:3–4).

Elijah obeyed, and miraculously *the ravens would bring him bread and meat in the morning and bread and meat in the evening* (1 Kings 17:6), recalling the wondrous stories of the manna and quail with which God had sustained the Israelites morning and evening.[15] Eventually, though, the prophet himself experienced the dire effects of the drought he had imposed: *The wadi dried up, for there was no rain in the land* (1 Kings 17:7).

God then instructs Elijah to journey to Phoenician territory—to Zarephath, a town on the Mediterranean coast, a little north of the Israelite border. God assures his prophet, *Look, I have ordered a certain widow there to sustain you* (1 Kings 17:9). At the entrance to the town, Elijah sees a widow gathering sticks to build a fire. (Apparently, he recognizes her by "her widow's garb.")[16] He asks her to bring him some water,[17] and as she is going to fetch it, he calls to her, asking too for a morsel of bread. She responds by describing her desperate situation: *By the life of YHVH your God, I have no loaf but only a handful of flour in the jar and a bit of oil in the jug, and here I am gathering a couple of sticks, so I can go in and make it for me and my son, and we will eat it and die* (1 Kings 17:12).

Immediately Elijah reassures her: *Fear not. Come, do as you have spoken; but first make me from there a little loaf and bring it out to me, and for you and for your son make afterward. For thus YHVH God of Israel has said: "The jar of flour will not go empty nor the jug of oil be drained until the day YHVH sends rain upon the land"* (1 Kings 17:13–14).

It seems strange—even perverse—that Elijah would ask the starving widow to prepare food for him first and only afterward for herself and her son. After all, she has just told Elijah that there isn't enough flour for even mother and child. Is this an example of Elijah's self-concern? Alternatively, he is challenging the woman to place her faith in him as God's prophet.

Elijah the miracle worker has appeared. From now on, throughout his biblical career, he is characterized by wonders. In fact, he and his disciple-successor, Elisha, are the only prophets in the Hebrew Bible especially noted for performing miracles. Subsequently, in Elijah's endless postbiblical career, miracles multiply.

After some time, the widow's son became ill, so severely that *no breath was left in him* (1 Kings 17:17). This somewhat ambiguous wording may mean that the boy actually died or that he was critically ill, in a comatose state, with his breathing barely detectable.[18] In any case, the distraught mother lashes out at Elijah: *What is between you and me, O man of God, that you have come to me to recall my sin and to put my son to death?* (1 Kings 17:18).

What sin of hers is she referring to? Probably none in particular. Rather, in accordance with widespread belief, she assumes that her suffering stems from some wrongdoing. The very presence of Elijah, the *man of God*, has exposed to divine attention some transgression, for which she is now being punished by the death of her only son.[19]

Elijah replies simply, "*Give me your son.*" Then,

> *he took him from her bosom and brought him to the upper chamber where he was staying and laid him on his bed. He called out to YHVH, saying, "YHVH my God, have You brought evil even upon the widow with whom I lodge, putting her son to death?"*
>
> *He stretched out over the child three times and called out to YHVH, saying, "YHVH my God, let this child's life-breath return into him."*
>
> *YHVH heeded Elijah's voice, and the child's life-breath returned into him, and he revived. Elijah took the child and brought him downstairs from the upper chamber and gave him to his mother, and Elijah said, "See, your son is alive."*
>
> *The woman said to Elijah, "Now I know that you are a man of God, and the word of YHVH in your mouth is truth."* (1 Kings 17:19–24)

The harsh prophet here challenges God Himself. Whereas first Elijah conveyed the divine attribute of stern judgment—stopping the rain and bringing ruinous drought—now he embodies compassion, praying forcefully for the widow and her lifeless son and winning back the boy's life.[20]

Elijah acts by "stretching himself" over the child three times. The Hebrew verb—*va-yitmoded*—means literally "he measured himself." The Greek Septuagint renders this freely and contextually as "he breathed," and similarly some interpreters view Elijah's act as bringing the child back to life by mouth-to-mouth resuscitation. In the parallel miracle story about Elijah's disciple, Elisha, who revives the dead child of the Shunammite woman, the text reads: *He climbed up and lay upon the child, putting his mouth over his mouth, his eyes over his eyes, and his palms over his palms,* va-yighar, *and he stretched out, over him, and the child's body grew warm. He went back and walked in the house this way and that, and he climbed up and stretched out over him, and the lad sneezed a full seven times, and the lad opened his eyes* (2 Kings 4:34–35). The biblical author probably conceives of Elijah (as well as Elisha) conveying the warm vitality of his own body, enhanced by his prophetic aura, to the breathless boy.[21]

The prophet has overcome death, prefiguring his triumph over his own death as he is transported to heaven.

The two miracles performed by Elijah—providing a continual supply of nourishment for the widow and her son, and reviving the boy—take place in foreign territory, in the kingdom of Sidon, from which Jezebel came and where Baal reigned supreme. Right in the heart of Baal's domain, Elijah demonstrates that it is the omnipotent YHVH who bestows sustenance and life—not Baal, the false god of fertility, who was thought to disappear into the realm of death each summer when vegetation dies, only to be resurrected in the autumn as the rains return.[22]

THE CONTEST ON MOUNT CARMEL

Elijah had "parched the world" for several years, when God commanded him, *Go, appear before Ahab, that I may send rain upon the land* (1 Kings 18:1).[23] Elijah set out and encountered Obadiah, the royal majordomo, *who was appointed over the palace* (1 Kings 18:3). The name *Ovadyahu* (Obadiah) means "servant (or worshiper) of YHVH," and Ahab's steward was true to his name: *Obadiah revered YHVH greatly. When Jezebel was exterminating the prophets of YHVH, Obadiah took a hundred prophets and hid them, fifty men to a cave, sustaining them with bread and water* (1 Kings 18:3–4). Jezebel's devotion to Baal and Asherah had impelled her to persecute and slaughter the entire guild of prophets of YHVH, or as many as she could find. She may have held them culpable for the drought.[24] In hiding a hundred of them from the queen, Obadiah risked his life.

Normally, Obadiah would have been occupied in the royal palace, but Elijah found him on the road because, due to the severe drought, Ahab had sent him on an urgent mission:

> *Ahab said to Obadiah, "Go through the land to all the water-springs and to all the wadis. Perhaps we will find grass and we can keep horse and mule alive and will not lose all our beasts."*
>
> *So they divided the land between them to pass through—Ahab went one way by himself and Obadiah went another way by himself.*
>
> *Now as Obadiah was on the way, suddenly Elijah was coming toward him. He recognized him and flung himself on his face, saying, "Is that you, my lord Elijah?"*
>
> *He replied, "It is I. Go, tell your lord* [i.e., Ahab], *'Elijah is here!'"*
>
> *He said, "What wrong have I done, that you should hand your servant* [i.e., me] *over to Ahab to put me to death? By the life of YHVH your God, there is no nation or kingdom to which my lord* [i.e., Ahab] *has not sent to search for you. And when they said, 'He is not here,' he made that kingdom or nation swear that they could not find you. And now you say, 'Go, tell your lord: Elijah is here'? When I leave you, the spirit of YHVH will carry you off to I know not where; and when I come to tell Ahab and he doesn't find you, he will kill me!" . . .*
>
> *Elijah replied, "By the life of YHVH of Hosts, whom I serve, today I will appear before him."* (1 Kings 18:5–12, 15)

Obadiah may have recognized the prophet by his distinctive appearance, recorded later on: *a hairy man, with a leather loincloth bound round his waist* (2 Kings 1:8). The royal steward also knew Elijah's elusive nature: how the fugitive prophet had avoided Ahab and Jezebel's wrath for several years, how he appeared and disappeared, seemingly transported by a supernatural force—how *the spirit of YHVH will carry you off to I know not where.*[25]

Reassured by Elijah that the prophet intends to meet Ahab that very day, Obadiah conveys the message to the king. Ahab immediately sets out to confront the man who had predicted the drought and then vanished, leaving the entire kingdom to suffer famine:

> *Ahab went to meet Elijah. And when Ahab saw Elijah, he said to him, "Is that you, troubler of Israel?"*
>
> *He replied, "I have not troubled Israel; but you and your father's house have, by your forsaking YHVH's commands and following the Baalim."* (1 Kings 18:16–18)[26]

Elijah declares that the time has arrived for a fateful competition between Baal and YHVH. He tells the king, "*Now, send out, gather for me all Israel at Mount Carmel, and the four hundred fifty prophets of Baal and the four hundred prophets of Asherah, who eat at Jezebel's table*" (1 Kings 18:19).

The bold promontory of Mount Carmel juts into the Mediterranean Sea, forming to the north the Bay of Acre (Akko) along with the modern harbor of Haifa. Its range of hills and mountains extends eastward from the coast. The name Carmel means "orchard, vineyard, garden," reflecting the fertility of its slopes, which catch the Mediterranean moisture from the westerly sea breezes. Its lofty beauty is reflected in the lover's exclamation in Song of Songs: *Your head upon you like Carmel* (Song of Songs 7:6).[27]

Long before Elijah, the mountain was revered as a holy site. Seafarers and locals alike venerated the conspicuous landmark as the seat of Baal of the Promontory. (The modern Bahá'í garden shrine retains some of the verdant and sacred character of the mountain.) In Elijah's time, the Carmel range may have marked the boundary between the kingdom of Tyre (home to Jezebel) and the kingdom of Israel.[28] By staging the contest between Baal and YHVH on Mount Carmel, Elijah was challenging the rival god right on his border.

Responding to Elijah, *Ahab sent out among all the Israelites and gathered the prophets at Mount Carmel. Elijah approached all the people and said, "How long will you keep hopping between the two branches? If YHVH is God, follow Him; and if Baal, follow him!" But the people answered him not a word* (1 Kings 18:20–21).

Elijah demands that the people stop wavering and straddling two opposite sides, dividing their allegiance between YHVH and Baal—like a bird hopping between two branches, hesitating to choose which to perch on. Syncretism or polytheistic pluralism would enable dual worship; but Elijah, the radical monotheist, rejects any such eclectic devotion, insisting that the Israelites choose now.[29]

The people do not respond to Elijah, perhaps because they don't understand why they can't worship both Baal and YHVH. So Elijah proposes a contest to determine which god is worthy of their sole loyalty:

> *Elijah said to the people, "I alone remain a prophet of YHVH,*[30] *and the prophets of Baal are four hundred fifty men.*[31] *Let two bulls be given to us, and let them choose for themselves one bull and cut it up and set it on the wood—but let them set no fire. And I on my part will prepare the other bull and put it on the wood—but I will set no fire. You shall call on the name of your god,*[32] *and I on my part will call on the name of YHVH, and it shall be that the god who answers with fire, he is God."*
>
> *All the people answered, saying, "The matter is good!"* (1 Kings 18:22–24)

Finally the people respond, because, after all, everyone loves a contest. Having set the terms of the competition, Elijah turns to the prophets of Baal:

> *Elijah said to the prophets of Baal, "Choose one of the bulls for yourselves and go first, for you are the majority, and call on the name of your god—but set no fire."*
>
> *They took the bull that was given to them,*[33] *and they pre-*

> *pared it and called on the name of Baal from morning till noon, saying, "O Baal, answer us!" But there was no sound and no one answering. They hopped about the altar that they had made.*[34]
>
> *At noon, Elijah mocked them, saying, "Call out loudly, for he is a god. Maybe he is defecating or urinating,*[35] *or off on a journey.*[36] *Perhaps he is sleeping—and will wake up."*[37]
>
> *They called out loudly and gashed themselves with swords and spears, as was their custom, till blood spilled upon them. When noon passed, they flung themselves into a frenzy*[38] *until the hour of the meal offering, but there was no sound and no one answering and no attention.* (1 Kings 18:25–29)

All the intense efforts of the prophets of Baal have yielded nothing but silence. Now, Elijah prepares for his attempt:

> *Elijah said to all the people, "Draw near me." And all the people drew near him. Then he mended the wrecked altar of YHVH. Elijah took twelve stones, corresponding to the number of the tribes of the sons of Jacob—to whom the word of YHVH came, saying, "Israel shall be your name."*[39] *With the stones he built an altar in the name of YHVH, and around the altar he made a trench with a capacity of two* seahs *of seed. He laid out the wood and cut up the bull and placed it on the wood. He said, "Fill four jugs with water and pour it on the offering and on the wood." He said, "Do it a second time," and they did it a second time. He said, "Do it a third time," and they did it a third time. The water ran around the altar, and the trench, too, was filled with water.* (1 Kings 18:30–35)

The altar of YHVH may have been destroyed as a result of Jezebel's campaign against the worship of YHVH.[40] Elijah rebuilt it with twelve stones, *corresponding to the number of the tribes of the sons of Jacob*. Whereas in his time, in the ninth century BCE, the Northern Kingdom (of Israel) and the Southern Kingdom (of Judah) were rivals, Elijah sought their reunion, which he represented by combining twelve stones. By soaking the offering and the wood with water, he magnified the fiery miracle that he expected momentarily.[41]

The fact that Elijah rebuilt an altar outside of Jerusalem indicates that this narrative was composed before the revolutionary regulation in Deuteronomy limiting sacrificial worship to one central sanctuary: *the place that YHVH your God will choose* (Deuteronomy 12:5), namely, the Temple in Jerusalem. In the pre-Deuteronomic era (including Elijah's lifetime), multiple altars were the rule.[42]

The rabbis of the Talmud, however, believed that Deuteronomy recorded Moses's last words—several centuries before Elijah—and that its restriction against altars outside of Jerusalem had long pertained. Consequently, they had to explain how Elijah could violate this *mitsvah* by building an altar on Mount Carmel. One solution was offered by Rabbi Simlai, based on Elijah's remark a few verses later in this chapter: *By Your word have I done all these things* (1 Kings 18:36), which Rabbi Simlai interpreted as, "By Your [explicit] utterance have I done [this]."[43] Elijah's abnormal act was justified because he was obeying God's clear command.

According to a related tradition, Elijah's act of sacrificing outside of Jerusalem exemplifies how a prophet is empowered to advocate transgressing one of the *mitsvot*—though only temporarily: "Even if [an authentic prophet] tells you to violate one of the *mitsvot* in the Torah—like Elijah on Mount Carmel—obey him in accordance with the need of the hour [or, temporarily]."[44] Here, "the need of the hour" was to extricate Israel from the rampant, pernicious sin of idolatry.

Having grandly set the stage, Elijah prays to God: *At the hour of the meal offering, Elijah the prophet approached and said, "YHVH, God of Abraham, Isaac, and Israel! This day let it be known that You are God in Israel and I am Your servant, and by Your word have I done all these things. Answer me, YHVH, answer me, that this people may know that You, YHVH, are God, and it is You who turned their heart backward!"* (1 Kings 18:36–37).

Here, for the first time in his career, Elijah is called by his enduring title: *Eliyyahu ha-Navi*, Elijah the prophet—a title that appears nowhere else in the biblical saga.[45] Previously, when the son of the widow of Zarephath lay lifeless, Elijah had challenged God, virtually demanding that the boy be revived. Now, at this dramatic moment, Elijah the prophet steps forward and calls upon God to demonstrate His power, eliminating the illusory dominion of Baal.

Elijah's concluding words are startling: *It is You who turned their heart backward* (aḥorannit)—implying that God caused Israel to sin, succumbing to idolatry. Various attempts have been made to interpret the statement in the opposite sense: "It is You who turned their heart back from believing in Baal," or "back toward You."[46] But the simple sense of the word *aḥorannit* is neither "back toward" nor "back from," but simply "backward."[47]

The prophet's bold accusation against God is clarified by the medieval commentator Rashi (acronym for Rabbi Shelomoh Yitsḥaqi): "You enabled them to desert You, whereas it was in Your power to set their heart firm toward You."[48] Maimonides explains that because of Israel's persistent idolatry, God prevented them from engaging in repentance.[49]

Elijah's indictment is affirmed in the Talmud by Rabbi El'azar: "Elijah flung words against Heaven, as is said: *It is You who turned their heart backward!*"[50] Another rabbinic tradition mitigates the shock of Elijah's statement by inserting a conditional clause: "What did Elijah say? '. . . *Answer me, YHVH, answer me, that this people may know that You, YHVH, are God.* And if You do not answer me, then I will say, *It is You who turned their heart backward!*'"[51]

The simple sense of Elijah's extreme formulation undermines the principle of free will, making God responsible for Israel's idolatry. However, the biblical author is not concerned here with the conflict between human free will and the divine will. From a theological perspective, Elijah's accusation accords with his visceral belief in divine omnipotence. Everything is caused by God; only His hidden providence could be responsible for Israel's sinful backsliding.[52]

The prophet's passionate words evoke an immediate response: *Then the fire of YHVH came down and consumed the offering, the wood, the stones, and the soil, and it licked up the water that was in the trench. And all the people saw and fell on their faces and said, "YHVH, He is God; YHVH, He is God!"* (1 Kings 18:38–39).[53]

As Elijah was preparing the contest, he confronted the Israelites: *"How long will you keep hopping between the two branches? If YHVH is God, follow Him; and if Baal, follow him!"* Then, in describing the contest, he announced, *"The god who answers with fire, he is God."* Now, awestruck, the people acknowledge that YHVH—not Baal—is the true God, committing themselves to abandon idolatry. As indicated by a midrash, their declaration on Mount Carmel parallels the opening words of divine revelation at Mount Sinai: "On Carmel, the name of the blessed Holy One was sanctified and upon it was said *YHVH, He is God; YHVH, He is God!*—corresponding to *I am YHVH your God* (Exodus 20:2)."[54] The people's proclamation also echoes the name of the prophet who has restored their faith: *Eliyyahu*, "My God is YHVH."

God's fiery response to Elijah's prayer has stunned the people into submission. The prophet's immediate reaction is to enlist their help in eradicating his rivals: *Elijah said to them, "Seize the prophets of Baal. Let not one of them escape." They seized them, and Elijah took them down to the wadi of Kishon and slaughtered them there* (1 Kings 18:40).

The verb *va-yishḥatem* means literally "and he slaughtered them," though some commentators interpret this to mean that Elijah commanded the Israelites to slaughter them. In any case, here the prophet displays his ruthless zeal, following the example of Moses at the incident of the golden calf and outdoing the zealous Phinehas (Aaron's grandson) and the prophet Samuel.[55] The medieval rabbi Isaac Arama criticizes Elijah for acting here "impulsively," in "boiling rage."[56]

The divine fire had consumed the offering, thereby defeating Baal, and with his fiery zeal Elijah had exterminated Baal's prophets. But the entire chapter began with God's promise of water: *Go, appear before Ahab, that I may send rain upon the land.* Now, Elijah proceeds to complete his task, addressing the king, who had silently witnessed the contest on Mount Carmel: *Elijah said to Ahab, "Go up, eat and drink, for there is a rumbling sound of rain." So Ahab went up to eat and drink, while Elijah went up to the top of Carmel, crouched on the ground, and put his face between his knees* (1 Kings 18:41–42).

The prophet adopts a posture of humility, supplication, and mental absorption. The same prayerful, meditative position—placing one's head between the knees—appears in rabbinic, Jewish mystical, and Sufi traditions. It corresponds to the fetal position.[57] At this critical moment, Elijah withdraws into primal solitude, immersed in communion with God, intensely dedicated to healing his people's distress. As one medieval commentator wrote, "By placing his face between his knees, he intended to shift his attention from all of creation and to strip away his thought, focusing entirely on his immediate purpose."[58]

Earlier, Elijah had prayed demandingly for the revival of the widow's child; now he prays soundlessly for the revival of the whole people and the land. His silent prayer surpasses the power of words.[59]

No rain has yet arrived. Elijah sends his servant to the mountaintop to catch sight of any approaching clouds:

> *He said to his lad, "Go up, look toward the sea." He went up and looked, and said, "There's not anything."*
>
> *Seven times* [Elijah] *said, "Go back." On the seventh time,* [the lad] *said, "Look, a cloud as small as a man's hand is rising from the sea."*
>
> [Elijah] *said, "Go up, say to Ahab, 'Harness* [your chariot]

and go down, so that the rain will not hold you back.'" Meanwhile, the heavens grew dark with clouds and wind, and there was heavy rain. Ahab mounted up and went to Jezreel. And the hand of YHVH came upon Elijah, and he girded his loins and ran before Ahab all the way to Jezreel. (1 Kings 18:43–46)

Elijah's wordless prayer is answered, and the long drought ends dramatically, demonstrating to the assembled people along with their king the victory of YHVH over Baal, the supposed storm god. Empowered by divine spirit, the prophet sprints triumphantly in the pouring rain ahead of the royal chariot all the way to Ahab's palace in Jezreel, outstripping the galloping horses.[60]

WHAT ARE YOU DOING HERE, ELIJAH?

Elijah's jubilant success is short-lived. In the recesses of the winter palace, Ahab reports to Jezebel what happened on Mount Carmel, and the outraged queen lashes out, seeking to avenge the slaughter of her prophets of Baal: *Ahab told Jezebel all that Elijah had done and how he had killed all the prophets by the sword. And Jezebel sent a messenger to Elijah, saying, "So may the gods do to me, and even more, if by this time tomorrow I do not make your life like the life of one of them"* (1 Kings 19:1–2).[61]

Elijah's great triumph is ruined by the imperious queen, whose loyalty to Baal is invulnerable to his miraculous displays. Rather than seizing the prophet immediately, she prefers for some reason to simply threaten him; thereby, intentionally or not, she "provides him an opening" to escape:[62] *He was afraid, and he arose and fled for his life. He came to Beer-sheba, which is in Judah, and he left his lad there. He himself went a day's journey into the wilderness, and he came and sat under a broom bush, and he wished that he might die. He said, "Enough! Now, YHVH, take my life, for I am no better than my ancestors"* (1 Kings 19:3–4).[63]

Elijah flees outside of Ahab's realm and beyond the reach

of Jezebel—to the southern edge of the kingdom of Judah and then on into the wilderness. His situation is desperate. He had convinced himself that his miraculous victory on Mount Carmel converted the king and the people from idolatry, bending them to his charismatic authority and the divine will. But he had not reckoned with Jezebel's fierce implacability. Now he feels that his spectacular public triumph on the mountain was ephemeral and his mission to extirpate the worship of Baal has failed. Falling into a deep depression, he sees no purpose to his life, since his prophetic identity is the core of his being. Why go on? Why suffer any more? Temporarily he may have escaped from the queen who threatens his life, but he has sunk so low that he begs God to *take* his life.[64]

Physically and emotionally drained, all Elijah can do is fall asleep; but God refuses his request:

> *He lay down and slept under a broom bush; and look, an angel was touching him, and said to him, "Arise, eat."*
>
> *He looked, and there, at his head, was a loaf baked on hot stones and a jug of water. He ate and drank, and he lay down once more.*
>
> *The angel of YHVH came back again and touched him and said, "Arise, eat, for your way is long."*
>
> *He rose and ate and drank, and by the strength of that food he walked forty days and forty nights as far as the mountain of God, Horeb.* (1 Kings 19:5–8)

Elijah is not told where to go, but his inner compass directs him toward *the mountain of God* (known as both Horeb and Mount Sinai). Elijah's journey recalls Moses's stay on Mount Sinai. In fact, he is the only biblical figure after Moses to reach this mountain. Fortified by his meal of bread and water, Elijah *walked forty days and forty nights*, while Moses reports: *I stayed on the mountain forty days and forty nights, no bread did I eat nor water did I drink* (Deuteronomy 9:9). This is one of many parallels between Elijah and Moses. Whoever composed the early legendary accounts of Elijah (later incorporated into the biblical saga) intended to portray him as a sort of Moses redivivus (reborn).[65]

At Mount Sinai, God hid Moses *in the cleft of the crag* (Exodus 33:22) before revealing Himself to him. Now, on the same mountain Elijah enters a cave before encountering God:

> *There he went into a cave,*[66] *where he spent the night. And, look, the word of YHVH came to him and said to him, "What are you doing here, Elijah?"*
>
> *He replied, "I have been so zealous for YHVH, God of Hosts, for the Israelites have forsaken Your covenant—Your altars they have destroyed, Your prophets they have killed by the sword, and I alone remain, and they have sought to take my life."* (1 Kings 19:9–10)

God asks, *What are you doing here, Elijah?* This may imply: "What are you—Elijah the prophet—doing here, retreating all alone to the desert, so far away from your people? A prophet should be tending his flock. Why have you abandoned them, deserting your post and mission?"[67]

Defensively, Elijah proclaims his zealousness, complaining, *I alone remain, and they have sought to take my life.* He feels that he has been fighting the battle for God's honor all by himself.[68]

Jolting him out of his self-absorption, God commands Elijah: *Go out and stand on the mountain before YHVH. Look, YHVH is passing by, with a great and mighty wind tearing out mountains and shattering rocks before YHVH. Not in the wind is YHVH. And after the wind, an earthquake. Not in the earthquake is YHVH. And after the earthquake, fire. Not in the fire is YHVH. And after the fire, a sound of sheer stillness* (1 Kings 19:11–12).[69]

Several hundred years earlier, on this same mountain, God revealed Himself to Moses and Israel with thunder, lightning, cloud, and fire, *and the whole mountain trembled greatly* (Exodus

19:16, 18).[70] And on Mount Carmel, God had just brought down fire from heaven. Now, however, the revelation is subtle and refined—not in the forces of nature (wind, earthquake, or fire), but rather in *qol demamah daqqah*, "a sound of sheer stillness (or, silence)."[71]

The description here may convey a polemic against Baal, who was believed to bring lightning, storm, and rain.[72] Some commentators detect, as well, a veiled criticism of Elijah, as if God is demonstrating that in order to eliminate idolatry and turn Israel back to God, Elijah should overcome his fiery fanaticism and stormy zeal, and instead coax the people gently and lovingly.[73]

Various interpretations are possible, but note that the elements of wind, earthquake, and fire are not entirely rejected. They all precede the revelation of God—like runners heralding His arrival. Ultimately, the divine presence is not manifested in any of these precursors, but uniquely in *qol demamah daqqah*. From out of the stillness—a pregnant, vibrant silence—Elijah hears God's voice:[74]

> *When Elijah heard, he wrapped his face in his mantle, and he went out and stood at the entrance of the cave. And look, a voice came to him, saying, "What are you doing here, Elijah?"*
>
> *He replied, "I have been so zealous for YHVH, God of Hosts, for the Israelites have forsaken Your covenant—Your altars they have destroyed, Your prophets they have killed by the sword, and I alone remain, and they have sought to take my life."* (1 Kings 19:13–14)

God's question and Elijah's response are identical to their exchange just a few verses earlier. This duplication may be simply a scribal error; or else, it is intentional: a symmetrical framing of the prophet's divine encounter, before and after the *sound of sheer stillness*.[75]

Assuming that the repetition is deliberate, why does God

pose the question again?—*What are you doing here, Elijah?* The implication may be: "Has this revelation had any effect on you? Have you changed? Do you now understand why you have been brought here?"

On this same mountain, Moses had pleaded to God on behalf of Israel for mercy, but Elijah persists in proclaiming his zeal and condemning the people. Apparently, he wants God to avenge the wrongs that Israel has committed. Repeating himself, Elijah clings to the fantasy that he is the only remaining faithful one. Zealots rarely change.[76]

According to the Midrash, God criticizes Elijah's excessive zeal and self-concern:

> *I have been so zealous for YHVH, God of Hosts, for the Israelites have forsaken Your covenant.* The blessed Holy One said to him, "Is it My covenant or yours?"
>
> *Your altars they have destroyed.* He said to him, "Are they My altars or yours?"
>
> *Your prophets they have killed by the sword.* He said to him, "They are My prophets—why does it concern you?"[77]

In the biblical narrative, God responds to Elijah by sending him on a further mission:

> *YHVH said to him, "Go, return on your way to the wilderness of Damascus. You shall come and anoint Hazael as king over Aram, and Jehu son of Nimshi you shall anoint as king over Israel, and Elisha son of Shaphat from Abel-meholah you shall anoint as prophet in your place. Whoever escapes the sword of Hazael, Jehu shall slay, and whoever escapes the sword of Jehu, Elisha shall slay. I will leave in Israel seven thousand, every knee that has not bowed to Baal and every mouth that has not kissed him."* (1 Kings 19:15–18)

Apparently, God is accepting Elijah's condemnation of the people, assuring him that all the Israelites who cling to Baal will be killed, with only a loyal remnant spared. Elijah's successor, Elisha, will complete the bloody task.

The rabbis, however, perceive a different tone here:

> The blessed Holy One said to Elijah, "*What are you doing here, Elijah?*" (1 Kings 19:9). [Elijah] should have said to Him, "Master of the universe, they are Your children, the children of those who have been tested by You, the children of Abraham, Isaac, and Jacob, who have done Your will in the world." But he did not do so. Instead he said to Him, "*I have been so zealous for YHVH, God of Hosts, [for the Israelites have forsaken Your covenant—Your altars they have destroyed, Your prophets they have killed by the sword, and I alone remain, and they have sought to take my life]*" (1 Kings 19:10). . . .
>
> For three hours He waited for him [to ask for mercy for Israel]; but he persisted in his previous words: *I have been so zealous for YHVH, God of Hosts* (1 Kings 19:14).
>
> At that moment, the Holy Spirit said to Elijah, "*Go, return on your way to the wilderness of Damascus . . . and Jehu son of Nimshi you shall anoint as king over Israel, and Elisha son of Shaphat [from Abel-meholah you shall anoint as prophet in your place]*. What you have in mind [namely, to destroy Israel], I cannot do."[78]

Eventually, Israel will be punished; but for now, Elijah is to be relieved of his prophetic duties, since he has failed to defend the people. An early midrash expresses this critique forcefully:

> Elijah demanded the honor due the Father, but did not demand the honor due the son, as is said: *I have been so zealous for YHVH, God of Hosts, [for the Israelites have forsaken Your covenant—Your altars they have destroyed, Your prophets they have killed by the sword, and I alone remain, and they have sought to take my life]* (1 Kings 19:14). So what is said there? *Go, return on your way . . . and Elisha son of Shaphat from Abel-meholah you shall anoint as prophet in your place.* The wording *in your place* indicates: "I do not want your prophesying."[79]

According to this view, the word *taḥtekha*, "in your place," implies "to replace you!" Elijah is so focused on God and on his own troubles that he has failed to plead for Israel or to respect them. He is no longer fit to be a prophet.

A different perspective is offered by the medieval commentator David Kimḥi, according to whom God is responding to Elijah's earlier desperate plea to die: "Since you want to depart from the world—having said, '*Enough! Now, YHVH, take my life*' (1 Kings 19:4)—you must leave behind a prophet *in your place* and appoint *Elisha son of Shaphat* and teach him."[80]

Elijah leaves *the mountain of God* and proceeds northeast, toward the Jordan Valley, where he encounters his successor-to-be:

> *He went from there and found Elisha son of Shaphat while he was plowing with twelve yoke of oxen in front of him, and he was with the twelfth. Elijah went over to him and flung his mantle upon him. He abandoned the cattle and ran after Elijah and said, "Let me kiss my father and my mother, and I will follow you."*
>
> [Elijah] *said to him, "Go, return. For what have I done to you?"*
>
> *He turned back from him and took the yoke of oxen and slaughtered them, and with the wood from the gear of the oxen he cooked the meat and gave it to the people, and they ate. He arose and followed Elijah and served him.* (1 Kings 19:19–21)

The detail of *twelve yoke of oxen* indicates that Elisha is a prosperous farmer. Yet he is willing to abandon his cattle, wealth, and family in order to follow Elijah, who casts his prophetic mantle upon him. All Elisha asks is to kiss his parents good-bye.

Elijah's reply—*Go, return. For what have I done to you?*—is ambiguous, as we will see later, when we compare this story with one in the New Testament about Jesus and a potential follower.[81] In any case, Elisha sees no conflict between kissing his parents good-bye and following Elijah. He slaughters his oxen and prepares a farewell feast for those plowing with him, his family, and perhaps other residents of the town. In turning the yokes into firewood, Elisha is burning his bridges behind him, as he sets off after Elijah.

HAVE YOU MURDERED AND TAKEN POSSESSION, TOO?

Elijah's biblical career is drawing to a close, but he still has work to do. Queen Jezebel has committed a lethal crime against an innocent man named Naboth, a resident of Jezreel. Ahab and his queen resided in the capital of Samaria, where Ahab had built an *ivory house* (1 Kings 22:39)—an ostentatious palace whose paneling and furniture were inlaid with ivory. The royal couple also had a winter palace in Jezreel, and there King Ahab clashed with his neighbor Naboth:

> *It happened after these things that Naboth the Jezreelite had a vineyard in Jezreel near the palace of Ahab king of Samaria. Ahab spoke to Naboth, saying, "Give me your vineyard, so that I may have it as a vegetable garden, for it is close to my house, and I will give you in exchange a better vineyard. Or if you prefer, I will give you its price in silver."*
>
> *Naboth replied to Ahab, "YHVH forbid that I should give you the inheritance of my ancestors!"* (1 Kings 21:1–3)

For Naboth, the plot of land is not simply a vineyard but *naḥalat avotai*, "the inheritance of my ancestors"—too precious to be exchanged or sold, even at the king's request. In fact, the biblical narrative seems to identify Naboth with the importance of inherited land, providing the phrase *naḥalat avot* (ancestral inheritance) as a midrashic complement of the name *Navot* (Naboth).[82]

Ahab does not dare to simply seize Naboth's vineyard, because the principle of preserving tribal and family inheritance was deeply embedded in both law and custom. Even the king could not appropriate a person's inherited property against his will. Although by this time urban civilization was developing and land was being exchanged and sold, Naboth's response reflects the traditional system. Retaining his inherited land is a sacred obligation.[83]

Realizing that his royal powers are limited, Ahab feels deeply frustrated:

> *Ahab came home sullen and angry over what Naboth the Jezreelite had told him: "I will not give you the inheritance of my ancestors." He lay down on his bed, turned away his face and would not eat.*
>
> *Jezebel his wife came to him and said, "Why is your spirit sullen and you do not eat?"*
>
> *He told her, "I spoke to Naboth the Jezreelite and said to him, 'Give me your vineyard for silver, or if you wish, I will give you a vineyard in exchange.' But he said, 'I will not give you my vineyard.'"* (1 Kings 21:4–6)

In repeating his conversation with Naboth, Ahab makes several changes. He pretends that he first proposed buying Naboth's vineyard, whereas actually he began with a more generous offer: *I will give you in exchange a better vineyard.* Now the offer to exchange follows the offer to purchase, and "a better vineyard" has turned into simply "a vineyard." Apparently, Ahab wants to present himself to Jezebel as being more businesslike than he was. Then when he quotes Naboth's response, Ahab omits any mention of the sacred obligation to retain *the inheritance of my ancestors*, thereby making Naboth seem merely obstinate.[84]

Jezebel construes Naboth's stubborn refusal as an act of lèse-majesté and her husband's reaction as weakness: *Jezebel his wife said to him, "You, now, must act like a king over Israel! Rise, eat, and cheer up! I myself will give you the vineyard of Naboth the Jezreelite!"* (1 Kings 21:7).

Jezebel does not tell her husband how she will transfer Naboth's vineyard. On her own, she concocts a scheme, in effect usurping his power, "acting like a king" instead of him:[85]

She wrote letters in Ahab's name and sealed them with his seal and sent the letters to the elders and the nobles of his town, who dwelled with Naboth. In the letters she wrote as follows: "Proclaim a fast and seat Naboth at the head of the people. And seat two worthless men opposite him, and have them testify against him, saying, 'You have cursed God and king!' Then take him out and stone him to death."

The men of his town—the elders and the nobles who dwelled in his town—did as Jezebel had sent to them, as was written in the letters she sent them. They proclaimed a fast and seated Naboth at the head of the people. The two worthless men came and sat opposite him, and the worthless men testified against Naboth in front of the people, saying, "Naboth has cursed God and king!" They took him outside the town and stoned him to death. Then they sent to Jezebel, saying, "Naboth has been stoned to death."

When Jezebel heard that Naboth had been stoned to death, she said to Ahab, "Rise, take possession of the vineyard of Naboth the Jezreelite, which he refused to give to you for silver; for Naboth is not alive, he is dead." When Ahab heard that Naboth was dead, he set out to go down to the vineyard of Naboth the Jezreelite to take possession of it. (1 Kings 21:8–16)

At the show trial, the two scoundrels offer false testimony against Naboth, accusing him of cursing God and King Ahab. Their allegation may have been that Naboth uttered an abusive remark against the king reinforced by the name YHVH. According to biblical law, two witnesses are required in order to convict someone, and the punishment for blaspheming God is death by stoning. So the process engineered by Jezebel, although based on perjury, is otherwise proper, seeming to justify Naboth's execution.[86]

Just as Ahab omitted certain details when conveying to Jezebel his exchange with Naboth, so Jezebel now skips several details. She makes no mention of the false accusation nor of Naboth's being stoned to death. It is enough to tell her husband that Naboth is dead and that Ahab should seize the vineyard.

At this point, God directs Elijah to intervene:

Then the word of YHVH came to Elijah the Tishbite, saying, "Rise, go down to meet Ahab king of Israel, who resides in Samaria. Look, he is in the vineyard of Naboth, where he has gone down to take possession of it. Speak to him, saying, 'Thus says YHVH: "Have you murdered and taken possession, too?" Thus says YHVH: "Where the dogs licked Naboth's blood, they will lick your blood, too!"'"

Ahab said to Elijah, "Have you found me, my enemy?"

He replied, "I have found you. Because you have given yourself over to doing evil in the eyes of YHVH, I am about to bring evil upon you, and I will sweep you away. I will cut off from Ahab every pisser against the wall, bound or free in Israel. I will make your house like the house of Jeroboam son of Nebat and like the house of Baasha son of Ahijah, for the vexation with which you have vexed Me, causing Israel to sin.

"Concerning Jezebel, too, YHVH has spoken, saying, 'The dogs shall devour Jezebel in the field of Jezreel. Those of Ahab's kin who die in the town, the dogs shall devour; and those who die in the open country, the birds of heaven shall devour.'"

Surely there was no one like Ahab, who gave himself over to doing evil in the eyes of YHVH, enticed by Jezebel his wife. He acted so abominably, following filthy fetishes, just as the Amorites had done, whom YHVH had dispossessed before the Israelites.

When Ahab heard these words, he tore his garments and put sackcloth on his flesh and fasted and lay in sackcloth and walked about subdued. The word of YHVH came to Elijah the Tishbite, saying, "Have you seen how Ahab has humbled himself before Me? Because he has humbled himself before Me, I will not bring the evil in his days. In his son's days will I bring the evil upon his house." (1 Kings 21:17–29)

Elijah's proclamation of doom pertains to Ahab's idolatry; but when God instructs the prophet to confront the king, He condemns Ahab to death specifically for killing and dispossessing Naboth: *Thus says YHVH: "Have you murdered and taken possession, too? . . . Where the dogs licked Naboth's blood, they will lick your blood, too!*" The nefarious murder of Naboth seals Ahab's fate. Elijah has now become a champion of ethical demands, advocating for justice and human rights. He exhibits the moral conscience that develops further in the classical prophets of the next century: Amos, Hosea, Micah, and Isaiah. As we will see, this sterling quality characterizes the postbiblical Elijah.

It was Jezebel, of course, not Ahab, who engineered the treacherous judicial murder of Naboth. Here, however, Ahab is blamed, for one or more reasons: he motivated Jezebel by complaining to her; he enabled her scheme by entrusting her with the royal seal; he did not protest afterward but rather set out immediately to seize the victim's vineyard.[87]

Eventually, Ahab's son, King Jehoram, will be assassinated by his army commander, Jehu, who is prompted to do so by Elijah's successor, Elisha. Fittingly, Jehoram's corpse is flung into the field of Naboth (2 Kings 9:24–26). Jehu then has Jezebel killed, by being thrown down from the window of her palace:

> *He said, "Push her out." They pushed her out, and her blood spattered against the wall and on the horses, and they trampled her. . . . They went to bury her, but all they found of her were the skull, the feet, and the palms of the hands. They came back and told him, and he said, "It is the word of YHVH that He spoke through His servant Elijah the Tishbite, saying, 'In the field of Jezreel the dogs shall devour the flesh of Jezebel. And Jezebel's carcass shall be like dung upon the ground in the field of Jezreel, so that they cannot say, This is Jezebel.'"* (2 Kings 9:33, 35–37)[88]

Jehu proceeds to murder Ahab's seventy descendants, his other relatives, and the prophets and followers of Baal. As Scripture states (with a little exaggeration), *Jehu destroyed Baal from Israel* (2 Kings 10:28).

Although the full severity of Ahab's punishment is postponed until his son's reign, he himself does not die peacefully. In a battle between a coalition of the Northern and Southern

Kingdoms (Israel and Judah) and their common enemy, Aram, Ahab is pierced by an arrow while riding in one of his many chariots. His death spreads panic among the troops:

> *He died in the evening, and the blood of the wound spilled out into the bottom of the chariot. A cry passed through the camp as the sun was setting: "Every man to his town! Every man to his land!" So the king died and was brought to Samaria, and they buried the king in Samaria. They flushed out the chariot at the pool of Samaria, and the dogs licked his blood, and the whores bathed, in accordance with the word of YHVH that He had spoken.* (1 Kings 22:35–38)

Elijah had prophesied that Ahab's blood would be lapped up in Jezreel: "*Where the dogs licked Naboth's blood, they will lick your blood, too!*" (1 Kings 21:19). Here, instead, Samaria becomes the scene of Ahab's postmortem humiliation. The description *and the whores bathed* taints the deceased king further, implying that when they bathed in *the pool of Samaria*, the harlots were immersing themselves in Ahab's diluted blood.[89]

WIELDING FIRE

The disgraced Ahab was succeeded by his son Ahaziah, who reigned little more than one year. Having no sons, Ahaziah was succeeded by his brother Jehoram. Elijah plays a dramatic role in Ahaziah's brief reign:

> *Ahaziah fell through the lattice in his upper chamber at Samaria and was injured. So he sent messengers, saying to them, "Go, inquire of Baal-zebub, god of Ekron, whether I will survive this injury."*
>
> *The angel of YHVH spoke to Elijah the Tishbite: "Rise, go up to meet the messengers of the king of Samaria and speak to them: 'Is it for lack of a God in Israel that you go to inquire of Baal-zebub, god of Ekron? Therefore, thus says YHVH: From the bed*

> *you mounted you shall not come down, for you are doomed to die.'"*
> *And Elijah set out.* (2 Kings 1:2–4)

King Ahaziah seeks to inquire of a pagan oracle in Ekron, a major city of the Philistines on their border with Judah. The name of this local manifestation of Baal—Baal-zebub—means "Lord of the flies," which is probably an intentional, pejorative misspelling of the original divine name Baal-zevul, meaning "Baal the Prince" or "Lord of glory."[90]

To the royal messengers, Elijah conveys God's outrage that an Israelite king would consult the oracle of a foreign god rather than the God of Israel:

> *The messengers went back to* [Ahaziah], *and he said to them, "Why have you come back?"*
>
> *They replied, "A man came up to meet us and said to us, 'Go back to the king who sent you, and speak to him: Thus says YHVH—Is it for lack of a God in Israel that you send to inquire of Baal-zebub, god of Ekron? Therefore, from the bed you mounted you shall not come down, for you are doomed to die.'"*
>
> [Ahaziah] *said to them, "What is the manner of the man who came up to meet you and spoke these words to you?"*
>
> *They replied, "A hairy man, with a leather loincloth bound round his waist."*
>
> *He said, "That's Elijah the Tishbite!"* (2 Kings 1:5–8)

Finally, near the end of the biblical tale of Elijah, we are offered a glimpse of his roughhewn appearance. The messengers' description (along with their report of the prophetic indictment) is enough for King Ahaziah to identify the man they encountered as his father Ahab's nemesis, Elijah.[91] Immediately, the king dispatches a military unit to apprehend him:

> *He sent to him a captain of fifty with his company of fifty. He went up to him, and look, he was sitting on a hilltop. He spoke to him: "Man of God! The king has spoken: 'Come down!'"*

> *Elijah replied to the captain of fifty, "If I am a man of God, may fire come down from heaven and consume you and your company of fifty!" And fire came down from heaven and consumed him and his company of fifty.* (2 Kings 1:9–10)

In the contest with the prophets of Baal on Mount Carmel, Elijah entreated God to send down fire to consume his sacrifice. Now, he does not need to pray; like a sorcerer, celestial fire comes at his bidding, consuming the soldiers. Yet, this spectacular display does not deter the king:

> [Ahaziah] *persisted and sent him another captain of fifty with his company of fifty, and he went up and spoke to him: "Man of God! Thus says the king: 'Quick, come down!'"*
>
> *Elijah replied, "If I am* ish ha-Elohim, *a man of God, may fire come down from heaven and consume you and your company of fifty!" And* esh Elohim, *a fire of God, came down from heaven and consumed him and his company of fifty.*
>
> *He persisted and sent a third captain of fifty with his company of fifty, and the third captain of fifty went up and came and fell on his knees in front of Elijah and pleaded with him, saying, "Man of God! May my life and the lives of these fifty servants of yours be precious in your eyes. Look, fire has come down from heaven and consumed the first two captains of fifty and their companies of fifty—so now may my life be precious in your eyes!"*
>
> *The angel of YHVH spoke to Elijah: "Go down with him. Do not fear him."*
>
> *He rose and went down with him to the king. He spoke to* [Ahaziah]*: "Thus says YHVH: 'Because you sent messengers to inquire of Baal-zebub, god of Ekron—is it for lack of a God in Israel to inquire of His word?—therefore from the bed you mounted you shall not come down, for you are doomed to die.'"*
>
> *And he died in accordance with the word of YHVH that Elijah had spoken.* (2 Kings 1:11–17)

As decreed by the prophet, Ahab and his son have both died. Two verses later, we see that it is now Elijah's time to depart from earth. Having brought down fire, he is about to ascend in the same element.

ELIJAH WENT UP IN A WHIRLWIND TO HEAVEN

We are informed ahead of time that Elijah will be taken to heaven. Knowing that he is about to disappear from earth, the prophet sets out on a farewell tour:

> *When YHVH was about to take Elijah up in a whirlwind to heaven, Elijah and Elisha set out from Gilgal. Elijah said to Elisha, "Stay here, please, for YHVH has sent me on to Bethel."*
>
> *Elisha said, "By the life of YHVH and by your life, I will not leave you."*
>
> *So they went down to Bethel. The guild of prophets who was in Bethel came out to Elisha and said to him, "Do you know that today YHVH is taking your master away from you?"*
>
> *He replied, "I know, too. Keep silent!"* (2 Kings 2:1–3)

Elijah's imminent departure is known to *the guild of prophets*, one of various brotherhoods living together in the towns of northern Israel. Elisha is also aware of the momentous event, but he wants it kept secret. Loyal and devoted to his mentor, he refuses to leave Elijah's side, although Elijah prefers, as usual, to be alone:

> *Elijah said to him, "Elisha, stay here, please, for YHVH has sent me to Jericho."*
>
> *He said, "By the life of YHVH and by your life, I will not leave you."*
>
> *So they came to Jericho. The guild of prophets who was in Jericho approached Elisha and said to him, "Do you know that today YHVH is taking your master away from you?"*
>
> *He replied, "I know, too. Keep silent!"*
>
> *Elijah said to him, "Stay here, please, for YHVH has sent me to the Jordan."*
>
> *He said, "By the life of YHVH and by your life, I will not leave you."*

So the two of them went on. Fifty members of the guild of prophets went and stood opposite at a distance, and the two of them stood by the Jordan. Elijah took his mantle, rolled it up, and struck the water, and it parted in two, and the two of them crossed over on dry land. As they were crossing, Elijah said to Elisha, "Ask what I may do for you before I am taken from you."

Elisha said, "Please, let a double share of your spirit come upon me."

He said, "You have asked a difficult thing. If you see me being taken from you, this will be granted to you; and if not, it will not be." (2 Kings 2:4–10)

Elijah strikes the waters of the Jordan and they part—reenacting on a small scale the miracle performed by Moses, when he stretched out his hand and rod over the Sea of Reeds *and the waters were split apart . . . and the Israelites came into the sea on dry land* (Exodus 14:21–22).[92]

In requesting *a double share*, Elisha is not asking for twice the spirit of Elijah. Rather, the phrase alludes to the share of the eldest son, who inherits a portion twice that of his brothers. So Elisha is seeking the larger amount due the eldest; he wants to be recognized and endowed as Elijah's true successor.[93] He assumes that the divine spirit within Elijah can be transmitted to him, as in a previous generation the seventy elders were invested with the spirit that had settled upon Moses.[94]

The prophet and his devotee proceed: *As they went along, walking and talking, suddenly a chariot of fire and horses of fire appeared, separating the two of them, and Elijah went up in a whirlwind to heaven. Elisha was watching and kept crying out, "My father, my father! Israel's chariots and horsemen!" And he saw him no more. Then he grasped his garments and tore them in two* (2 Kings 2:11–12).

Fire is Elijah's medium and instrument, flashing at key moments in his biblical lifetime. Now it becomes his wondrous vehicle, a fiery chariot transporting him to heaven.

When Elisha was initially designated by Elijah, he asked to bid farewell to his father and mother before leaving home and going off with the prophet. Now he acknowledges that ever since, Elijah has been his paternal guide: *My father, my father!* The conclusion of his exclamation—*Israel's chariots and horsemen!*—could be Elisha's response to the fiery vision he beholds. Primarily, though, it is an honorific title bestowed upon Elijah, who represents Israel's true power, just as chariots and horsemen are the driving power of an army. This notion is expressed by the Aramaic Targum on the verse: "My master, my master, who by his prayer is better for Israel than chariots and horsemen."[95] Here we find a hint of Elijah's eventual role as harbinger of Israel's redemption.

Elisha assumes that Elijah has died, so he tears his own clothes in mourning.[96] Then, literally and figuratively, he takes up Elijah's mantle:

> *He lifted up Elijah's mantle, which had fallen from him, and he went back and stood on the bank of the Jordan. He took Elijah's mantle . . . and struck the water and said, "Where is YHVH, God of Elijah?" He, too, struck the water, and it parted in two, and Elisha crossed over. The guild of prophets who was in Jericho saw him from the other side and said, "The spirit of Elijah has settled upon Elisha!" They came to meet him and bowed down before him to the ground.*
>
> *They said to him, "Look, please, your servants have fifty valiant men. Let them go and search for your master. Perhaps the spirit of YHVH has carried him off and flung him onto some mountain or into some valley."*
>
> *He replied, "Do not send them!"*
>
> *They urged him incessantly, until he said, "Send them!"*
>
> *So they sent fifty men, who searched for three days but did not find him. They came back to him while he was staying in Jericho, and he said to them, "Didn't I tell you, 'Do not go'?"* (2 Kings 2:13–18)

Like Elisha, the members of the guild of prophets also think that Elijah has died, his body cast away by *ruaḥ YHVH*, "the spirit [or, wind] of YHVH." This image dovetails with what King Ahab's steward said to Elijah: *When I leave you, the spirit of YHVH will carry you off to I know not where* (1 Kings 18:12).[97] Finally, Elisha gives in to the acolyte prophets, letting them search for the missing master, though he knows they will fail. With his own eyes he has seen Elijah riding off to heaven in a chariot, swept away in a whirlwind.

WHAT HAPPENED TO ELIJAH?

Did the passionate prophet die a spectacular death, ending his life supernaturally? Or did he overcome death? Although Elisha assumes that his master has died, the biblical description leaves us wondering.

As Elijah evolves in rabbinic literature, the nearly unanimous view is that he became immortal. "Elijah lives and endures forever"; he "did not taste the taste of death." Rather, he was translated—body and soul—to heaven or paradise.[98] Yet for some medieval Jewish rationalists, such as Gersonides, it seemed "impossible that . . . [God] raised [Elijah] to heaven, because these bodies cannot ascend there," since physical existence is incompatible with the ethereal realm above. "Rather, the meaning of [God taking Elijah *up to heaven*] is 'up in the air.' . . . The spirit of God carried him by angelic power to a place still unknown, where he lives."[99]

The biblical account leaves no doubt that Elijah entered heaven—*When YHVH was about to take Elijah up in a whirlwind to heaven . . . Elijah went up in a whirlwind to heaven* (2 Kings 2:1, 11)—but Gersonides and others tone this down. In the Septuagint, Elijah is not exactly taken *up to heaven*, but rather *taken up as into heaven.* Similarly, in the Aramaic Targum, he is taken *le-tseit shemayya*, "toward heaven."

How close did Elijah come? In its typical fashion, the Talmud provides a precise measurement: "Rabbi Yose says, 'Shekhinah never descended to earth, nor did . . . Elijah ever ascend to heaven' . . . But didn't . . . Elijah ascend to heaven? Look at what is written: . . . *Elijah went up in a whirlwind to heaven!*—That was below ten [handbreadths from heaven]."[100]

For the historian Josephus, Elijah's departure remains a mystery. In retelling the story for his Hellenistic readers, he omits all mention of heaven: "At that time Elijah disappeared from among human beings, and no one knows of his end to this very day. . . . Of Elijah, as well as of Enoch, who lived before the Flood, it is written in the sacred books that they disappeared, and nobody knows anything about their death."[101]

In the Middle Ages, some thinkers explicitly denied Elijah's physical immortality. According to David Kimḥi, who often explained biblical miracles rationalistically, "Elijah became spirit, and the body perished."[102] Elaborating, he writes: "A whirlwind raised him from the earth to the atmosphere . . . on the sphere of fire, and there his clothes were burned except for the mantle, and his flesh and substance perished, and the spirit returned to God who gave it."[103] Kimḥi admits, however, that this represents a minority view: "The opinion of our masses, as well as our Sages, is that God brought him into the Garden of Eden in his body, as Adam existed before he sinned."[104]

For Moses Naḥmanides, who was more mystically inclined, Elijah's body and soul remained united: "The body was not cast away from him nor separated from the soul, but rather endured from then on forever. . . . The prophet said, *Look, I am sending to you Elijah the prophet before the coming of the day of YHVH, great and awesome* (Malachi 3:23), which proves that his soul was not separated from the holy body and endured in human existence."[105]

For Naḥmanides, Elijah's immortality becomes a model and goal for spiritual seekers:

> Those who abandon all matters of this world and pay no attention to it, as if they possess no body, and all their thoughts and intentions are focused only on their Creator—as was the case with Elijah—[such people], by cleaving with their soul to the Glorious Name, will live forever in body and soul, as seen by what is written of Elijah and as is known of him in *qabbalah* (tradition), and as appears in the *midrashim* about Enoch and about those destined for the world to come who rise in the resurrection.[106]

According to the philosophers (and most traditionalists), the soul is liberated from the body at death; but for Naḥmanides, Elijah demonstrates the possibility of living "forever in body and soul."

Both Elijah and Enoch are "taken" by God. The verb *lqḥ* (to take) appears four times in this biblical chapter concerning Elijah's departure.[107] Enoch's disappearance is recorded enigmatically in a single verse: *Enoch walked with God, and he was no more, for God took him* (Genesis 5:24). This could mean simply that Enoch died, but the wording *God took him* was later interpreted to mean that he was taken alive to heaven and transformed into an angel, enjoying everlasting intimacy with God. While Elijah's postbiblical portrayal is similar, he differs from Enoch in one essential way: Enoch never returns to earth from his heavenly perch, but Elijah frequently does.

The geographical location of Elijah's ascent—in the Transjordan opposite Jericho—is near Mount Nebo, where Moses departed from this world. Unlike Elijah, Moses actually died, though he was supposedly buried by God Himself: *Moses, the servant of YHVH, died there in the land of Moab by the word of YHVH, and He buried him in the valley in the land of Moab opposite Beth-Peor, and no one knows his burial place to this day* (Deuteronomy 34:5–6).[108] In this respect, Elijah outshines Moses, for he is the only figure in the Hebrew Bible of whom it is explicitly stated that he *went up to heaven*. Perhaps in reaction to Elijah's apparent superiority, a minority view insisted that "Moses did not die, but rather stands ministering above."[109]

In his first biblical mention, Elijah appears suddenly, confronting Ahab—without a trace of his lineage or early life—and from then on, he is elusive, evading Ahab and Jezebel for years, surprising those he encounters. Fittingly, he departs from earthly existence in mystery, leaving everyone, including us, to wonder where he has gone.

Even if the account of his sailing off in a fiery chariot was never intended to imply that Elijah escaped death, this striking image stimulated others to invest him with eternal life. After all, near the start of his prophetic career, he already overcame death by reviving a lifeless child.

LOOK, I AM SENDING TO YOU ELIJAH THE PROPHET

Outside of the book of Kings, Elijah resurfaces twice in the Hebrew Bible—in a famous passage and in another, relatively unknown one.

The latter appears in the book of Chronicles, which reports that during the reign of King Jehoram of Judah, *a letter came to him from Elijah the prophet* (2 Chronicles 21:12). This letter castigates the king for worshiping idols and for murdering his brothers to consolidate his rule. Elijah predicts affliction for the people of Judah and death for Jehoram himself by a ghastly intestinal disorder.[110]

This brief episode seems rather strange. Nowhere else in the Bible does a prophet castigate kings by correspondence. Furthermore, throughout the book of Kings, Elijah never confronts the rulers of Judah, only of the Northern Kingdom of Israel. The letter is likely invented by the author of Chronicles, based on Elijah's role as the zealous champion of YHVH, in opposition to Baal, during the reign of Ahab, and because King Jehoram of Judah was married to Ahab's daughter, Athaliah.[111]

Apparently, the author of Chronicles thought that Elijah had not yet ascended in the fiery chariot, unless he assumed that Elijah composed this prophetic letter some years earlier, before disappearing in the whirlwind.[112] According to the chronology of the early rabbinic work *Seder Olam*, Elijah had already been "hidden away" in heaven for seven years before his letter reached Jehoram.[113]

But if Elijah did not die and remains alive in heaven, then he can continue to be an active force in the world, capable of intervening in the course of history. Perhaps the Chronicler already knew of the tradition that Elijah did not entirely disappear.[114] According to medieval commentators, Elijah composed the letter of chastisement to King Jehoram directly from his heavenly abode.[115] This, then, becomes the first sign of Elijah's revelation after his ascent.

Elijah is featured in the final prophecy of the Hebrew Bible, in the closing verses of Malachi, composed around 500 BCE, after Israel's return from the Babylonian exile. This climactic passage indicates that Elijah endures, ready to return to earth:

> *Remember the Torah of Moses My servant that I commanded him on Horeb for all Israel—statutes and laws.*
>
> *Look, I am sending to you Elijah the prophet before the coming of the day of YHVH, great and awesome. He will bring fathers' hearts back to their children and children's hearts to their fathers, lest I come and strike the land with sacred destruction.* (Malachi 3:22–24)[116]

Malachi insists that Moses and his Torah are to be remembered—but Elijah will be directly encountered. He will herald the *day of YHVH*, namely, the day of judgment and redemption. By reconciling the older generation with the younger, Elijah will assuage God's wrath. Returning to earth, the fiery prophet will rekindle the natural love between parent and child. Elijah's emotional mandate is broadened by the Septuagint's paraphrase of this verse: *He will bring a father's heart back to his son and a man's heart back to his neighbor.*

In the Talmud, the day of *YHVH* is described as "the birth-pangs of the Messiah."[117] For the rabbis, Malachi's prophecy implied that Elijah would announce not just the day of judgment but the arrival of the Messiah. A step in this direction appears in the Wisdom of Ben Sira, composed near the beginning of the second century BCE and included in the Apocrypha. The final major section of this book, titled "Praise of the Ancestors," includes this description of Elijah: "Until a prophet like fire arose . . . How awesome are you, Elijah! Who is as glorious as you? . . . Taken up in a whirlwind, by a battalion of heavenly fire. Inscribed and destined to end divine wrath before it rages, to turn fathers' hearts back to their children and to reestablish the tribes of Israel. Happy is one who sees you before he dies!"[118]

Here Elijah is destined to gather the dispersed of Israel, in preparation for the day of YHVH. The castigator of his people—*troubler of Israel,* as Ahab called him—will return to protect, reunify, and reconcile them. The role of paving the way for redemption becomes prominent in the next phase of Elijah's endless life, as he is reshaped by the rabbis.

2

The Compassionate Super-Rabbi: Elijah in the Talmud and Midrash

As envisioned by the rabbis, Elijah differs from his stark biblical portrait. The zealous prophet of God—who parched the land with drought and slaughtered his pagan rivals—now develops his compassion. Having ascended to heaven, Elijah does not remain there constantly, awaiting his messianic mission; he returns to earth ahead of time, frequently—to save those in danger, fight for justice, champion the innocent, heal the sick, gladden the miserable, fortify the weak, and stimulate both the wicked and the average to engage in *teshuvah* ("turning back" to God). He becomes gracious and generous, helping those in need and ultimately heralding salvation.

The biblical Elijah, of course, already knew how to be compassionate. He miraculously nourished the starving widow of Zarephath and later revived her child. Conversely, the rabbinic Elijah never entirely loses his harsh quality. According to one midrashic fragment, at the end of days, "The blessed Holy One will seize the prince [of Esau] by the lock of his hair, and Elijah will slaughter him—his blood splattering on [God's] clothes."[1] In a sense, however, Elijah is transformed from a biblical zealot into a Jewish bodhisattva. In Mahayana Buddhism, a bodhisattva is one who refrains from entering nirvana so that instead he or she can save others. Elijah, transported to heaven, refrains from basking eternally in celestial bliss and instead makes himself available to humanity. His passionate nature endures, conveying love, demanding and inspiring ethical behavior.[2]

Although no longer confined to earth, Elijah still feels connected to its inhabitants. He becomes a supernatural mediator, bridging this world and the beyond. He delivers messages from above, reports the proceedings of the Divine Court, and transmits spirited debates from the Academy of Heaven. He knows what God is doing—and discloses this to worthy sages. To an inquiring rabbi on the road, as we will see, he reveals God's intimate feelings.

MULTIPLE IDENTITIES

Elijah knows so much, and about him we know so little. Since the Bible never identifies his parents, birthplace, or background, the rabbis naturally wondered about his origin and lineage. The opening verse of the Elijah saga describes him as *one of the inhabitants of Gilead* (1 Kings 17:1), and some authorities assigned him to the tribe of Gad, who settled in the Transjordan, in or near the hills of Gilead.[3] Others claimed he was descended from Levi (born to Jacob's wife Leah) or from Benjamin (born to his other wife, Rachel). Fortunately, since for the rabbis he never died, Elijah was able to participate in the matter:

> One time our Masters were sitting and discussing where Elijah came from. Some of them said: "[He came] from the seed of Rachel." Some said: "[He came] from the seed of Leah." While they were sitting and discussing the matter, Elijah

> came and stood before them. He said to them, "My Masters, I am surely from the seed of Rachel! Is it not written as follows in the genealogy of Benjamin: *Adashah, Elijah, and Zichri were the sons of Jeroham?*" (1 Chronicles 8:27).[4]

The Elijah mentioned in that verse from Chronicles is someone else entirely, but Elijah the prophet, employing midrashic license, locates himself there.

One of the alternative views—that Elijah was descended from the tribe of Levi—accords with the tradition that he was a priest. (All Jewish priests are descended from the first Israelite priest, Aaron, who was a Levite.) In a midrashic source, he declares, "I am Elijah the priest."[5] A talmudic rabbi, Rabbah son of Avuha, is surprised to find Elijah in a graveyard, since priests are forbidden to be near the dead. Rabbah asks him, "Isn't my master a priest?"[6]

Whatever his earthly origins, Elijah's destiny was transcendent. As pictured by the rabbis, when his chariot ride reached heaven, he turned into a unique angel. As mentioned earlier, the mysterious figure Enoch was also transfigured after *God took him*. Enoch and Elijah are a pair, both of whom "ascended and ministered above."[7] In the mystical version of Enoch's ascent, he becomes the chief angel Metatron. Kabbalistic tradition later identifies Elijah as another prominent angel, Sandalphon.[8] Both Enoch and Elijah are pictured as the heavenly scribe, recording all human deeds. Yet despite their similarities, there is a crucial difference between them. Once Enoch ascends to heaven, he never leaves. Why leave paradise? But Elijah has a reason to leave, to move continually back and forth. He is on an endless mission: to rescue, teach, and inspire.

Often Elijah displays his angelic talents. He is "a winged creature," "flying through the world like a bird."[9] He flies almost as effortlessly as Michael and Gabriel, the two principal archangels: "Michael [traverses the world, reaching his destination] in one [glide, or stroke of his wings], Gabriel in two, Elijah in four, and the Angel of Death in eight."[10]

Spanning all of space, Elijah also spans time, since for the rabbis, he never died. Elijah is included in all of the various lists of those select humans who entered the Garden of Eden alive.[11] Moreover, he is one of seven long-living humans whose lifetimes overlapped, so that together they form a chain of being, extending from creation to the end of time: "Seven humans span eternity: Adam saw Methuselah; Methuselah saw Shem [son of Noah]; Shem saw Jacob; Jacob saw Serah [daughter of Asher]; Serah saw [the prophet] Ahijah [of Shilo]; Ahijah saw Elijah; and Elijah lives and endures until the Messiah comes."[12]

As a member of the celestial family, Elijah moves about freely in heaven. Each morning he glides to earth, attending to the patriarchs in the cave of Machpelah, waking them from their graves, one at a time, for morning prayer.[13] When certain sages depart from earth, he ushers them into paradise.[14]

Although he has become angelic, Elijah remembers his humanity and descends to earth to associate with people, conversing with the sages in the house of study or even in the marketplace. He is not always perfect, and his supernatural knowledge is limited. For example, he knows when the Messiah will come, but not precisely:

> Elijah said to Rabbi Yehudah, the brother of R. Salla the Ḥasid, "The world will exist for no fewer than eighty-five jubilees [of fifty years each, totaling 4,250 years], and in the final jubilee the [Messiah] son of David will come."
>
> He asked [Elijah], "At the beginning or at the end [of that final jubilee]?"
>
> [Elijah] replied, "I don't know."
>
> [He asked,] "Will [the final jubilee] be completed or not?"
>
> [Elijah] replied, "I don't know."[15]

He retains a measure of his human nature and personality, which affords him greater freedom of action than other angels, who are directly controlled by God. Unlike them, Elijah can be spontaneous, expressing his individuality and emotions. If his zealotry has waned, his passion still surges: fighting injustice, rescuing those in distress, and championing ethical ideals. At times he seems more human than angelic, a super-rabbi.[16]

Among his human traits is an appreciation of humor, when employed for a holy purpose. Once, in a certain Babylonian marketplace, he revealed himself to Rabbi Beroka Ḥoza'ah, who immediately asked him, "Is there anyone in this market who is worthy of the world to come?" Elijah replied, "No." But after a while, two brothers came along, whom the prophet identified as deserving of eternal bliss:

> [Rabbi Beroka] approached them and asked, "What is your occupation?"
>
> They replied, "We are jesters. We cheer up the depressed. Also, when we see two people quarreling, we try hard to make peace between them."[17]

Although Elijah has become angelic, he readily assumes various human forms. He can appear as an ordinary person or especially an old man, the archetype of wisdom. But often he appears in disguise, adopting whatever personality is appropriate to the situation. He impersonates a horseman, an Arab, a Persian, a slave, a royal minister of a gentile ruler, a Roman dignitary. Already in the biblical narrative, he could turn up or disappear at any moment. In his postbiblical adventures, he can turn into someone else. Elijah is a shape-shifter, able to mold his angelhood into any identity he needs.

To the rabbis, he usually appears as a fellow sage. When necessary he can impersonate a specific rabbi—as when he came to Rabbi Yehudah the Prince in the guise of Rabbi Ḥiyya, a target of Yehudah's anger. Pretending to be Ḥiyya, Elijah assuaged

Yehudah, thereby reconciling the two rabbis. How did he do so? By curing Yehudah's severe toothache.[18]

On one occasion, Elijah assumed the guise of a biblical character in the book of Esther. At a dramatic point in the scriptural tale, Harbonah (a eunuch in the palace of King Ahasuerus) advises the king to hang the Jews' arch-enemy, Haman. The Midrash attributes this counsel to Elijah, who was impersonating Harbonah.[19]

Another time, Elijah made an appearance before the Roman emperor. He did so in the company of the sage Naḥum of Gimzo, whose title is based on his town, located in the center of the land of Israel. In a pun on this place-name, the sage became known as Naḥum of Gam Zo:

> Why was he called Naḥum of Gam Zo? Because whatever happened to him, he would say, "*Gam zo le-tovah* (This too is for the best)."
>
> Once the Jews wished to send a gift to the emperor. They said, "Who should go? Let Naḥum of Gam Zo go, for he is experienced in miracles." They sent with him a chest full of jewels and pearls.
>
> He set out, and he spent the night at a certain inn. During the night, the occupants of the inn arose and emptied the chest and filled it with earth. In the morning, when [Naḥum] saw what had happened, he said, "*Gam zo le-tovah.*"
>
> When he reached his destination, they opened the chest and saw that it was full of earth. The king then wanted to kill all of them [all the Jewish emissaries, or all the Jews], saying, "The Jews are mocking me!" [Naḥum] said, "*Gam zo le-tovah.*"
>
> Elijah came and appeared before [the emperor] as one of [his ministers]. He said to [the emperor], "Perhaps this is some of the earth of their father Abraham; for when [Abraham] threw earth [against the enemy], it turned into swords, [and when he threw] stubble, it turned into arrows." . . .
>
> Now, there was a certain province that [the Romans]

> were unable to conquer. When they tried [throwing] some of [this earth against that province], they conquered it. So they went into the royal treasury and filled [Naḥum's] chest with jewels and pearls, and sent him off with great honor.[20]

Elijah saves Naḥum and the Jews by turning himself into a Roman minister and turning worthless dirt into magic dust.

Of his many transfigurations, perhaps the most shocking one involves Rabbi Me'ir, a leading sage of the second century. Me'ir had boldly rescued his sister-in-law from a Roman brothel, to which she had been condemned. Consequently, the Roman authorities posted Me'ir's "wanted" picture on the city gates: "They went and engraved Rabbi Me'ir's image at the entrance of Rome and proclaimed, 'Anyone who sees this face—bring him!' One day [some Roman officers] saw him and ran after him; he ran away from them. . . . Some say that Elijah appeared to [the pursuing officers] as a prostitute and embraced [Rabbi Me'ir]. [The officers] said, 'Perish the thought! If this were Rabbi Me'ir, he wouldn't have done that.' [Thereby he was saved.]"[21]

To rescue Rabbi Me'ir, Elijah fashions himself into a whore and behaves accordingly. For the rabbi in distress—and for his oppressed and colonized people—Elijah breaks the rules of the game, in which the Romans governing Palestine (or the Persians governing Babylonia) always win and the Jews always lose. Elijah in disguise opens unpredictable possibilities. He comes as a benign trickster, making fools of gentile oppressors; he is champion of the Jews in a risky world.[22]

An expert in the unexpected, Elijah motivates others to emulate him. Here he saves Rabbi Me'ir by ruining Me'ir's dignity; on another occasion he stimulates the same sage to sacrifice his dignity:

> Once Rabbi Me'ir was sitting and expounding [on Friday night. There was a woman there sitting and listening to him.

> His discourse went late, and she waited until he finished.] She went home, it being Sabbath evening, and found that her [Sabbath] light had gone out. Her husband asked her, "Where have you been until now?"
>
> She replied, "I've been listening to Rabbi Me'ir's discourse."
>
> Now, that man was a scoffer. He said to her, "I swear, no matter what, you will not enter my house until you go and spit in the face of Rabbi Me'ir!"
>
> She left his house. Elijah (gratefully remembered) appeared to Rabbi Me'ir, and said to him, "Look, because of you that woman has left her house." Then Elijah (gratefully remembered) informed him of what had happened.[23]
>
> What did Rabbi Me'ir do? He went and sat down in the Great House of Study. When that woman came to pray, he saw her and pretended to be blinking. He asked, "Who knows how to recite an incantation to cure an eye?"
>
> That woman replied, "I have come to recite an incantation." And she spat in his face.[24]
>
> [Rabbi Me'ir] said to her, "Tell your husband, 'I spat in the face of Rabbi Me'ir.'" And he added, "Go and be reconciled with your husband."[25]

Here the prophet destined to *bring fathers' hearts back to their children and children's hearts to their fathers* (Malachi 3:24) brings a husband's heart back to his wife, inspiring Rabbi Me'ir to do so in a startling way.

Inspiration is Elijah's specialty; he embodies *ruaḥ ha-qodesh* (the Holy Spirit). Remarkably, in the original versions of this story it is not Elijah who inspires Rabbi Me'ir to save the couple's marriage but the Holy Spirit. By the ninth century (when this revised version was composed), a midrashic author felt free to personalize *ruaḥ ha-qodesh* as Elijah.

ENCOUNTERING ELIJAH

In early rabbinic literature, Elijah rarely leaves heaven. In fact, according to the chronology of the early historical work *Seder Olam*, ever since his ascent to heaven, Elijah has remained hidden: "Ahaziah son of Ahab ruled for two years. In the second year of his reign Elijah was hidden away, and he will not appear until the Messiah arrives. In the days of the Messiah he will reappear and then be hidden away again, and he will not reappear until Gog arrives. Now he records the deeds of every single generation."[26]

In accord with this description, in all Tannaitic literature (through the second century) we never find Elijah appearing to a rabbi. Only in the Amoraic sources (third–sixth centuries) does he begin to appear, and then more frequently, until the Talmud and Midrash are peppered with his rabbinic interactions.[27]

When he appears to the common folk, Elijah's identity is unknown, revealed as an astonishment or after he has disappeared. However, the sages whom he regularly visits recognize him—though even for them such a meeting is unpredictable.[28]

Regarding such sages, we never hear why Elijah started meeting with them. But we sometimes hear why he *stopped* meeting with them: because they did something unethical or unkind. By staying away, Elijah makes it clear that such conduct taints a person. Sometimes the erring party becomes painfully aware of Elijah's absence and mends his ways. Elijah promotes and enforces ethical values among laypeople and scholars alike.

"There was a certain pious man with whom Elijah used to converse. But when [the man] built a gatehouse, [Elijah] did not converse with him again."[29] Why? Because the gatehouse was intended to prevent the poor from entering the man's courtyard or home.

Elijah's presence is a reward for those who are generous; it is unavailable to those who are not:

> [It is told about] Avuha son of Ihi and Minyamin son of Ihi, that one gave [his waiter a portion] of every kind of dish [as it was served], while the other gave [his waiter a portion] of one kind only. With the former, Elijah conversed; with the latter, he did not.
>
> [It is told about] two pious ones—some say about Rabbi Mari and Rabbi Pinḥas, sons of Rabbi Ḥisda—that one of them gave [a share to his waiter] first [i.e., before he tasted it himself], while the other gave to him last. With the one who gave first, Elijah conversed; with the one who gave last, Elijah did not converse.[30]

One talmudic rabbi enjoyed a particularly close relationship with Elijah: the third-century Palestinian *amora* Rabbi Yehoshu'a son of Levi. He and Elijah were study partners.[31] Once Elijah showed him the hidden jewels that will become the building blocks of the restored city of Jerusalem.[32] The winged prophet also gave him a personal tour of the torments of hell.[33] Eventually, Elijah heralded Rabbi Yehoshu'a's arrival in paradise, proclaiming "Make room for the son of Levi, make room for the son of Levi!" Like Elijah his mentor, Yehoshu'a escaped normal death, entering paradise while still alive.[34]

But even Rabbi Yehoshu'a could be shunned by Elijah: "A man was devoured by a lion some three parasangs from the town where Rabbi Yehoshu'a son of Levi lived, and consequently Elijah did not converse with [Rabbi Yehoshu'a] for three days."[35] Apparently, Yehoshu'a should have prayed that nothing like this would happen in his vicinity, or he should have guided the sinner (since the victim must have sinned to deserve his grisly punishment) to repent, thereby preventing the tragedy.

One action by Rabbi Yehoshu'a repulsed Elijah longer:

> It was taught: If a group of [Jews] are threatened by heathens who declare, "Surrender one of yourselves and we will kill him; and if not, we will kill all of you"—they should all be killed and not surrender one soul of Israel. But if [the enemy]

> specified a particular person . . . , they should surrender him and not all be killed. . . .
>
> Ulla son of Qosher was wanted by the government. He arose and fled to Rabbi Yehoshu'a son of Levi at Lydda, and officers were dispatched after him. Rabbi Yehoshu'a son of Levi went to him and urged him [to surrender], saying, "Better that you should be killed rather than that the whole community be punished on account of you." [Ulla] was persuaded and was handed over to them.
>
> Now, Elijah used to speak with [Rabbi Yehoshu'a], but once he did this, [Elijah] stopped coming to him. [Rabbi Yehoshu'a] fasted thirty days, and finally [Elijah] appeared to him. [Rabbi Yehoshu'a] asked him, "Why were you absent, Master?"
>
> He replied, "Am I a companion of informers?"
>
> He said, "But is this not a Tannaitic statement: 'If a group of [Jews are threatened by heathens who declare, "Surrender one of yourselves and we will kill him; and if not, we will kill all of you"—they should all be killed and not surrender one soul of Israel. But if (the enemy) specified a particular person . . . , they should surrender him and not all be killed']?"
>
> [Elijah] replied, "Is that *mishnat ḥasidim* (an instruction for the devout)? This should have been done by others, not by you!"[36]

Rabbi Yehoshu'a was simply following the established teaching: that one life may be sacrificed in order to save all the rest of a threatened group. But Elijah insists that by handing over Ulla to the Roman oppressor, Rabbi Yehoshu'a has violated a higher standard—beyond the law. Elijah's ethical paradigm—*mishnat ḥasidim*—is incumbent upon anyone truly devoted.[37]

In another encounter with Elijah, Rabbi Yehoshu'a asked him about the Messiah:

> Rabbi Yehoshu'a son of Levi encountered Elijah standing by the entrance of Rabbi Shim'on son of Yoḥai's tomb. He asked him . . . "When will the Messiah come?"

[Elijah] replied, "Go and ask him."

[Rabbi Yehoshu'a asked,] "Where is he sitting?"

[Elijah replied,] "At the entrance of Rome."

[Rabbi Yehoshu'a asked,] "By what sign will I recognize him?"

[Elijah replied,] "He is sitting among the poor who suffer from disease; and all of them untie their bandages [for dressing their sores] all at once and then [after treating each sore] rebandage them all at once, whereas he unties each bandage separately and [after treating that sore] rebandages it [before treating the next sore], thinking, 'Perhaps I will be needed [as the Redeemer at any moment], so I must not be delayed [by having to rebandage a number of open sores].'"

So [Rabbi Yehoshu'a] went to [the Messiah] and said to him, "Peace unto you, my Master and Teacher."

[The Messiah] replied, "Peace unto you, son of Levi."

[Rabbi Yehoshu'a] asked, "When are you coming, Master?"

[The Messiah] replied, "Today."

[Rabbi Yehoshu'a] returned to Elijah, who asked him, "What did he say to you?" . . .

[Rabbi Yehoshu'a] replied, "Surely he lied to me, for he said, 'I am coming today,' and he did not come!"

[Elijah] replied, "This is what he was saying to you: *Today, if you heed His voice*" (Psalms 95:7).[38]

Elijah will herald the redemption at the end of days, but inhabiting eternity, he knows that the messianic moment could be now.

A contemporary of Rabbi Yehoshu'a son of Levi's, the Babylonian *amora* Rabbi Anan, was also virtuous enough for Elijah to frequently visit. According to legend, the prophet began dictating to Anan an entire book, which came to be known as *Seder Eliyyahu* (The Arrangement of Elijah) or *Tanna de-Vei Eliyyahu* (The Lore of Elijah's School). One day, however, Anan caused a miscarriage of justice, and although he did this inadvertently and indirectly, Elijah stopped coming. Seeking to win back the prophet's presence, "[Anan] fasted and prayed for mercy, and [Elijah] reappeared. But when he appeared, he frightened [Anan] intensely. So [Anan] made a box and sat in it before him until [Elijah] had conveyed his Arrangement to him."[39]

The Arrangement of Elijah includes two parts, which according to this talmudic passage Anan received from Elijah over two distinct periods: before his peccadillo when he could face Elijah directly, and then afterward, shielding himself in the box.

The exact relation between Elijah's book as described here in the Talmud and the book in its present form is unclear, but *The Lore of Elijah's School* as we now possess it was likely composed in the ninth century. Whoever its author was, he may have felt that Elijah appeared to him in the guise of a sage imparting wisdom. Alternatively, he may have named his school and its discourses after Elijah. Or the head of a certain school was himself named Elijah, and he extended his name to the school, from which this book stemmed. Gradually, the authorship may have been attributed no longer to this later Elijah but back to Elijah the prophet. Fittingly, Elijah's book refuses to yield the secret of its origin.[40]

Occasionally in the book Elijah appears as the main character of a story, or he offers an interpretation or is cited as an authority. But throughout he is mentioned in the third person, never depicted as the author. As for the anonymous author, his style is a blend of midrash and ethical literature, spiced with mystical ingredients.[41] In one famous passage, he links the ethical and mystical realms, insisting that inspiration is unrestricted, available to anyone who earns it: "I call heaven and earth to witness that whether it be gentile or Jew, man or woman, manservant or maidservant, the Holy Spirit settles upon a person entirely in accordance with the deeds he performs."[42]

"WHAT IS THE BLESSED HOLY ONE DOING?"

Elijah knows the deepest secrets and follows the learned discussions in the Heavenly Academy. To certain sages, he divulges highlights of these discussions, including God's participation:

> Rabbah son of Sheila encountered Elijah. He said to him, "What is the blessed Holy One doing?"
>
> [Elijah] replied, "He is uttering traditions in the name of all the Rabbis except for Rabbi Me'ir."
>
> [Rabbah] asked him, "Why?"
>
> [Elijah replied,] "Because [Rabbi Me'ir] learned traditions from the mouth of Aḥer."

"Aḥer" (meaning "the Other") is a nickname for Elisha son of Avuyah, the most famous heretic in the Talmud. Obviously, Aḥer has no place in the Heavenly Academy; but according to Elijah, God refuses to quote even the teachings of Rabbi Me'ir simply because he learned from Aḥer. Hearing this, Rabbah objects to Elijah:

> [Rabbah] said to him, "Why? Rabbi Me'ir found a pomegranate; the fruit within he ate, its peel he threw away!" [That is, Rabbi Me'ir learned what was valuable from Aḥer, while rejecting his heretical views.]
>
> [Elijah] replied, "Now [the blessed Holy One] says, 'Me'ir, My son, says, "When a person suffers [capital punishment imposed by a judicial court], what does *Shekhinah* utter? 'My head feels heavy! My arm feels heavy!' If the blessed Holy One feels such sorrow over the blood of the wicked, how much more so over the blood of the righteous that is shed!"'"[43]

Elijah reports that God has changed His mind, on the basis of Rabbah's pithy defense, and will no longer exclude Rabbi Me'ir. A mere human, Rabbah has persuaded God to be more compassionate. Back in the Heavenly Academy, the blessed Holy One is already reciting a teaching of Rabbi Me'ir's on the theme of God's empathy for human suffering—the suffering of one punished by the court, the suffering of the righteous, and the suffering of "Me'ir, My son," whom God neglected simply because his teacher strayed.[44]

Without Elijah, of course, none of this would have happened. If he hadn't revealed to Rabbah what God was reciting in the Heavenly Academy, Rabbah would never have evoked divine compassion, altering God's will. Nor would Rabbah have known how he affected God if Elijah hadn't reported it.[45]

Elijah's membership in the Heavenly Academy enables him to disclose not only what God is teaching but also what He is *studying*—because even God delves into Torah:

> Rabbi Evyatar encountered Elijah and asked him, "What is the blessed Holy One doing?"
>
> [Elijah] replied, "He is engaged in [studying the episode of] the concubine in Gibeah."

On this particular day, God is studying a gruesome story in the book of Judges, accounting the brutal rape-murder of a certain Levite's concubine. This outrage was perpetrated by a gang of men in the city of Gibeah while the couple was staying there.[46] Rabbi Evyatar wonders what God has discovered about this tragic event:

> [Rabbi Evyatar asked him,] "And what is He saying?"
>
> [Elijah] replied, "[God is saying,] 'Evyatar, My son, says this; and Yonatan, My son, says that.'"

In the biblical story, before the Levite and his concubine traveled together to Gibeah, she had deserted him and fled to her father's house. In the talmudic passage, Rabbi Evyatar and Rabbi Yonatan offer different opinions regarding the cause of the marital dispute. Elijah tells Rabbi Evyatar that God is quoting both of their views. But this puzzles Rabbi Evyatar: Doesn't God know which one is correct?

> [Rabbi Evyatar] said to him, "Perish the thought! Is there doubt in the mind of the Heavenly One?"
>
> [Elijah] replied, "Both these and those are words of the Living God."[47]

How can God uphold two contrary views? Elijah reveals that divine truth embraces multiple and conflicting possibilities of meaning. God does not merely tolerate the varieties of truth; He commends them by quoting both differing interpretations and calling each rabbi "My son." By reporting God's study habits, Elijah affirms the sages' innovative exegesis.[48]

In a similar talmudic passage, Elijah shows that a biblical verse is not confined to a single meaning. Here the rabbis are discussing a pivotal passage in the book of Esther in which the queen invites the wicked Haman to a banquet:

> *Let the king and Haman come [today] to the banquet [that I have prepared for him]* (Esther 5:4). Our rabbis have taught: What prompted Esther to invite Haman?
>
> Rabbi El'azar said, "She was setting a trap for him [planning to expose him during the banquet] . . ."
>
> Rabbi Yose said, "So that he would constantly be close by [and she could accuse him]."
>
> Rabbi Shim'on son of Menassiah said, "[Esther thought,] 'Perhaps the Omnipresent will notice [how popular Haman has become, and how vulnerable the Jews are] and He will perform a miracle for us.'" . . .
>
> Rabban Gamliel said, ". . . She made the king jealous of him, and she made the ministers jealous of him." . . .
>
> Rabbah son of Avuha encountered Elijah and asked him, "In accord with whose opinion did Esther see fit to do so [i.e., to invite Haman to the banquet]?"
>
> He replied, "In accord with all of those *tanna'im* and all of those *amora'im*."[49]

What really motivated Esther to invite Haman? For Elijah, any or all of these talmudic answers are valid. Each is one of the "seventy facets of Torah," treasured by the prophet, who here again bolsters rabbinic creativity and hermeneutic pluralism.[50]

In the aggadic realm, differing views can be legitimate; but in the halakhic realm, communal cohesion requires a single, normative view. God delights in both of these scenarios, and fittingly it is Elijah who tells how God acts and feels about each of them. We have seen how the prophet describes the blessed Holy One quoting two conflicting aggadic opinions. In another passage, Elijah reveals God's emotions toward the halakhic process and its human participants.

This is the famous talmudic story known as "The Oven of Akhnai." The setting is the rabbinic house of study, where the sages are engaged in a legal dispute concerning a technical matter: whether a certain type of oven, built from detachable sections, is subject to ritual impurity. Rabbi Eli'ezer has tried to persuade his colleagues that such an oven is not subject to impurity, but the majority of sages have decided that it is. Still, Rabbi Eli'ezer does not relent:

> It has been taught: On that day Rabbi Eli'ezer brought forward all the arguments in the world, but they did not accept them.
>
> [Rabbi Eli'ezer] said to them, "If the halakhah is as I say, let this carob tree prove it!" The carob tree was uprooted from its place and it moved a distance of one hundred cubits—some say, four hundred cubits. They responded, "One does not bring proof from a carob tree." The carob tree returned to its place.
>
> [Rabbi Eli'ezer] said to them, "If the halakhah is as I say, let the aqueduct prove it!" The water in the aqueduct flowed backwards. They responded, "One does not bring proof from water." The water returned to its place.

> [Rabbi Eli'ezer] said to them, "If the halakhah is as I say, let the walls of the academy prove it." The walls of the academy inclined and were about to fall. Rabbi Yehoshu'a rebuked them, saying, "When scholars grapple with one another in a halakhic dispute, what does it have to do with you?"
>
> It has been taught: [The walls] did not fall, in deference to Rabbi Yehoshu'a; and they did not stand upright, in deference to Rabbi Eli'ezer. They still remain inclined.
>
> [Rabbi Eli'ezer] said to them, "If the halakhah is as I say, let it be proved from Heaven!" A Heavenly Voice issued, saying "What do you have against Rabbi Eli'ezer, since the halakhah agrees with him everywhere!"
>
> Rabbi Yehoshu'a arose and said, "*It is not in heaven* (Deuteronomy 30:12)." What does this mean? Rabbi Yirmeyah said, "One pays no attention to a Heavenly Voice, since You already gave [the Torah] to us on Mount Sinai and it is written there: *Follow the majority* (Exodus 23:2)."
>
> Rabbi Natan encountered Elijah, and asked him, "What did the blessed Holy One do at that moment?"
>
> He replied, "He laughed and smiled, and said, 'My children have defeated Me! My children have defeated Me!'"[51]

Rather than intervening any further, God yields to the halakhic process, accepting its fallible human reasoning, confirming that the sages can ignore the divine will. This remarkable surrender to the rabbis affirms their power as they wrestle with Torah. Yet we know of God's surrender only through Elijah—who straddles heaven and earth, conveying secrets to the worthy, including the secret of how God feels.

God feels most deeply about humanity, especially His people Israel. He shares in the sorrow of their exile, as emphasized by Elijah in another rabbinic encounter:

> Rabbi Yose said, "I was once walking on the road, and I entered one of the ruins of Jerusalem to pray. Along came Elijah (gratefully remembered) and waited for me at the entrance

until I finished my prayer. After I finished, he said to me, 'Peace unto you, my master!'

"I replied, 'Peace unto you, my master and teacher!'

"[Elijah] said to me, 'My son, why did you enter this ruin?'

"I replied, 'To pray.'

"He said to me, 'You should have prayed on the road.'

"I replied, 'I feared that I might be interrupted by passersby.'

"He said to me, 'You should have recited an abbreviated prayer.'

"At that time I learned from [Elijah] three things: I learned that one should not enter a ruin; and I learned that one can pray on the road; and I learned that one praying on the road should recite an abbreviated prayer.

"And he said to me, 'What voice did you hear in this ruin?'

"I replied, 'I heard a heavenly echo, cooing like a dove, saying, "Woe to Me that I destroyed My house and burned My temple and exiled My children among the nations of the world!"'

"[Elijah] said to me, 'By your life and by your head! Not at this moment alone does it exclaim so, but three times every single day! Moreover, whenever the people of Israel enter the synagogues and houses of study and respond [in the Kaddish], "May His great name be blessed!," the blessed Holy One shakes His head and says, "Happy is the king who is thus praised in his house! [i.e., when the Temple still stood. But now,] Woe to the father who has banished his children, and woe to the children who have been banished from their father's table!"'"[52]

In the ruins of Jerusalem, Rabbi Yose hears a heavenly voice echoing, bemoaning the destruction of the Temple and Israel's exile. Elijah informs him that God constantly feels and vents sorrow.

The dialogue between Elijah and Rabbi Yose is marked by mutual respect. Elijah greets him politely ("Peace unto you, my master!"), and Rabbi Yose, in turn, salutes Elijah as a senior sage ("Peace unto you, my master and teacher!"). Elsewhere, too, Elijah seems more like a rabbi than an angel. He functions as an esteemed colleague, to whom one may pose legal or exegetical questions.

When Rabbah son of Avuha meets Elijah and asks three halakhic questions, the prophetic sage does not respond with a message from heaven but rather with biblical prooftexts, just as any rabbi would. Toward the end of their encounter, though, Elijah's supernatural powers resurface. He wonders why Rabbah himself doesn't know the answer to the last of his three questions, which can be solved by a rabbinic teaching about the laws of purity. Rabbah explains that he is "hard-pressed" financially, so he was unable to study those particular traditions. Elijah remedies this situation:

> [Elijah] led him into the Garden of Eden and said, "Remove your cloak, gather some of these leaves and take them." So [Rabbah son of Avuha] gathered and took them.
>
> As he was leaving [the Garden of Eden], [Rabbah son of Avuha] heard a voice exclaiming: "Who consumes his share of the world to come like Rabbah son of Avuha has done [taking the merit awaiting him in the future world and using it up now]?"
>
> He shook out his cloak, throwing [the leaves] away. Even so, when he brought his cloak back, it had absorbed the fragrance. He sold it for twelve thousand dinars, which he distributed among his sons-in-law.[53]

In the Garden of Eden, the fallen leaves are still suffused with an aroma of the paradisal trees, so much so that even Rabbah's cloak retains the rich fragrance.

Elijah responds to questions about God's activity ("What is

the blessed Holy One doing?") and about redemption ("When will the Messiah come?"). But he can also explicate the meaning of a biblical verse:

> Rabbi Yose encountered Elijah and said to him, "It is written [*YHVH Elohim said, 'It is not good for the human to be alone;*] *I will make him a helper* [*alongside him*]' (Genesis 2:18). How does a woman help a man?"
>
> [Elijah] replied, "A man brings wheat; does he chew [raw] wheat? Flax—does he wear [unprocessed] flax? Isn't she the one who brightens his eyes and stands him on his feet?"[54]

In one of Elijah's dialogues with an individual rabbi, he sheds the role of teacher and instead seeks to learn from his human colleague, asking Rabbi Nehorai the meaning of a biblical verse.[55] As we have seen, although he is angelic, Elijah retains a vestigial humanness. For example, he can be irritable even when rescuing someone—as when he saves the life of Rabbi Kahana, who tried to commit suicide rather than succumb to sexual sin:

> Rabbi Kahana was selling baskets. A certain matron propositioned him. He said to her, "Let me go and adorn myself." He climbed up to the roof and threw himself down toward the ground.
>
> Elijah came and caught him. [Elijah] said to him, "You've troubled me [to fly] four hundred parasangs [to save you]!"
>
> [Rabbi Kahana] replied, "What made me [sell baskets to women]—wasn't it poverty?"
>
> [Elijah] gave him a bushel of gold coins.[56]

The biblical zealot has not mellowed completely. Although according to a rabbinic tradition, Elijah says, "I appear only to one who is not hot-tempered,"[57] he himself is still irascible. After all, this is the same Elijah who angrily confronted King Ahab, slaughtered the 450 prophets of Baal, and called down fire to consume 100 soldiers. One rabbi who merely mentioned Elijah's biblical temperament immediately became its target:

> Rabbi Yose taught in Sepphoris: "Father Elijah was hot-tempered." Now, [Elijah] used to visit him regularly, but [after this] he concealed himself from [Rabbi Yose] for three days and did not come. When he finally came, [Rabbi Yose] said to him, "Why didn't you come, Master?"
>
> He replied, "You called me hot-tempered!"
>
> He responded, "Look here in front of us! For Master, you're displaying your temper!"[58]

By staying away from Rabbi Yose for three days simply because the rabbi mentioned his infamous temper, Elijah has demonstrated the persistence of that trait. Elijah felt insulted by being called irascible, but Rabbi Yose does not feel chastened by Elijah's abandoning him. Rather, he holds his ground, teaching Elijah a lesson.

"UNTIL ELIJAH COMES": THE PROPHET AND HALAKHAH

Elijah joins with the rabbis in searching for the meaning of Torah, and his opinion does not automatically outweigh that of other sages. While many medieval authorities relied on Elijah's views, some did not.[59]

Elijah's power is limited, because traditionally a prophet cannot invoke his own authority to establish the halakhah: "*These are the commandments* [*that YHVH gave Moses for the Israelites on Mount Sinai*] (Leviticus 27:34)—from now on [i.e., after Moses], a prophet is not allowed to innovate anything."[60]

Elijah cannot even overrule a widely accepted custom.[61] Yet in certain halakhic matters he dares to innovate. In one late midrash, we find him carrying the corpse of the martyred Rabbi Akiva, despite the fact that Elijah identifies himself there as a priest, whom a corpse would render impure. Elijah explains that "impurity does not inhere in the righteous [such as Rabbi Akiva] nor in their disciples."[62]

Such halakhic innovations by Elijah are rare. After all, he participated in the famous story of the oven of Akhnai (quoted above), whose message was that the Torah is not in heaven, but rather in the hands and minds of the rabbis. In fact, Elijah himself conveyed the divine punch line, in which God joyously confessed, "My children have defeated Me!"[63]

As an angelic rabbinic sage, Elijah participates in the halakhic process and is still obligated to fulfill halakhic norms. When he responds to questions from his merely mortal colleagues, he employs the standard techniques of rabbinic hermeneutics, such as *gezerah shavah* (similarity of a phrase, verbal analogy).[64]

When Elijah returns to herald the arrival of the Messiah, he will clarify halakhic doubts, explain problematic verses in the Bible, and harmonize rabbinic disputes. But even then, he will not intervene directly in matters of halakhah, except in rare instances to safeguard family purity. According to an ancient tradition, if a certain family had been illegally declared fit or unfit, Elijah will eventually reverse those decrees:

> Rabbi Yehoshu'a said, "I have received a tradition from Rabban Yoḥanan son of Zakkai, who heard from his teacher—and his teacher from his teacher—as a halakhah given to Moses at Sinai, that Elijah will not come to declare pure or impure, or to declare unfit or fit [literally, to remove afar or to bring near]. Rather, to declare unfit those [families] that were declared fit illegally [literally, by force], and to declare fit those [families] that were declared unfit illegally. . . . Such will Elijah come to declare pure or impure, to declare unfit or fit."
>
> Rabbi Yehudah says, "To declare fit, but not to declare unfit [even those declared fit illegally]."
>
> Rabbi Shim'on says, "To harmonize disputes."

> And the Sages say, "Neither to declare unfit nor to declare fit, but to make peace in the world, as is said: *Look, I am sending to you Elijah the prophet . . . and he will bring fathers' hearts back to their children and children's hearts to their fathers*" (Malachi 3:23–24).[65]

The limitation on Elijah's destined legal role is described succinctly by Rashi: "Permitting and forbidding do not depend on [Elijah], since *it is not in heaven* (Deuteronomy 30:12)."[66]

How will Elijah contribute to the future halakhic process? Primarily, by clarifying doubts and by establishing the facts pertaining to a talmudic dispute. If the sages declared something forbidden, invalid, or impure due to a certain doubt—since the facts were concealed from them—Elijah will clarify those facts. Wielding his mental superpowers, Elijah will reveal something hidden from common knowledge, some piece of information that simple mortals could not ascertain. Thereby he will help to determine the law—without negating any biblical or rabbinic tradition.[67]

For example, if the ritual status of a priestly offering is uncertain, Elijah will clarify whether it is pure or impure.[68] In the interpersonal realm too, his clairvoyance will be decisive: "If two people deposited money with a third—one of them 100 *zuz* and the other 200 *zuz*—and afterward one says, 'The 200 is mine,' and the other says, 'The 200 is mine,' he should give each of them 100 *zuz*, and the rest must remain until Elijah comes."[69]

Elijah will identify who the real owner is and who the deceiver. Similarly, if a precious object has been lost, he alone will know the owner's identity: "If one finds . . . vessels of silver or copper, he may make use of them for their own good, but not so as to wear them out. If [one finds] vessels of gold or glass, he may not touch them until Elijah comes."[70]

He knows nearly everything, from celestial secrets to mundane reality. When someday he returns, he will be able to answer questions that baffle the rabbis. For example, in the opening tractate of the Talmud, the sages discuss the grace after meals, and they wonder whether drinking wine constitutes a meal by itself. If it does, then after drinking, one should recite the full grace. However, it is noted that "people do not base their meals on [wine]":

> Rabbi Naḥman son of Yitsḥaq asked Rava, "If a person based his meal on it, what then?"
>
> He replied, "When Elijah comes, he will say whether or not it can serve as the basis for a meal. Now, in any case, such a person's intention is nullified vis-à-vis that of all other people."[71]

Since wine is not considered a main course, for now it does not require the complete grace after meals. Someday Elijah, who knows the nature of things, will clarify the matter.[72]

As the ultimate teacher, he will also be able to explain certain contradictions in the Bible: "*The priests shall not eat anything, whether bird or animal, that dies of itself or is torn by beasts* (Ezekiel 44:31). Is it only priests who may not eat these, whereas Israelites may?! [After all, any animal that dies of itself or is torn by beasts is forbidden to all Israelites.] Rabbi Yoḥanan said, 'This passage will be interpreted by Elijah in the future.'"[73]

Elijah will resolve contradictions and eliminate doubt. In the Babylonian Talmud, when a legal matter is left undecided, the discussion often concludes with the formula תיקו (*teiqu*), "Let it stand," that is, "Let the matter remain unresolved." This expression appears in the Talmud more than three hundred times. Centuries later, *teiqu* was interpreted imaginatively as an acronym referring to Elijah the Tishbite: תשבי יתרץ קושיות ואבעיות (*Tishbi yetarets qushyot ve-av'ayot* [or, *ve-ibba'yot*]), "The Tishbite will resolve difficulties and questions." Though this meaning of *teiqu* was never intended by the Talmud, it fits Elijah's image.[74]

Despite Elijah's wisdom and brilliance, the rabbis limit his present and future teaching, on the basis of the principle, "A prophet is not allowed to innovate anything."[75] The normative view, expressed by Maimonides, is that Elijah "will neither add to nor detract from the Torah."[76] Yet occasionally a more radical possibility emerges, linked with the notion of a messianic Torah, as described in this late midrash: "One day the blessed Holy One will be sitting in the Garden of Eden and discoursing there, with all the righteous of the world sitting before Him and the celestial family [of angels] standing erect. The blessed Holy One will be expounding before them the reasons of the new Torah that He will one day give them by the hand of the Messiah."[77]

Elijah is not mentioned here, but in another midrash describing the messianic revelation, Elijah plays a prominent role: "At that time, [Elijah] will bring forth *Sefer ha-Yashar*, of which this entire Torah is but one song."[78] The title *Sefer ha-Yashar* (Book of the Upright) can refer to a lost work, which is quoted twice in the Bible. From these quotations, it seems to have been an anthology of archaic Hebrew poems or epics. Here the scope of *Sefer ha-Yashar* expands, turning it into the immense primordial Torah, of which our current Torah is just a single sample. As the Messiah arrives, Elijah will transmit the full pristine text, whose contents match the dawning eon.[79]

Long ago, Elijah hinted at his messianic role of revealing a new Torah when he opened fresh perspectives for the talmudic sages, adding a dimension to their discourse. He showed how conflicting opinions can each be "words of the Living God" and how various meanings of a single verse can all be true. Elijah bends the rules of the interpretive game.[80]

ELIJAH AND THE MESSIAH

As we have seen, the prophet Malachi predicted that Elijah would return before the climactic *day of YHVH*, the day of judgment and redemption. Malachi makes no mention of a messianic figure, but this final prophecy of the Hebrew Bible gradually inspired the belief that Elijah would herald the Messiah. By the first century of the Common Era, Elijah was widely expected to return as the messianic harbinger. The rabbinic history of the world, *Seder Olam*, records this matter-of-factly: "In the second year of the reign of [King Ahaziah son of Ahab], Elijah was hidden away, and he will not appear until the Messiah arrives."[81]

Some Jews believed that Elijah would anoint the Messiah, as attested by the second-century church father Justin Martyr.[82] Medieval Jewish authors mention this too, though in rabbinic literature the general view is that the Messiah will not be anointed. Yet Elijah's anointing role may be reflected in the midrashic prediction that when he reappears, he will restore to Israel "the vessel of anointing oil."[83]

As the herald, Elijah will appear before the Messiah himself. According to the Talmud, Elijah will precede him by one day.[84] A midrashic description has him come several days earlier:

> Three days before the Messiah arrives, Elijah comes and stands atop the mountains of Israel, crying and mourning over them. . . . and his voice is heard from one end of the world to the other. Afterward he says to them, "Peace has come to the world." . . . On the second day he comes and stands atop the mountains of Israel and says, "Goodness has come to the world." . . . On the third day he comes and says, "Salvation has come to the world." . . . At that moment, the blessed Holy One displays His Glory and Dominion to all inhabitants of the world and redeems Israel.[85]

Several apocalyptic midrashim add to the picture. According to *The Prayer of Rabbi Shim'on son of Yoḥai*, "At that time [the archangel] Michael the Great Prince will stand and blow the shofar three times . . . and Messiah son of David and Elijah will be revealed. Both of them will go to Israel who are in the wilderness of the nations, and Elijah will declare to them, 'This is the Messiah!'"[86]

Another such midrash pictures Elijah as sounding four blasts on the shofar, each of which will have a spectacular effect:

> The Messiah son of David, Elijah, and Zerubbabel will climb to the top of the Mount of Olives, and the Messiah will command Elijah to blow the shofar. The light of the seven days of Creation will reappear, *and the light of the moon will be like the light of the sun* (Isaiah 30:26), and God will send complete healing to all the sick of Israel.
>
> The second blast blown by Elijah will resurrect the dead. They will rise from the dust, and each person will recognize his fellow. A man and his wife, a father and his son, one brother and another—all will come to the Messiah from the four corners of the earth, from east and west, from north and south. Upon the wings of an eagle the Israelites will fly and reach the Messiah. A pillar of fire will issue from the Temple, becoming a portent to all who see it, that they may know for certain that now the Temple has been firmly established.
>
> At the third blast blown by [Elijah], the glory of God will appear. At the fourth blast, the mountains will become a valley, and the face of the whole earth a plain. . . . The Temple will appear, as prophesied by Ezekiel.[87]

With his second shofar blast, Elijah will resurrect the dead. This role fits him, since he never died—but also because in his biblical phase he revived a widow's lifeless boy. That miracle, according to the Midrash, proves the possibility of resurrection: "God says, 'If someone tells you that the dead cannot come to life, tell him, "Look at Elijah! . . . [who] testifies that through him I have already revived the dead in this world—namely, the son of the woman of Zarephath."'"[88]

Despite his proven ability, when Elijah appears and announces himself, he may be tested by those longing to reunite with their loved ones:

> *At our door, all luscious fruit* (Song of Songs 7:14). Rabbi Yose said, "This alludes to Elijah, who will come and say to Israel, 'I am Elijah.'
>
> "They will say to him, 'If you are Elijah, revive the dead for us—not the dead whom we don't name, but rather the dead whom we name [i.e., whom we knew personally].'"[89]

Perhaps even the dead, but certainly the living, eagerly await Elijah's messianic return. But when will he come? As we have seen, even Elijah doesn't know the exact date. Still, a clue is provided by the Midrash, which guarantees that Israel's final redemption will take place on the anniversary of their original redemption from Egyptian slavery: the first night of Passover.

> On that [night], Messiah and Elijah will appear. . . . A parable. This may be compared to a woman awaiting her husband who crossed the ocean. He had told her, "Let this sign be in your possession. When you see this sign, know that I am coming, that I am about to arrive."
>
> So Israel has been awaiting [redemption] ever since Edom [i.e., the Roman Empire] came to power. The blessed Holy One said, "Let this sign be in your possession: On the day when I wrought salvation for you [on Passover in Egypt]—know that on that very night I will redeem you."[90]

The Passover timing of the messianic redemption helps to explain the most mysterious object on the seder table: the Cup of Elijah. In the course of the seder, it is hoped that the immortal prophet will appear at the front door, drink wine from his goblet, and announce the imminent arrival of the Messiah. As we will see, though, other elements contributed to the custom of preparing a cup for Elijah and opening the door to welcome him.

Although Passover would be an appropriate time for the final redemption, the general view is that Elijah could appear, heralding the Messiah, at any time—or nearly anytime. According to the Talmud, he will not arrive on Friday, so as not to bother people, since they are busily preparing for Shabbat![91]

Elijah and the Messiah are a team. The immortal prophet serves as *mevasser tov*, herald of goodness, paving the way for the redeemer:

> *The voice of my beloved, here it comes* (Song of Songs 2:8)—the voices that are destined to come before the Messiah.
>
> *Bounding over mountains, leaping over hills* (Song of Songs 2:8)—Elijah, of whom is said: *How lovely on the mountains the feet of the herald: announcing peace,* mevasser tov, *heralding goodness, announcing salvation* (Isaiah 52:7).[92]

Elijah carries out various preparatory tasks, after which the Messiah himself will gather the exiles, vanquish Israel's enemies, and rebuild the Temple. However, in some descriptions, Elijah fulfills what is normally the Messiah's task. Or the two figures merge—as in a late midrash, where Elijah is listed as one of the seven names of the Messiah, based on that final verse in the prophetic canon: *Look, I am sending to you Elijah the prophet before the coming of the day of YHVH* (Malachi 3:23).[93]

According to one prediction, Elijah himself will eventually overcome Israel's foes: "The blessed Holy One said, 'In this world I sent an angel before them, and he cut down the nations of the world; but in the world to come it is Elijah (gratefully remembered) whom I will send to you,' as is said: *Look, I am sending to you Elijah the prophet before the coming of the day of YHVH, great and awesome.*"[94]

The key prerequisite for Israel's redemption is *teshuvah* ("turning back" to God). After the murder of Naboth, the biblical Elijah stimulated Ahab to engage in *teshuvah*. In paving the way for the Messiah, he will motivate all of Israel to do so:

> Rabbi Yehudah says, "If Israel does not engage in *teshuvah*, they will not be redeemed; and Israel engages in *teshuvah* only

> out of distress, oppression, wandering, and lack of sustenance. Israel will not excel in *teshuvah* until Elijah (gratefully remembered) comes, as is said: *Look, I am sending to you Elijah the prophet before the coming of the day of YHVH, great and awesome;* ve-heshiv, *and he will bring back, fathers' hearts to their children and children's hearts to their fathers* (Malachi 3:23–24)."[95]

For Rabbi Yehudah, the word *ve-heshiv*, "and he will bring back," alludes to *teshuvah*, which Elijah will inspire Israel to achieve, thereby assuring their salvation.

ELIJAH AND MOSES

In his messianic role, Elijah resembles an earlier hero: "Moses redeemed [Israel] from Egypt . . . , and Elijah will redeem them in the time to come."[96] In fact, the two redeemers may make a joint appearance: "The blessed Holy One said to him, 'Moses, by your life! Just as you gave your soul for [the Israelites] in this world, so in the time to come, when I bring them Elijah the prophet, the two of you will appear together.'"[97]

The two prophets share numerous traits and experiences, nearly justifying the midrashic hyperbole, "You find that Moses and Elijah are equivalent in everything."[98] Both are *ish ha-Elohim*, "man of God."[99] At Mount Sinai, *Moses went up to God* (Exodus 19:3), while *Elijah went up in a whirlwind to heaven* (2 Kings 2:11). Moses fled from Pharaoh after killing an Egyptian, and Elijah fled from Jezebel after killing the prophets of Baal. Moses (with God's help) parted the Red Sea with his outstretched arm so that the Israelites could cross over on *dry ground* (Exodus 14:21), while Elijah parted the Jordan so that he and Elisha could cross on *dry ground* (2 Kings 2:8). Both were zealots—Moses ordering the Levites to kill many of the Israelites who worshiped the golden calf, and Elijah slaughtering the prophets of Baal. Both were in a cave (or crevice) at *the mountain of God* at Sinai (Horeb).[100] Moses spent forty days and forty nights on

Mount Sinai, while Elijah journeyed forty days and forty nights to the same site.[101] At Mount Sinai, Moses inspired Israel to declare, *All that YHVH has spoken we will do and we will heed* (Exodus 24:7), while on Mount Carmel, Elijah inspired Israel to declare, *YHVH, He is God; YHVH, He is God!* (1 Kings 18:39). At Sinai, Moses built an altar and erected *twelve pillars for the twelve tribes of Israel* (Exodus 24:4), while on Mount Carmel, Elijah built an altar of *twelve stones, corresponding to the number of the tribes* (1 Kings 18:31). Both—in moments of desperation due to the burdensome stubbornness of the Israelites—asked God to take their lives.[102] Both ended their earthbound lives in the same vicinity: east of the Jordan River, across from Jericho. Regarding Moses, *no man knows his burial place to this day* (Deuteronomy 34:6). As for Elijah's disappearance, among those who did not realize that he *went up in a whirlwind to heaven* (2 Kings 2:11), *fifty men . . . searched for three days but did not find him* (2 Kings 2:17).

But, of course, here lies one major difference between the two prophets. Whereas Moses died a natural death in sight of the promised land, Elijah, it is told, never died, but rather ascended to heaven in the fiery chariot and ever since has been returning intermittently to earth to help those in need. In this sense, Elijah surpassed Moses.

In a crucial way, however, Moses outshone Elijah. After Israel committed idolatry at Mount Sinai by worshiping the golden calf, God proposed exterminating the people entirely and forming a new nation from Moses's own descendants. However, Moses pleaded with God to spare Israel, saying: *Now, if You would bear their sin! And if not, please wipe me out of Your book that You have written* (Exodus 32:32). Whereas Moses offered to die in order to win forgiveness for Israel, Elijah despaired so deeply over his failure to eradicate the worship of Baal that he asked God to take his life: *He said, "Enough! Now, YHVH, take my life, for I am no better than my ancestors"* (1 Kings 19:4). Then, when he reached Horeb—the very place where Moses had defended and pleaded for his people—Elijah failed to imitate his model and instead accused Israel, complaining, *The Israelites have forsaken Your covenant . . . , and I alone remain, and they have sought to take my life*" (1 Kings 19:10).[103]

Moses was rewarded with divine intimacy, whereas Elijah was relieved of his prophetic duties for failing to defend Israel. The contrast between the two is displayed by juxtaposing God's words to each of them at Mount Horeb (Sinai): "In one matter, we find that Moses surpassed Elijah. For to Moses, [God] said, *And you, stand here with Me* (Deuteronomy 5:28); whereas to Elijah He said, *What are you doing here, Elijah?* (1 Kings 19:9)."[104] Now the rhetorical question implies, "Why have you deserted your mission and abandoned your people?" Consequently, Elijah is, roughly speaking, fired.[105]

ELIJAH AND JONAH

If Elijah is linked to Moses, he also shares several elements with another biblical prophet: Jonah. Elijah fled from Jezebel, abandoning his prophetic mission, while Jonah fled before his mission even began. God had commanded him to go to Nineveh, the capital of the Assyrian Empire, *and call out against it, for their evil has risen before Me* (Jonah 1:2). Immediately Jonah sailed off in the opposite direction—out of fear of the Assyrian enemy, or perhaps because he foresaw that the Ninevites would repent and that God would forgive them.

Eventually, after spending three harrowing days and nights in the belly of a whale (or great fish), Jonah delivered the divine chastisement to Nineveh, and sure enough, the residents repented and were forgiven by God the compassionate. Jonah became so upset and angry that he prayed, *Now, YHVH, please take my life, for I would rather die than live* (Jonah 4:3). As we recall, when Elijah fled, he too *wished that he might die. He said,*

"Enough! Now, YHVH, take my life, for I am no better than my ancestors" (1 Kings 19:4).[106]

Elijah is criticized by the rabbis for his lack of compassion for Israel; Jonah is criticized by God for lacking compassion for the Ninevites.

Beyond these parallels, the two prophets were more intimately connected—at least according to one tradition, which claims that Jonah was none other than the son of the widow of Zarephath, miraculously revived by Elijah. The little boy whom Elijah saved grew up to become a prophet himself. No wonder that he shared not only his savior's prophetic gift but also some of his faults.[107]

Cryptically, the *Zohar* alludes to the identification of Jonah with the revived child by interpreting the biblical verse *Who has gone up to heaven and come down?* (Proverbs 30:4): "*Who has gone up to heaven?* Elijah. *And come down*—Jonah, who descended to the abyss, to the depths of the sea. Jonah derived from the power of Elijah. Elijah ascended, Jonah descended. One prayed that he might die, and the other prayed that he might die. So he is called *son of Amittai* (Jonah 1:1), and it is written: *The word of YHVH in your mouth is* emet, *truth* (1 Kings 17:24)."[108]

The *Zohar* connects Jonah's full name—*Jonah son of Amittai*—with the final word spoken by the grateful mother to Elijah after he hands her revived son back to her: *Now I know that you are a man of God and that the word of YHVH in your mouth is* emet, *truth*. Since Elijah brought little Jonah back to life, he assumed the role of Jonah's father, and the opening verse of Jonah's book now implies that *Jonah* was *son of Amittai* (*the True One*), son of Elijah.

Elijah shares his messianic role with the revived child, since this child is identified as Messiah son of Joseph, who will precede Messiah son of David, who will himself be heralded by Elijah. Since the child was understood to be Jonah, the latter likewise became associated with Messiah son of Joseph.[109] Similarly, in Christianity, Jonah became the archetype of Jesus. Just as Jonah was spewed out of the fish after three days, so Jesus was cast forth from his tomb and resurrected after three days.[110] Later we will explore the close relationship between Elijah and Jesus.

"PHINEHAS IS ELIJAH"

If Elijah is linked to Moses and Jonah, he is more closely linked with Phinehas, grandson of Aaron the high priest. Elijah and Phinehas are the two great zealots of the Hebrew Bible, each fighting ruthlessly to extirpate idolatry and champion the sole divinity of YHVH.

For both, pious zeal becomes violent. After defeating the prophets of Baal on Mount Carmel, Elijah slaughtered all 450 of them. Later, after delivering a prophetic message of doom to King Ahaziah, he confronted a hundred royal troops who had been sent to apprehend him. Calling down fire from heaven, he burned them all up.[111]

As for Phinehas, he acted zealously when Israel strayed and worshiped the heathen god Baal Peor (meaning "the Baal venerated at Peor"), related to the Canaanite Baal. This was Israel's first encounter with Baal, several hundred years before Elijah's contest on Mount Carmel. The scandal occurred at Israel's final stop on their forty-year trek through the wilderness of Sinai—at Abel Shittim (Brook of the Acacias), close to the Jordan River, as they verged on entering the promised land. There, many of the Israelite men went *whoring with the daughters of Moab* (Numbers 25:1) and worshiped Baal Peor. God's anger flared against the people, and He inflicted a plague upon them. In the midst of the plague, Phinehas saw a tribal Israelite chieftain fornicating with a Midianite princess. Fueled by righteous zeal, Phinehas killed the sinning couple by stabbing them both with a spear, and the plague ceased.

By taking the law into his own hands and killing impulsively, Phinehas set a dangerous precedent. According to one tradition, Moses and others sought to excommunicate Phinehas, but God prevented them by immediately praising His zealot:

> *YHVH spoke to Moses, saying, "Phinehas son of Eleazar son of Aaron the priest turned away My wrath from the Israelites by zealously enacting My zeal in their midst, so I did not annihilate the Israelites by My zeal. Therefore say: I hereby grant him My covenant of peace. And it shall be for him and for his seed after him a covenant of eternal* [or, *perpetual*] *priesthood in recompense for his acting zealously for his God and atoning for the Israelites."* (Numbers 25:10–13)[112]

The doublet describing Phinehas's act—*be-qan'o et qin'ati*, "by zealously enacting My zeal"—resembles the doublet employed by Elijah: Qanno qinneiti, *I have been so zealous, for YHVH, God of Hosts, for the Israelites have forsaken Your covenant* (1 Kings 19:10, 14). Nowhere else in the Bible is this root duplicated in a single phrase; no one was as zealous as Elijah and Phinehas, each an extremist in restoring Israel's heart to God.

The connection between the two zealots eventually yielded a saying: *Pinḥas hu Eliyyahu*, "Phinehas is Elijah."[113] This wording could simply indicate their shared defining trait: they were both so zealous that they were virtually identical.

Or might there be a mystical explanation—that Elijah was a reincarnation of Phinehas? Some have thought so, but the concept of reincarnation was unknown to Jews before medieval times, whereas the identity of Phinehas and Elijah is attested as early as the first century CE. No, their psychological affinity did not result from Phinehas's soul transmigrating into the body of Elijah. The situation is simpler and yet stranger. The saying "Phinehas is Elijah" means that they were actually the same person!

Given biblical chronology, this is far-fetched. Phinehas was likely born toward the end of the thirteenth century BCE, whereas Elijah appeared nearly four hundred years later. And yet, the life of Phinehas was unusually long. After everyone else in his generation had died, he was still on the scene. In the words of the *Zohar*, "He was privileged to exist longer than all those who came out of Egypt."[114] Toward the end of the book of Joshua (22:13–34), Phinehas appears as a zealous priest. Subsequently during the period of the Judges, he officiated at the national shrine of Shiloh: *Phinehas son of Eleazar son of Aaron was ministering before Him in those days* (Judges 20:28). According to the chronology of the early historical work *Seder Olam*, he prophesied to Israel at least 188 years after they entered the promised land.[115] On the basis of these biblical and rabbinic traditions, several medieval commentators reckoned that Phinehas lived for more than 300 years.[116]

If, in the Jewish imagination, Phinehas lived for centuries, then perhaps he never died. After all, the Bible never records his death.[117] Meanwhile, it also never records the birth of Elijah, who appears for the first time suddenly, fully grown, confronting King Ahab. Conceivably, in the ninth century BCE, the quite elderly Phinehas adopted a new name—Elijah—and the two zealots share a single, immortal personality.[118]

As we have seen, Elijah's ascent to heaven in a fiery chariot was interpreted to mean that he never died. With a little creativity, Phinehas's immortality, too, could be certified by a biblical prooftext. Recall God's reward for Phinehas's zealous act: *I hereby grant him My covenant of peace. And it shall be for him and for his seed after him a covenant of* kehunnat olam, *eternal* [or, *perpetual*] *priesthood, in recompense for his acting zealously for his God and atoning for the Israelites* (Numbers 25:13). The simple meaning of *eternal priesthood* is that Phinehas's descendants would inherit his role endlessly, but the phrase might imply that Phinehas himself would be priest forever. Like Elijah, he is described in rabbinic sources as "still existing."[119]

The earliest reference to the identity of Phinehas and Elijah appears around 100 CE in *Biblical Antiquities*, an anonymous retelling of parts of the Hebrew Bible.[120] The startling notion that "Phinehas is Elijah" is never stated explicitly in the Talmud nor in early midrashic literature and seems to have been suppressed. Yet it must have been widespread, since several of the early church fathers refer to it as a Jewish tradition. At the beginning of the third century, Origen writes that the Hebrews "conceived Phinehas and Elijah to be the same person, whether they judged soundly in this or not."[121]

An explicit identification of the two-as-one appears in *Targum Yerushalmi* (an Aramaic paraphrase of the Torah), where we read that Aaron's grandfather, Kohath, lived long enough to see his great-great-grandson "Phinehas, who is Elijah the high priest, who is destined to be sent to the diaspora of Israel at the end of days."[122] According to one view, Elijah was descended from the tribe of Levi, and in various sources he appears as a priest or high priest, which matches the tradition that Elijah and Phinehas are one and the same.[123]

As an immortal figure, Phinehas the high priest continually expiates the sins of Israel. In the words of an early midrash, likely alluding to his identity with Elijah: "Until now [Phinehas] has not budged. Rather, he continues atoning [for Israel] until the dead will be revived."[124] A later midrashic fragment states explicitly: "*Hu Pinḥas hu Eliyyahu*, Phinehas is none other than Elijah (gratefully and blessedly remembered). Were it not for him, we would have no existence in wicked Edom [i.e., among Israel's oppressors]. That is what our rabbis have said: 'Ever since the Temple was destroyed, he offers two sacrifices daily to atone for Israel, and on their skins he records the deeds of every single day.'"[125]

One could say, then, that Phinehas and Elijah are different in name only—as is stated explicitly in another midrash: "The blessed Holy One turned Phinehas's name into Elijah (gratefully remembered)."[126] Another passage in the same work simply assumes that the two are identical:

> The blessed Holy One revealed Himself to [Elijah] and said, "*What are you doing here, Elijah?*"
>
> He replied, "Qanno qinneiti, *I have been so zealous, [for YHVH, God of Hosts, for the Israelites have forsaken Your covenant . . .]*" (1 Kings 19:9–10).
>
> The blessed Holy One said to him, "You are always zealous! You were zealous in Shittim on account of fornication, as is said: *Phinehas son of Eleazar [son of Aaron the priest turned away My wrath from the Israelites* be-qan'o et qin'ati, *by zealously enacting My zeal, in their midst, so I did not annihilate the Israelites by My zeal]* (Numbers 25:11). And here too you are zealous. By your life! Israel shall not enact the covenant of circumcision until you see it with your eyes."
>
> Because of this, the Sages instituted the practice of preparing a seat of honor for the Angel of the Covenant [identified with Elijah], as is said: *And the angel of the covenant, whom you desire—behold, he is coming!* (Malachi 3:1).[127]

Elijah—who accused Israel of forsaking the covenant—will now appear at every ritual circumcision to witness the fact that Israel *keeps* the covenant: the covenant of circumcision. The phrase "preparing a seat of honor" refers to the custom of arranging a special chair at the circumcision, known as the Chair of Elijah, which we will later discuss.

The author of this midrash felt no need to explain that "Phinehas is Elijah," which shows that this notion was familiar to his readers. In the Middle Ages, it was widely accepted, although several authorities did not hesitate to reject the wild idea. The rationalistic biblical commentator Abraham ibn Ezra remarked simply, "[Phinehas] is not Elijah at all!" Another scholar wrote acerbically, "Whoever says 'Phinehas son of Eleazar is Elijah' is devoted to lies. . . . Phinehas is not Elijah."[128]

Yet despite the implausibility of Phinehas being Elijah, their fusion into a single personality makes psychological, if not historical, sense. The two biblical heroes share a covenantal zeal, which characterizes and defines them. For Elijah, this identification with a figure from the past demonstrates his timelessness and the elasticity of his nature.

Given his multiple identities, who is Elijah? And what does it mean to encounter him? The answers unfold further as the perennial prophet evolves in mystical Judaism, to which we now turn.

3

Inspiring the Mystics: Elijah in the Kabbalah

Already in talmudic times, Elijah began visiting worthy sages, exploring Torah with them and occasionally conveying what he had heard in the Heavenly Academy, of which he was an esteemed member. In Kabbalah, Elijah develops into a mystagogue, initiating seekers into the orchard of wisdom.

If he is to be trusted as a guide to wisdom, it is important to know who *his* teacher was. According to one tradition, it was none other than Moses.[1] This may mean not that Elijah was literally Moses's student, but that he received and passed on the Torah of Moses. The literal sense seems chronologically impossible, unless one accepts the fanciful notion we have just discussed—that Elijah is identical with Phinehas, grandson of Aaron and thus Moses's grandnephew, whom Moses could plausibly have tutored.

A more likely candidate for the role of Elijah's teacher is mentioned in the Talmud: Ahijah of Shiloh, the great prophet of the preceding generation, famous for announcing that Solomon's kingdom would be split.[2] Ahijah and Elijah can be imagined as two vital, consecutive links in the chain of tradition extending back to Moses, which is how Maimonides described them:

> Although the Oral Torah was not written, Moses our Rabbi taught all of it in his court to the seventy elders. . . . To Joshua, his servant, Moses transmitted the Oral Torah and instructed him on it. . . . Many elders learned from Joshua, and Eli [the high priest] received from the Elders . . . , and Samuel received from Eli . . . , and David received from Samuel . . . , and Ahijah of Shiloh was among those who left Egypt, and he was a Levite, and he heard from Moses—being young in the days of Moses—and he received from David . . . , and Elijah received from Ahijah of Shiloh . . . , and Elisha received from Elijah.[3]

Ahijah, Elijah's mentor, is pictured as a master of the inner meaning of Torah and as one who immersed himself in secret wisdom, specifically in the mysteries of the divine chariot described by Ezekiel (although Ahijah preceded Ezekiel by several centuries).[4] The image of Ezekiel's fiery chariot evokes Elijah's chariot of fire, in which he flew off to heaven, and the rabbinic imagination links the two celestial vehicles. According to the book of Kings, immediately before the chariot appeared, Elijah and his disciple, Elisha, *went along, walking and talking*. But what were they talking about? Well, the two prophets must have been discussing Torah, and various talmudic rabbis speculate about the topic they were exploring in their final conversation:

> One should not take leave of his friend by chatter or laughter or frivolity or idle talk, but rather by a word of Torah. . . . Elijah, too, took leave of Elisha only by a word of Torah: *As they went along, walking and talking, [suddenly a chariot of fire and horses of fire appeared, separating the two of them, and Elijah went up in a whirlwind to heaven]* (2 Kings 2:11).

In what were they engaged? Rabbi Aḥava son of Rabbi Ze'eira said, "They were engaged in [discussing] the recitation of the *Shema*. . . ."

Rabbi Yehudah son of Pazi said, "They were engaged in [discussing] the creation of the world. . . ."

Rabbi Yudan son of Rabbi Aibu said, "They were engaged in the consolations over [the destruction of] Jerusalem. . . ."

And our rabbis say, "They were engaged in [discussing] the chariot [of Ezekiel], as is said: *suddenly a chariot of fire and horses of fire appeared*. . . ."[5]

By exploring the theme of the divine chariot with his disciple, perhaps Elijah conjured up another chariot, which then transported him above. Unlike his disciple (Elisha) and his teacher (Ahijah), he became more than a link in the chain of tradition. Based in heaven and able to manifest anywhere, Elijah gradually turned into a source of revelation for spiritual seekers, fueling the growth of Kabbalah. Literally, Kabbalah means "receiving," hence "that which has been received," or the esoteric "tradition." For the kabbalists, Elijah is the one who conveys this secret wisdom.

GILLUI ELIYYAHU: A REVELATION OF ELIJAH

Several of the earliest kabbalists reportedly experienced *gillui Eliyyahu*, "a revelation (or apparition) of Elijah," an epiphany of Elijah. According to one account, Elijah revealed certain secrets to the twelfth-century talmudist Abraham ben Isaac of Narbonne, who revealed them to his son-in-law, the Rabad, Abraham ben David of Posquières. The Rabad, who began disseminating Kabbalah in Provence, revealed these secrets to his son, Isaac the Blind, who has been called "the father of Kabbalah."

In another version of the chain of transmission, Elijah revealed the secrets to Jacob ha-Nazir (the Nazirite), one of a group of kabbalistic hermits in Provence, who transmitted them to the Rabad, who in turn passed them on to Isaac the Blind. In all the early accounts of this chain, Elijah is the source.[6]

Kabbalah is boldly innovative yet staunchly traditional. Its formulations are a blend of what the *Zohar* calls "new-ancient words." If a kabbalist discovered new meaning in an ancient verse or prayer, was this his own invention or had he experienced some type of revelation from above? According to an early rabbinic text, "With the death of the last [biblical] prophets—Haggai, Zechariah, and Malachi—the Holy Spirit ceased from Israel. Even so, [prophetic revelation] was conveyed to them by means of a heavenly echo." Nearby, the same text associates Elijah, in particular, with the Holy Spirit: "Until Elijah was hidden away [i.e., taken to heaven], the Holy Spirit was widespread in Israel. Once Elijah was hidden away, it disappeared from them." The presence of Elijah guaranteed the manifestation of the Holy Spirit throughout his biblical lifetime—so much so that according to one sage, the number of prophets in the days of Elijah surpassed one million.[7]

If Elijah's being "hidden away" in heaven signified the removal of the Holy Spirit, his eventual reappearance to usher in the Messiah will signal the spirit's return:

> *I lie down and I sleep.* [*I awake, for YHVH has sustained me*] (Psalms 3:6). The Assembly of Israel said, "*I lie down*—deprived of prophecy. *And I sleep*—deprived of the Holy Spirit.
>
> "*I awake*—through Elijah, as is said: *Look, I am sending to you Elijah the prophet* [*before the coming of the day of YHVH, great and awesome*] (Malachi 3:23). *For YHVH has sustained me*—through King Messiah."[8]

How long would it be until Elijah returned? An early tradition insisted that he would remain concealed in heaven "until the Messiah arrives."[9] But as we have seen, the Talmud and Midrash contradict this statement, portraying an Elijah who is much more outgoing, manifesting himself to various rabbis. Awakening the worthy in this benighted, unredeemed era, Elijah conveys a measure of the Holy Spirit. He enacts that spirit.

By the Middle Ages, the notion of *gillui Eliyyahu* was familiar to anyone acquainted with rabbinic literature. The assertion that the founders of Kabbalah experienced "a revelation of Elijah" implied two claims simultaneously: a new teaching had suddenly emerged, and this newly disclosed secret was rooted in sacred tradition. The prophet Elijah, guardian of that tradition, would never reveal anything controverting or undermining it. If an innovative teaching came from Elijah, it was automatically acceptable and beyond any suspicion of foreign influence or heresy. The phenomenon of *gillui Eliyyahu* shows how Kabbalah combines conservative and novel tendencies.[10]

The earliest kabbalistic testimonies about "a revelation of Elijah" do not record the prophet's specific words, but they appear in texts discussing *kavvanah*, mystical "intention" or meditation during prayer.[11] On this topic, who could be a more reliable authority than Elijah, the Master of Prayer? After all, by imploring God, he revived the child of the widow of Zarephath; and later, on Mount Carmel he called forth fire from heaven. Soon after the fire consumed the sacrificial offering, *Elijah went up to the top of Carmel* to pray for rain. There, *he crouched on the ground, and put his face between his knees* (1 Kings 18:42)—a meditative pose that eventually became a technique for attaining mystical vision.[12]

When a kabbalist encounters Elijah, is he meeting the genuine eternal prophet or imagining him in his mind? According to Moses Cordovero (in the sixteenth century), the two possibilities are not distinct:

> Sometimes Elijah clothes himself in a person's mind, revealing to him hidden matters. To the person, it seems as if he pondered those things on his own, as if that innovation sud-

> denly entered his mind. This may relate to matters of Torah or to worldly matters, with [Elijah] informing him what will happen and what will not happen. This comes in a concealed manner. The person feels a certain heaviness in the head but no ringing in the ears . . . ; it feels as if he said it himself.[13]

Cordovero's view is shared by his contemporary, Judah Loew ben Bezalel (the Maharal of Prague). Discussing a talmudic story in which Rabbi Yehoshu'a son of Levi meets Elijah, the Maharal writes: "It makes no difference whether [Elijah] was revealed to [Rabbi Yehoshu'a son of Levi] in a vision or whether he was revealed as such, not in a vision. For frequently Elijah would speak words to someone, and that person did not know where they came from. It seemed to him as if those words came from himself—but they were the words of Elijah, speaking to him."[14]

The encounter with Elijah takes place deep within. In the words of Abraham Joshua Heschel, it is "an inner experience, a fact in the soul, a rung that the treasured few believed they attained."[15]

Whereas some kabbalists convey the interior quality of the experience, others describe journeying with Elijah to destinations both earthly and celestial. In the preface to *Sefer ha-Peli'ah* (a mystical interpretation of the biblical account of creation), the author reports that Elijah appeared to him in the form of an old man, led him to a house of study and then to a certain "holy place":

> Immediately fire issued from heaven and surrounded me, and [Elijah] studied with me the Torah of truth, the Torah of love. He sat with me for many days and I learned much from him. Every time he would ask, "Do you understand these words of mine, my son?" And when I didn't understand, he would clarify and explain for me.
>
> One time he led me to the cave of Machpelah [the tomb

of the patriarchs], to Abraham, Isaac, and Jacob, and from there he led me to the Heavenly Academy. . . . A very great trembling seized me, and I asked Elijah to bring me down from there, and he immediately did so. . . .

My soul nearly flew away, when Elijah came and told me, "Do not fear. Return to your studies." And he learned with me all the hidden secrets of creation . . . and the *mitsvot* and the intimations of the *mitsvot* . . . , according to how these were explained in the Heavenly Academy. . . . Regarding every single statement, Elijah would ask me if I understood.[16]

"HE IS OF A DIFFERENT NATURE": ELIJAH IN THE *ZOHAR*

In the *Zohar*, the masterpiece of Kabbalah, Elijah develops a relationship with the hero of the work, Rabbi Shim'on son of Yoḥai, the famous *tanna* of the second century who lived in the land of Israel. Already in a talmudic story about Rabbi Shim'on, Elijah makes a cameo appearance. The rabbi had criticized the Roman occupiers of the Holy Land, and after an informant relayed his words to the authorities, Rabbi Shim'on was sentenced to death:

> [Rabbi Shim'on and his son Rabbi El'azar] went and hid in a cave. A miracle occurred: a carob tree and a spring of water were created for them. They undressed and sat up to their necks in sand [so as not to be naked]. All day long they studied; when it was time for prayer they dressed, covered themselves, and prayed; and then they undressed again, so that [their clothes] would not wear out. For twelve years they dwelled in the cave.
>
> Then Elijah came and stood at the mouth of the cave. He said, "Who will inform the son of Yoḥai that the emperor is dead and his decree has been nullified?" [Rabbi Shim'on and his son] emerged.[17]

Elijah reveals that Rabbi Shim'on is free to leave the cave, but there is no further communication between the two. However, when the *Zohar* retells this tale, Elijah becomes more involved: "Rabbi Shim'on son of Yoḥai fled to the wilderness of Lydda and hid in a cave—he and his son, Rabbi El'azar. A miracle was performed for them: a carob tree sprouted up and a spring of water gushed forth. They ate from that carob tree and drank from those waters. Elijah (gratefully remembered) visited them twice a day and taught them, and no one else knew."[18]

Elijah, we recall, was also fed miraculously while in hiding, after he confronted King Ahab and declared that there would be no rain (1 Kings 17:1–6). A few years later, after slaughtering the prophets of Baal, Elijah fled Queen Jezebel's wrath and was again miraculously fed and then spent a night in a cave on Mount Horeb (1 Kings 19:1–9). Some medieval writers claimed that Elijah's cave and Rabbi Shim'on's cave were one and the same.[19] In any case, the author of the *Zohar* could not imagine that Elijah would appear at Rabbi Shim'on's cave without enlightening him with words of Torah. Soon after the *Zohar* appeared in Spain in the thirteenth century, it was claimed that long ago Rabbi Shim'on composed the masterpiece in that cave, inspired by Elijah.[20]

Actually, most of the *Zohar*'s narrative unfolds outside of any cave, often in the Galilean countryside. Occasionally, Rabbi Shim'on or one of his *ḥavrayya* (companions) encounters Elijah, who reveals secrets:

> Rabbi Shim'on wept and paused for a moment. Then he said, ". . . This mystery was only revealed one day when I was at the seashore. Elijah came and . . . said to me, 'Rabbi, the word was concealed with the blessed Holy One, and He revealed it in the Academy on High. Here it is. . . .' Then Elijah flew off."[21]

> Rabbi Pinḥas said, "Once I was walking on the way and I encountered Elijah. I said to him, 'May my master tell me a word that will benefit creatures.'"[22]

Sometimes, Elijah is invoked without any narrative structure: "This is lucidity of the matter, and so did the Holy Lamp [i.e., Rabbi Shim'on] learn it from Elijah."[23] But Elijah also learns from Rabbi Shim'on, as in the following account: "Rabbi Shim'on was traveling to Tiberias, and he encountered Elijah. [Rabbi Shim'on] said to him, 'Greetings, Master. What is the blessed Holy One engaged with in heaven?'" In asking this question, Rabbi Shim'on seeks to know what topic God is discussing in the Heavenly Academy.[24] Elijah responds that God is engaged in the topic of sacrificial offerings. However, a certain question on this topic cannot be resolved in the academy, and God has asked Elijah to come to Rabbi Shim'on for the solution. After Rabbi Shim'on provides the answer, "[Elijah] said to him, 'Rabbi, by your life! This very thing the blessed Holy One wished to say, but in order not to take credit for Himself . . . , He consigned it to you. Happy are you in the world, for your Lord prides Himself on you above!'"[25]

Although Elijah does not appear very frequently in the narrative portions of the main body of the *Zohar*, his unique nature and personality are discussed. While adopting the rabbinic view that Elijah never died, the *Zohar* wonders how a physical being can possibly abide in heaven. Rabbi Shim'on answers this question by invoking the theme of the garment, which pertains both to Elijah ascending in the fiery chariot and to Moses ascending Mount Sinai:

> *Who has gone up to heaven?* (Proverbs 30:4). They have established: this is Moses, as is written: *To Moses He said, "Go up to YHVH"* (Exodus 24:1). However, *Who has gone up to heaven?* Elijah, of whom is written *Elijah went up in a whirlwind to heaven* (2 Kings 2:11). Now, how could Elijah go up to heaven, when all the heavens cannot bear even as much as a mustard seed of a body of this world? Yet you say, *Elijah went up in a whirlwind to heaven!*

> However, like this: *YHVH came down upon Mount Sinai* (Exodus 19:20), and it is written *Moses entered within the cloud and went up the mountain* (Exodus 24:18). Now, the blessed Holy One was on Mount Sinai, and it is written *The sight of YHVH's glory was like consuming fire at the mountaintop* (Exodus 24:17); so how could Moses ascend to Him? Well, of Moses is written *Moses entered within the cloud*—entering the cloud as one dons a garment; thus he donned the cloud, entering it. In the cloud he approached the fire and was able to draw near. Similarly, of Elijah is written *Elijah went up in a whirlwind*—entering that whirlwind and donning it and thereby ascending.[26]

Just as Moses ascended Mount Sinai within the protective covering of the cloud, so Elijah ascended to heaven within a whirlwind. Yet Elijah's garment also explains his ability to descend again and appear on earth, as Rabbi Shim'on explains:

> I found a secret in the Book of Adam describing the generations of the world: "There will be a spirit that will descend to the world, on earth, and will don a body, and Elijah is his name. In that body he will ascend, and his body will persist and remain in the whirlwind, and another body—of light—will be prepared for him to be among the angels.
>
> "When he descends, he will don that body remaining in the whirlwind, and in that body he will manifest below, while in the other body he will manifest above."
>
> This is the mystery of *has gone up to heaven and come down* (Proverbs 30:4). There has never been a human whose spirit has gone up to heaven and afterwards come down except Elijah, for this is the one who ascended and descended.[27]

Originally, Elijah's spirit descended to earth and was clothed in a human body. At the end of his earthly life, when he ascended in the chariot of fire, his body remained suspended in the whirlwind, while his spirit donned a body of light, in which

Elijah entered the company of the angels. Whenever necessary, Elijah descends again, clothing himself in the body preserved in the whirlwind, in order to carry out missions here below.

The notion that Elijah became an angel accords with rabbinic tradition, but the *Zohar* alludes to a more radical view: Elijah was *originally* an angel, even before his biblical phase. He is "not from the aspect of father and mother."[28] The fact that the Bible does not mention Elijah's parents now implies that he *had* no human parents. Nor, according to a different passage, did he have a son:

> One day, Rabbi Natan asked Rabbi Yose son of Rabbi Ḥanina, "Did Elijah have a son?"
>
> He replied, "He is of a different nature altogether . . ." . . .
>
> Rabbi El'azar said in the name of Rabbi Shim'on, "*Who has gone up to heaven and come down?* (Proverbs 30:4). Elijah. *And come down*—previously. So he is of a different nature."[29]

Not only does Elijah *come down* to earth continually after having ascended to heaven in the chariot; he had already *come down* "previously" from his original celestial abode, becoming clothed in human form in the time of King Ahab. He was an angel to begin with, and his ascent was simply a return to his unique angelic status.

Elijah's heavenly background is explored further by the main composer of the *Zohar*, Moses de León, in his remarkable kabbalistic responsa:

> In the Secrets of Torah I have seen a great, extremely wondrous secret: You will not find any mention of Elijah's father or mother in the entire Bible, nor is he described as "son of so-and-so," but rather *Elijah the Tishbite, of the inhabitants of Gilead* (1 Kings 17:1). They have said that previously he descended from heaven, and he was an angel, and his name is known in the Secrets of Torah.[30]
>
> Furthermore, afterward he appeared to the Sages in

> many places and in many forms: sometimes as a wandering Arab, sometimes as a horseman, sometimes as one of the leaders of the generation—his form and appearance being manifold. So do not be surprised by this notion that Elijah occupies a higher rung than all other human beings.

Moses de León proceeds to explain that Elijah was one of the angels whom God consulted during creation:

> They have said that when the blessed Holy One sought to create a human being, He said to the angels, "*Let us make a human*" (Genesis 1:26).
>
> They replied, "Master of the Universe, *What is a human that You are mindful of him?*" (Psalms 8:5).
>
> He stretched out His little finger against them, and they were burned up. He called upon another cohort [of angels], who responded similarly; and He stretched out His finger against them, and they were burned up.
>
> Finally He called upon so-and-so and his cohort, and He said to him, "*Let us make a human.*"
>
> [So-and-so] replied, "Master of the Universe, for You it is fine; for us, all the more so! If it is acceptable in Your eyes, I will descend and serve him."
>
> The blessed Holy One said to him, "From now on, your name will no longer be so-and-so, but rather so-and-so."
>
> Although he did not descend at that time, later he did. In the time of [King] Ahab, he spread throughout the world the belief that *YHVH, He is God* (1 Kings 18:39). Shortly afterward, the Omnipresent raised him to the heavenly heights.[31]

The notion that Elijah was originally—and not just eventually—an angel was too extreme for some kabbalists, despite the allusions to this idea in the *Zohar*, the canonical text of Kabbalah. After quoting Moses de León's "wondrous secret," Moses Cordovero criticizes it: "All the sages of the Talmud . . . argued only about which tribe [Elijah] belonged to, but to say that he was [originally] an angel who [in the days of King Ahab] assumed bodily form—no one would agree with this."[32]

Cordovero fully accepts Elijah's angelic destiny, but he refuses to surrender the prophet's human roots. As for the *Zohar*, despite its occasional hints at Elijah's angelic origin, elsewhere it assumes that Elijah was born human and became an angel only after ascending in the fiery chariot. Still, Elijah's soul is exceptional. All human souls are engendered by the union of the divine couple, the masculine *Tif'eret* and the feminine *Shekhinah*. In Elijah's case, his soul issued at a moment when the divine husband—*Tif'eret* (symbolized by the Tree of Life)—was especially potent:

> When desire of Male issues passionately, those souls are of greater vitality, suffused with passionate desire of the Tree of Life. Elijah was vitalized by that passion more than other humans. . . . Because he was on the side of Male more than all other inhabitants of the world, he endured more vitally and did not die like all others, for he derived entirely from the Tree of Life, not from dust. So he ascended and did not die according to the way of all the earth, as is written: *Elijah went up in a whirlwind to heaven* (2 Kings 2:11).
>
> Come and see what is written: *suddenly a chariot of fire and horses of fire appeared [separating the two of them]* . . . (2 Kings 2:11)—for then body was stripped from spirit, and he ascended, unlike the rest of the earth, and endured as a holy angel, like other holy supernal beings. He carries out missions in the world, as has been established, for miracles performed in the world by the blessed Holy One are performed by him.[33]

Imbued with the streaming energy of the Tree of Life, "Elijah was vitalized," so he never died. He became pure spirit, transformed into an angel. But that excess of masculinity also generated Elijah's zealotry, fueling it throughout his fierce biblical career.

As we have seen, when God asks the prophet on Mount Horeb, *What are you doing here, Elijah?*, he replies: *I have been so zealous for YHVH, God of Hosts, for the Israelites have forsaken Your covenant—Your altars they have destroyed, Your prophets they have killed by the sword, and I alone remain, and they have sought to take my life* (1 Kings 19:13–14). According to this same *Zohar* passage, God responds: "How long will you be zealous for Me? You have locked the door so that death has no dominion over you, and the world cannot endure you along with human beings. . . . *Elisha son of Shaphat from Abel-meholah you shall anoint as prophet in your place* (1 Kings 19:16)—here is another prophet for My children. As for you, ascend to your site!'"[34]

God acknowledges that Elijah has "locked the door" against death, attaining immortality and barring the Angel of Death from attacking him. But his endless existence poses a threat to humanity, who cannot bear Elijah's zeal. Consequently, he must be replaced by Elisha, a more tolerable prophet. In the Midrash, this replacement signifies that Elijah is being rejected because of his zealotry. Here, however, the tone is ambivalent. Since Elijah's zeal is incompatible with human society, he must leave earth and ascend to the only place fitting for him, joining the angels in heaven.[35]

Elsewhere in the *Zohar*, God criticizes Elijah for not acting like Moses did when Israel sinned by worshiping the golden calf. Instead of accusing the people of abandoning the covenant, Elijah should have felt compassion and pleaded with God for them, as Moses did, saving the people from divine wrath:

> [God] said to Elijah, "This is what you should have done! What's more, you should have realized that they are My children—My beloved children who accepted My Torah at Mount Horeb!" . . .
>
> Elijah did not depart from there until he swore before the blessed Holy One that he would always advocate the merits of Israel. Whenever someone performs a meritorious

> act, he is the first to say before the blessed Holy One, "So-and-so did such and such!" He does not budge until that person's merit is recorded.[36]

Elijah responds to God's critique by promising to change. The harsh chastiser commits himself, from now on, to mend his ways.

"THROUGH THE TWO OF US": ELIJAH AND RABBI SHIM'ON

In the main body of the *Zohar*, Elijah interacts occasionally with Rabbi Shim'on and his companions. However, in the *Zohar*'s commentary on the Song of Songs, Rabbi Shim'on and Elijah are constant companions. Together they explore the opening verses of this biblical love song, revealing its mystical meaning. The scriptural lover and beloved (who are alternately together and apart) allude to the divine couple—*Shekhinah* and the blessed Holy One—who at times unite and at times separate.

In the Song of Songs, the lovers are in dialogue, so fittingly the Song's secret sense emerges only through further dialogue. Rabbi Shim'on interprets a verse, and Elijah responds with an alternative meaning:

> Elijah said to him, "Rabbi, utter your words and I will follow you, for through the two of us the matter will be clarified! Permission has been granted to us from the Most Ancient of All that these mysteries be revealed from below and above—you for those below and I for those above.
>
> "By your life, Rabbi! Your stature is superior, for all your words will be inscribed above before the Ancient of Days, whereas my words will not be inscribed above but only in this world by your hand. Your words will be inscribed above and my words below."[37]

Elijah predicts that his words will be recorded on earth by Rabbi Shim'on, which reflects the prophet's role of revealing secrets to the kabbalists. His authority is stamped at the beginning of each of his six long teachings: "Decreed by the mouth of Elijah."[38] Whereas Elijah decrees his words, Rabbi Shim'on simply speaks: "Rabbi Shim'on opened, saying. . . ." Yet remarkably, Elijah swears that the earthbound rabbi's innovations are more elevated than his own! They "will be inscribed above before the Ancient of Days." Elijah is not just praising Rabbi Shim'on; he's stimulating his partner's creativity: "Elijah said to him, 'Rabbi, open your mouth and let your words shine! For permission from above has been granted to you.'"[39]

Like the lovers in the Song of Songs, Elijah and Rabbi Shim'on seem thrilled to be in each other's presence. Following Elijah's final mystical decree, "Rabbi Shim'on rejoiced, saying, 'At first, before these words from Song of Songs were spoken or revealed, I wept in sorrow. Now that these words have been revealed, I rejoice, saying: How happy is my share for being here! Moreover, these lofty teachings from above have been revealed here by my master!'"[40]

Rabbi Shim'on and Elijah are close colleagues, and like talmudic scholars they can also disagree. When Elijah indicates that at certain times *Shekhinah* is inaccessible to the lower worlds, Rabbi Shim'on insists that She is never distant from Her children.[41] But the prophetic master and the earthly sage respect each other's wisdom, and their dialogue displays collegiality and conveys an intimacy befitting the Song of Songs.

"ELIJAH OPENED . . ."

Elijah plays a major role in later parts of the *Zohar*, namely, *Ra'aya Meheimna* (The Faithful Shepherd) and *Tiqqunei ha-Zohar* (Embellishments on the *Zohar*).

The title "Faithful Shepherd" refers to Moses, whom Rabbi Shim'on and his companions meet on a visionary journey. Moses explains the mystical meaning of numerous *mitsvot*, in the course of which he converses with Elijah and at several points seeks assistance from him: "Elijah, rise! Open your mouth about the *mitsvot* along with me, for you are my helper on every side."[42]

In earlier tradition, Moses was Elijah's teacher. Now Elijah appears as Moses's "expert student" and his "student-colleague." The bond between them extends to the messianic age, when the dead will arise, Moses will teach on earth again, and Elijah will serve as "his mouth," clarifying Moses's words.[43]

Tiqqunei ha-Zohar consists of a commentary on the first portion of the Torah, each section opening with a new interpretation of the first word: *be-reshit* (in the beginning). Elijah is one of the main participants (along with Moses and Rabbi Shim'on), and many manuscripts of the work begin with his oration on the process of emanation. He describes the relation between *Ein Sof* (the Infinite) and the ten *sefirot* (the various divine attributes), pictured here as "adornments" of the Infinite. Paradoxically, the *sefirot* reveal divine aspects, while concealing the ultimate divine reality.

Ein Sof transcends all personal qualities, but here Elijah addresses Him directly as "You." He concludes by encouraging Rabbi Shim'on to continue revealing the secrets. This passage became known by its opening words, *Petaḥ Eliyyahu* (Elijah opened), and under the influence of Isaac Luria, it was incorporated into the daily and pre-Sabbath Sephardic liturgy, thereby becoming one of the most famous passages of the *Zohar:*

> Elijah opened, saying, "Master of the worlds! You are one—but not in counting. You are higher than the high, concealed from the concealed. No thought grasps You at all. It is You who generated ten adornments—called by us the ten *sefirot*—by which concealed, unrevealed worlds, as well as revealed worlds, are conducted. By them You are concealed from human beings, while You are the one who binds and unites them. Since You are within, whoever separates one of these ten from another—it is as if he divided You.
>
> "These ten *sefirot* proceed in order. . . . It is You who

conducts them, and no one conducts You—neither above nor below nor in any direction. . . . These . . . are named according to this arrangement: *Ḥesed*, right arm; *Gevurah*, left arm; *Tif'eret*, trunk of the body; *Netsaḥ* and *Hod*, two legs; *Yesod*, consummation of the body, sign of the holy covenant; *Malkhut*, mouth—we call Her Oral Torah. *Ḥokhmah* is the brain, inner thought. *Binah* is the heart-mind, through which the [human] heart-mind understands. . . . The highest crown, *Keter Elyon*, is the royal crown, the skull . . . , inside of which is יהוה (*YHVH*—*yod*, *he*, *vav*, *he*), path of emanation, sap of the tree, spreading through its arms and branches—like water drenching a tree, which thereby flourishes.

"Master of the worlds! You are the Cause of causes, drenching the tree with that flow—a flow that is like a soul for the body, life for the body. In You there is neither likeness nor image of anything within or without. You created heaven and earth, bringing forth sun, moon, stars and constellations. And on earth: trees, grass, the Garden of Eden, animals, birds, fish, and human beings. So that the beyond might be known—how above and below are conducted and how they become known.

"About You, no one knows anything. Apart from You, there is no union above and below. . . . Every one of the *sefirot* has a name that is known . . . , but You have no known name, for You pervade all names; You are the fullness of them all. When You disappear from them, all those names are left like a body without a soul.

"You are wise—not with known wisdom. You understand—not with known understanding. You have no known place—just making known Your power and strength to human beings, showing them how the world is conducted by judgment and compassion . . . , according to human action. . . . But actually, You have no known judgment or compassion, nor any of these qualities at all.

"Rise, Rabbi Shim'on, and words will be renewed by you, for permission has been granted to you to reveal hidden mysteries—something not permitted to any human being until now!"[44]

Who but Elijah would presume to address *Ein Sof* directly? His intimacy with God enables him to know the unknowable and trace the indescribable. Later in *Tiqqunei ha-Zohar*, Elijah explores a realm that is barely touched upon anywhere else in the *Zohar:* the *shi'ur qomah* (measure of the stature) of *Shekhinah*, the various limbs and features of the female body of God. Invited by Rabbi Shim'on, Elijah begins as follows: "Master of the Universe! May it be Your will that I utter words on a straight path, fittingly—all gauged and weighed—concerning the *shi'ur qomah*, measure of the stature, of Your *Shekhinah*."[45]

In another passage, Elijah describes *Shekhinah*'s features in detail, beginning with Her hair and proceeding to Her eyes, face, nose, mouth, lips, neck, hands, shoulders, arms, fingers, breasts, genitalia, and feet.[46] His unique intimacy with Her is reflected elsewhere in *Tiqqunei ha-Zohar*, when after he expounds mystical teachings in Her presence, "*Shekhinah* rose from Her throne and kissed him."[47]

IN THE WAKE OF THE *ZOHAR*

The prominence of Elijah in the *Zohar* (especially in its later sections) enhanced his authority for all subsequent kabbalists, who immersed themselves in the holy *Zohar*, believing that it was composed not in medieval Europe but in early rabbinic times. Could Elijah appear to them too?

According to biographical accounts, the famous kabbalist Isaac Luria (the Holy *Ari*, 1534–1572) secluded himself for years by the Nile River, "and there he attained the Holy Spirit. Elijah (gratefully remembered) revealed himself to him constantly, disclosing secrets of Torah."[48] Several years later, Luria conveyed some of these secrets to a circle of disciples in the mountaintop town of Safed in Galilee, where he spent the last years of his short life. His bold theology featured the cosmic catastrophe of the Breaking of the Vessels (which is reflected in the unredeemed state of the world) and the human task of *tiqqun*, "mending" the brokenness by living virtuously. Luria's innovative teachings were not seen as opposing tradition since the authority of Elijah was claimed for them.[49]

Luria's closest disciple, Ḥayyim Vital (1542–1620), encouraged others to stimulate *gillui Eliyyahu* (a revelation of Elijah) through various preparations. These included *teshuvah* ("turning back" to God, repentance), fulfilling the *mitsvot*, sincere intention during prayer, intense study of Torah, an ascetic lifestyle (limiting food, drink, and sensual pleasures), seclusion, immersion in a ritual bath, meditation on the divine name, emptying one's mind of worldly concerns, and love of God. "Through these practices of devotion, Elijah (gratefully remembered) will reveal himself. The greater one's devotion, the greater [Elijah's] revelation."[50]

One of Luria's colleagues in Safed was Joseph Caro (1488–1575), author of the *Shulḥan Arukh*, the standard code of Jewish law. Caro was both a leading halakhic authority and a kabbalist. In his mystical diary, he recorded teachings, rules, advice, and predictions revealed to him by a *maggid* (heavenly mentor or "preacher"). This *maggid* manifested itself in the form of automatic speech—as a voice issuing from Caro's mouth, which could be heard by others nearby. Caro remembered the *maggid*'s messages and subsequently recorded them in his diary. The *maggid* tells Caro that by practicing certain mortifications, "you will merit to see Elijah while awake, face-to-face, and he will speak to you directly, greeting you. For he will be your teacher and rabbi, teaching you all the secrets of Torah." Such meetings, however, cannot be arranged in advance, since Elijah "will come to you only unexpectedly."[51]

The *maggid*'s voice apparently sounded different from Caro's own, normal voice, but this was not the case with Elijah's voice, as indicated elsewhere in the diary. According to the *maggid*, if Caro would contemplate Torah ceaselessly and live ascetically,

> I will make you worthy of seeing Elijah . . . clothed in white, sitting in front of you, speaking with you as a person speaks with his friend, and your eyes will behold your teacher. Even though your wife and other men and women will be in your house, he will speak with you and you will see him, whereas they will not see him, and his voice will appear to them as if it were your voice.[52]

Gillui Eliyyahu (a revelation of Elijah) represents a higher state than the phenomenon of the *maggid*. But in this higher state, whose voice is actually speaking, Elijah's or Caro's? As we have seen before, there is no sharp distinction between the inner depths of the seeker and *gillui Eliyyahu*. From a psychological point of view, both the *maggid* and Elijah are products of the unconscious, crystallizing on the conscious level of Caro's mind into psychic entities. But whereas the *maggid* is experienced as more "dissociated" from Caro—delivering a message from beyond in another voice—Elijah's voice is indistinguishable from Caro's own, conveying mystical intuition.[53]

ELIJAH AND SHABBETAI TSEVI

If someone believes he's the Messiah, he's likely to feel a bond with Elijah, the messianic herald. This was certainly so for Shabbetai Tsevi, the most famous messianic pretender of the Middle Ages. Shabbetai was born in Izmir, Turkey, in 1626, apparently on the ninth of (the Hebrew month) Ab—traditionally identified as the dark date on which both the First and Second Temples in Jerusalem were destroyed. According to a rabbinic source, on this same date the Messiah will be born, for out of tragic depths issues a ray of salvation.

Shabbetai grew into a young scholar seeking to lead a

saintly life. But he manifested symptoms of what used to be called manic-depression, fluctuating between enthusiasm and melancholy. Sometimes he acted like a child or a fool. He would run off to the mountains or caves, without his family knowing where he was; or he would withdraw to a small dark room, locking himself in and hardly emerging. He felt persecuted and possessed by demons. At times he openly transgressed the Torah, believing that this was part of his mission.

The year 1648 was momentous for Jews, including Shabbetai. The *Zohar* had mentioned that year as the time of the resurrection of the dead, but in that very year many Jews were murdered during a Cossack and peasant revolt in Poland and Russia. The uprising, led by Bogdan Chmielnicki (Khmelnitski), was aimed against Polish Catholic domination, but it was accompanied by mass atrocities committed against the Jews, who in their capacity as leaseholders and landlords were seen by the peasants as their immediate oppressors. As Jewish blood was shed, refugees fled as far south as Turkey. In the wake of the atrocities, agitation swept the Jewish world, and many interpreted the "Khmelnitski massacres" as the birth pangs of the Messiah.

In Izmir, Shabbetai Tsevi, torn between his extreme moods, was wounded by the shattering news and electrified by the messianic expectations. One day he heard a voice proclaiming his mission: "You are the savior of Israel. . . . You are the true redeemer."[54] According to several reports, he had a vision that the patriarchs Abraham, Isaac, and Jacob anointed him with oil. Later, either Shabbetai himself or his followers substituted Elijah for the patriarchs, and an exact Hebrew date was established in the Shabbatean festival calendar—21 Sivan 5408 (corresponding to June 11, 1648)—marking the day on which Shabbetai Tsevi "was anointed by the prophet Elijah."[55]

According to Shabbatean tradition, Elijah became Shabbetai's spiritual guide, instructing him to read the *Zohar* and "meditate on it day and night."[56] At the circumcision of his son, Shabbetai reportedly sat on the Chair of Elijah, "sitting in meditation for about an hour."[57]

In the early 1650s, Shabbetai was banished from his hometown because of certain "strange actions" that he performed, including publicly pronouncing the Ineffable Name of God, YHVH—something that the Talmud says would be permitted only "in the world to come."[58]

From Izmir, Shabbetai proceeded to Salonika, but there too he shocked the residents and was expelled, reportedly after hosting prominent rabbis at a banquet, where he erected a bridal canopy, had a Torah scroll brought in, and performed a marriage ceremony between himself and the Torah.[59]

Years later, in the spring of 1665, Shabbetai met a kabbalist named Nathan of Gaza, who recognized Shabbetai as the Messiah and became his prophet. In May of that year, in Palestine, Shabbetai publicly proclaimed himself as the Messiah. In December, he did so again in a synagogue back in his hometown of Izmir. Much of the Jewish world was seized with messianic fervor. Some families sold their homes, expecting to be imminently and miraculously transported to the land of Israel. Earlier there had been reports of Elijah appearing in a synagogue in Aleppo. Then, Elijah was spotted in the streets of Izmir. Dozens, even hundreds, had seen him: he was the anonymous beggar asking for alms, as well as the invisible guest at a banquet. Invited to a circumcision ceremony in Izmir, Shabbetai halted the proceedings for a while. Then, "after a good half hour, Shabbetai ordered them to proceed," explaining that he had "stopped the performance . . . [because] Elijah had not yet taken his seat." Numerous letters were sent from Izmir to Amsterdam, confirming this appearance of Elijah.[60]

Late in December 1665, Shabbetai sailed to Constantinople, accompanied by some of the "kings" he had appointed from among his supporters and devotees. In Constantinople, during the days of expectation preceding Shabbetai's arrival, there was a penitential awakening as well as apparitions of the prophet Elijah, "whom many have seen."[61] Numerous believers had given up their businesses and had left, or were about to leave, for the Holy Land. But in February 1666, Shabbetai was arrested by the Turkish authorities, who were alarmed by his growing popularity and who considered him a rebel. Even when he was in prison, there were reports that Shabbetai had seen Elijah and that the prophet had directed people to observe the neglected commandment of *tsitsit*, according to its original sense of making fringes on the hem of ordinary garments. "Everyone began to obey the vision by fringing their garments."[62]

In a synagogue in Amsterdam, a cantor changed the wording of the hymn chanted at the conclusion of Shabbat. Instead of "Elijah the prophet, . . . may he come to us speedily with the Messiah son of David," he sang, "Elijah the prophet has come to us with the Messiah son of David."[63] In the summer of 1666, the rabbis of Izmir issued a prohibition against keeping cats, dogs, or other unkosher animals, since Elijah would not enter a house in which these creatures were present.[64]

Finally, in September 1666, Shabbetai was summoned before the sultan's council and given the choice between being put to death or converting to Islam. He chose the latter, saving his life at the cost of apostasy. Subsequently, he led a dual existence, performing the duties of a Muslim while still observing various Jewish rituals. After being denounced for his double-faced behavior and sexual license, he was banished to a small village in Albania.

In his last extant letter, written in the late summer of 1676 to nearby Jewish friends, Shabbetai urged them to send him a *maḥzor* (festival prayer book) for the approaching High Holy Days. We don't know whether the *maḥzor* ever arrived; but with or without it, Shabbetai died on that Yom Kippur in obscurity. According to his prophet, Nathan, the Messiah's death was only apparent—an "occultation"—and he would reappear to redeem Israel. This claim may have been nourished by the similar belief about Shabbetai's mentor, Elijah, who never died but was only "hidden away" in heaven.[65]

4

Elijah and the Daughters of Judaism

Not constricted by mortal time nor by measured space, Elijah also overleaps religious boundaries. Beyond Judaism, his sway extends to its daughter faiths: Christianity and Islam.

Elijah is the only personality in the Hebrew Bible who became a popular Christian saint. Already in the New Testament, he plays a significant role, being associated with both John the Baptist and Jesus. John was an ascetic Jewish prophet who appeared in the Jordan valley, proclaiming, *Repent, for the kingdom of heaven is at hand!* (Matthew 3:2). The imminent, fiery judgment would engulf all of Israel; the only protection was to turn back to God, reform one's life, and receive baptism from John (hence his surname). John referred vaguely to an eschatological figure (*the one who is more powerful than I* or *the one who is coming after me*), who would show his superiority by baptizing not with mere water but with the Holy Spirit.[1] Many Jews, including Jesus, flocked to the Jordan for John's protective baptism. The ruler Herod wanted to execute John, but *he feared the crowd, because they regarded him* [John] *as a prophet* (Matthew 14:5). Before long, though, John was arrested, imprisoned, and beheaded.

The figure of John recalls Elijah. The Baptist is described as wearing *a garment of camel's hair with a leather loincloth around his waist* (Matthew 3:4). The hairy mantle typifies a prophet, but John's appearance also resembles Elijah's: *a hairy man, with a leather loincloth bound round his waist* (2 Kings 1:8).[2] The resemblance between the two prophets becomes something more when Jesus indicates that John the Baptist *is* Elijah. Speaking to the crowds about John, Jesus says, *If you are willing to accept it, he is Elijah who is to come* (Matthew 11:14). Jesus speaks more cryptically in the Gospel of Mark (9:13): *I tell you that Elijah has come, and they did to him whatever they pleased.* The parallel in Matthew explicates Jesus's hint: *"I tell you that Elijah has already come, and they did not recognize him, but they did to him whatever they pleased. . . ." Then the disciples understood that he was speaking to them about John the Baptist* (Matthew 17:12–13).[3]

For the early Christians, John the Baptist was Elijah, who had returned to earth to proclaim the Messiah. Yet in his own lifetime, the Baptist probably did not see himself as Elijah; in the Gospel of John, he denies the identification explicitly.[4] There is someone else, though, whom many considered as Elijah: Jesus himself. In all three of the Synoptic Gospels, when Jesus asks his disciples, "Who do people say that I am?" they reply that some say he is Elijah. When Jesus asks further, "But who do you say that I am?" Peter replies, "You are the Christ."[5]

Jesus came to be seen as Christ (the Anointed), the Messiah. But during his lifetime he acted and was thought of as a Jewish eschatological prophet (such as Elijah), and at least initially, this may be how he perceived himself. Like the Baptist, he proclaimed the imminent coming of the kingdom of heaven. Yet, unlike his predecessor, Jesus celebrated the kingdom as already present—in his teaching and actions. His emphasis was less on doom and more on the good news that God was about to restore His scattered people.

As an itinerant prophet in northern Israel, reputed to be working miracles, Jesus would naturally conjure up images of Elijah and his disciple, Elisha. In one account, he identifies with both of them. In his first sermon in his local synagogue in Nazareth, Jesus taught, *No prophet is accepted in his own hometown.* According to the Gospel of Luke, Jesus demonstrated this by recalling certain miracles of Elijah and Elisha.[6] Various New Testament stories of Jesus's own miracles are modeled on the tales of that earlier prophetic pair. Like Elijah, Jesus revives the son of a widow;[7] like Elisha, he feeds the multitude with a few loaves of bread and cures a leper.[8] Finally, Jesus's ascent to heaven (after temporarily dying) recalls the ascent of Elijah.[9]

Understandably, some of Jesus's contemporaries imagined that he *was* Elijah, or another prophet fulfilling Elijah's eschatological role of proclaiming the arrival of the kingdom. Before long, however, Jesus was "promoted" from prophet to Messiah, and the role of Elijah-like prophet was dissociated from him and transferred to John the Baptist, whose mission now focused on heralding Christ.[10]

Still, Jesus remained linked with Elijah, as illustrated in the dramatic account of the transfiguration. Having climbed a mountain with three disciples, Jesus *was transfigured before them, and his garments became glistening, intensely white* (Mark 9:2–3). The disciples then saw Elijah and Moses appear, speaking with Jesus, *and from the cloud there came a voice: This is My beloved Son; listen to him!* (Mark 9:7). The scene may be intended to demonstrate that Jesus is the fulfillment of the Torah (given to Moses) and the Prophets (represented by Elijah).[11]

Elijah is the only prophet in the Hebrew Bible who calls someone to leave everything—home, family, and work—in order to follow him. The story of his call of Elisha echoes in the Gospel stories of Jesus calling his disciples. In Kings, as we have seen, Elijah finds Elisha as a prosperous farmer hard at work: *plowing with twelve yoke of oxen in front of him. . . . Elijah went over to him and flung his mantle upon him.* Immediately, Elisha abandons the cattle and runs after Elijah, saying, *Let me kiss my father and my mother, and I will follow you.* To which, Elijah replies enigmatically, *Go, return. For what have I done to you?* After serving a farewell meal to his family, Elisha *arose and followed Elijah and served him* (1 Kings 19:19–21).[12]

When Jesus finds his first disciples, they too are engaged in their everyday work:

> *As he walked by the Sea of Galilee, he saw two brothers, Simon, who is called Peter, and Andrew his brother, casting a net into the sea—for they were fishermen. He said to them, "Follow me, and I will make you fish for people." Immediately they left their nets and followed him.*
>
> *As he went from there, he saw two other brothers, James son of Zebedee and his brother John, in the boat with their father Zebedee, mending the nets, and he called them. Immediately they left the boat and their father and followed him.* (Matthew 4:18–22)[13]

The two pairs of brothers do not hesitate to abandon everything and follow Jesus. In the case of Elisha, he asks only to kiss his parents farewell. Elijah's reply is ambiguous: *Go, return. For what have I done to you?* This could mean two different things. The first is: "Why shouldn't you say farewell to your parents? I'm not forcing you to follow me this instant." Alternatively, although granting permission, Elijah may be rebuking Elisha for hesitating—for failing to realize the significance of what Elijah just did by casting his prophetic mantle upon him. Elijah could be pretending to deny that his act meant anything: "*Go, return. For what have I done to you?* If your parents are more important to you than following me right here and now, then leave me. Maybe you're not worthy of becoming my disciple and successor."

This second interpretation of Elijah's reply matches what Jesus says to another potential follower:

> *As they were going along the road . . . [someone] said [to Jesus], "I will follow you, Lord, but let me first say farewell to those at my home."*
>
> *Jesus said to him, "No one who puts his hand to the plow and looks back is fit for the kingdom of God."* (Luke 9:57, 61–62)[14]

For Jesus, filial piety is trivial compared with the urgent call of the kingdom. Whether or not Elijah's reply conveys the same message, for him too, family relationships are subordinate to the covenantal relationship with God. For both prophets, their true family embraces all of Israel.

From the beginning of his career, Jesus was engaged with Elijah, and throughout his ministry he conveyed his prototype's charismatic authority, miraculous powers, and zeal. As he hung dying on the cross, *Jesus cried with a loud voice,* Eli, Eli, . . . *my God, my God, why have You forsaken me?* (Matthew 27:46). Some of the bystanders mistakenly thought that his desperate cry *Eli, Eli* was directed not to God but to *Eliyyahu,* and they waited to see if Elijah would come to save him.[15] At that moment, Jesus was not calling out for *Eliyyahu,* but his entire mission evoked Elijah. The bond between the two testifies to the inherent Jewishness of Jesus, which faded away as Christianity separated from its mother religion and the Galilean rabbi was transmogrified into a gentile guru.[16]

ELIJAH AND THE CARMELITES

Elijah became an inspiration for Christian spiritual seekers. Based on his portrayal in the book of Kings, he was reimagined as a religious hermit and the founder of monastic life. It seems strange to think of the fiery zealot Elijah as a humble monk, but he could be visualized as celibate, since he seems to have never married or had children. In his minimal dress, he also looked like a hermit: *a hairy man, with a leather loincloth bound round his waist* (2 Kings 1:8). One of the first things we hear about him is that after declaring the drought to King Ahab, he fled to the wadi of Cherith, where he lived alone for an extended time, surviving on water from the stream and on bread and meat delivered miraculously by ravens.[17] Throughout his life, prayer was his instrument, enabling him to revive a lifeless boy, call down fire from heaven, and restore the rain. Soon afterward, he wandered into the desert and trekked for forty days to Mount Horeb, where he encountered God in a vibrant stillness.

Although the biblical Elijah often interacts with other people—from kings to an impoverished widow to the Israelite masses—Christian thinkers reasoned that he sought solitude as his way of life. In the words of a fourth-century author, "Elijah was such a one who fled the tumult of human society and chose to live in the desert."[18]

Perhaps he lived in a cave. The only cave mentioned in the Bible in connection with Elijah is the cave on Mount Horeb, where he spent the night before meeting God. But a tradition developed about "a cave of Elijah" on another mountain—Mount Carmel, where the Man of Truth defeated the false prophets of Baal, calling down fire from heaven to consume his sacrifice.[19]

It's unclear when a certain cave on the slopes of Mount Carmel was first called the Cave of Elijah, but that name likely appears before the sixth century in *Toledot Yeshu* (The Life of Jesus), a Jewish polemical satire on Christianity. In this narrative, predictably, Jesus loses to the rabbis in a contest of magical powers, and then he flies away to Elijah's cave on Mount Carmel.[20]

Jews, Christians, and Muslims have all prayed in that cave—and still do—imagining that Elijah preceded them there. By the fifth century, individual Christian monks were dwelling on

Carmel, perhaps meditating in Elijah's cave, sensing his presence. Seven hundred years later, a group of crusader pilgrims from the West settled on the mountain as hermits, and they became known as the Carmelites. Long ago, some of them believed, Elijah had established a contemplative community there. Its members would have included "the guild of prophets," a brotherhood who appears in the book of Kings, interacting with Elijah, though primarily with his disciple, Elisha.[21]

Journeying through Palestine around 1170, the famous Jewish traveler Benjamin of Tudela describes what he saw on Carmel: "There on the mountain is the Cave of Elijah (peace unto him), and there the Edomites [i.e., the Christians] have made a place of worship, which they call San Elias [Saint Elijah]. At the top of the mountain, one can identify the site of the wrecked altar that Elijah repaired in the days of Ahab."[22]

Benjamin may or may not have encountered the Carmelites, but they were already there on the mountain, modeling themselves on Elijah while living more ascetically than he ever had. Their original rules prescribed owning nothing and dwelling in a "cell" apart from others, except when they all met in chapel for morning liturgy. Much of their time was spent in solitary prayer and meditation, along with some manual labor. Abstaining from meat, they ate their meals alone in their cells and frequently fasted. From evening till morning, they practiced silence, and throughout the day idle chatter was forbidden.

With the weakening of the crusader Kingdom of Jerusalem in the thirteenth century, many of the Carmelites had to abandon the Holy Land and migrate back to Europe. Any who remained were finally forced to leave when Acre, the kingdom's capital and major stronghold, fell to the Mamluks in 1291. Exiled from the Holy Land, the Carmelites reaching Europe found an active ascetic movement, and they thrived, reorganizing along the lines of mendicant friars (brothers). They became less stringent, able now to settle in cities and towns, where they preached and heard confessions. The Carmelites became one of the main mendicant orders of the Catholic Church, along with the Dominicans, Franciscans, and Augustinians. Of all these, the Carmelites could claim the most ancient origin, since their order was purportedly founded by Elijah, the hermit of Carmel.[23]

The two most famous Carmelites were Teresa of Ávila (1515–1582) and John of the Cross (1542–1591). Teresa's grandfather was a converso (a Jewish convert to Christianity). Growing up in Ávila, she was attracted to the local Carmelite convent, which she joined at the age of twenty. By this time, the discipline among the Carmelite friars and nuns had relaxed considerably; they lived rather comfortably and visited freely with outsiders. After some twenty years in the convent, Teresa experienced a "conversion," which inspired her to adopt a rigorous program of discipline and prayer. Her devotions culminated in frequent visions of Christ, whom she heard speaking to her. Moved by these visions, she began planning to establish a small Carmelite convent that would commit itself to the original strict Carmelite rule, as described above. Her fellow nuns and the church authorities were not enthused, but in 1562, after obtaining permission from Rome, she established a new convent in Ávila. During the next twenty years, she founded more than a dozen others, all adopting the Primitive Rule.

Teresa also opened a similar monastery for Carmelite friars, one of whom was named Juan, soon to be known as Juan de la Cruz, John of the Cross. (Both of his parents were from converso families.) Together, Teresa and John founded the Order of Discalced Carmelites. The term "discalced" (unshod) refers to their habit of going barefoot, which Teresa soon modified to the custom of wearing sandals. John went on to establish other such monasteries, until gradually the "Teresian Reform" was adopted by the majority of Carmelites.

The prose and poetry of Teresa of Ávila and John of the Cross include masterpieces of spiritual literature, such as Teresa's

Interior Mansions and John's *Ascent of Mount Carmel.* For them and their circle, all Christian monastic life sprang from that mountain, where Elijah restored Israel's belief. If Elijah eventually enlightened the kabbalists, as the patron saint of the Carmelites he also inspired two of the greatest Christian mystics.

ELIJAH AND AL-KHIḌR, THE VERDANT ONE

Jews, Christians, and Muslims all came to the Cave of Elijah on Mount Carmel to venerate the same prophet, seek similar blessings or cures, and worship in their own distinct ways. For Muslims, it became the Cave of al-Khiḍr, a mysterious, revered figure who is similar to—and at times identical with—Elijah.

The name al-Khiḍr means "the Green One, the Verdant One." His origins are unclear, and he could be seen as an Islamic version of the Green Man, a legendary symbol of rebirth. Related to vegetation deities, this figure appears from ancient times around the world, developing independently within separate cultures.

Green, the color of nature and rejuvenation, is the preeminent color of Islam. According to a saying attributed to Muḥammad, al-Khiḍr was given his name "because after he would sit on barren land, it became green with vegetation."[24] In shaping the personality of al-Khiḍr, Islam drew on various sources, including traditions of Elijah. The two figures are depicted with similar traits. In Islamic legend, al-Khiḍr drank from the River of Life and, like Elijah, became immortal. He is pictured as the Eternal Youth, yet, like Elijah, he can appear in numerous guises, frequently as an old man. Both can manifest anywhere at any time to rescue those in crisis and extend compassion, before suddenly vanishing.[25]

Al-Khiḍr never appears by name in the Qur'an, but interpreters discovered (or projected) him there, right in the middle of Islam's holiest book, in the *Surah* (chapter) of the Cave. (The centrality of this *surah* is reflected by the fact that in some circles it is traditionally recited every Friday.) There we hear of an enigmatic servant of Allah, gifted with divine knowledge, whom Moses encounters. "May I follow you," Moses asks, "so that you may teach me the guidance you have learned?"[26]

The nameless divine servant replies, "Indeed, you will not be able to have patience with me. How can you be patient concerning what your understanding does not encompass?" The enlightened servant doubts whether Moses can bear the ways of wisdom. But Moses promises to be patient, and he is then told, "If you would follow me, then do not ask me about anything until I mention it to you."

The two proceed, and Allah's servant performs three strange and troubling acts: scuttling a boat, killing a young man, and repairing a wall in a town of unworthy residents who had refused them hospitality. Each time Moses is appalled. Breaking his promise, he repeatedly questions what the servant has done. After Moses criticizes him for the third action, the servant declares, "This is the parting between me and you. But I will tell you the ultimate meaning of what you did not have the patience to endure."

The servant—a spiritual master—then explains his actions. Though these seemed absurd and so contrary to moral values, each one, it turns out, was destined to bring good out of an apparent evil. For example, beneath the collapsed wall lay a treasure, intended for two young orphans in town. The servant repaired the wall so that this treasure would not be exposed and stolen by the unworthy townspeople. Eventually, when the orphans matured, they would retrieve the buried treasure. The entire tale vindicates God's inscrutable ways, while also highlighting Moses's deficiency, perhaps to lessen his status compared with the prophet Muḥammad.[27]

Within a century after the Qur'an appeared, Muslim commentators identified the servant of Allah as al-Khiḍr. A few hundred years later, a similar story appeared in a Jewish collection of legends written in Judeo-Arabic by the eleventh-century North African scholar Nissim Gaon. In this Jewish version the cast of characters has changed. Moses is replaced by a talmudic sage, Rabbi Yehoshu'a son of Levi. And instead of the servant of Allah (or al-Khiḍr), we find Elijah. Rabbi Yehoshu'a and Elijah are a natural pair, since in rabbinic literature they have an ongoing relationship, which sometimes turns into a sort of lover's quarrel.[28]

As Nissim's narrative opens, Rabbi Yehoshu'a has not seen his prophetic colleague lately, so he fasts and prays in order to attain *gillui Eliyyahu* (a revelation of Elijah). Finally, one day the rabbi meets him on the road:

> Elijah asked him, "Is there anything that you desire?"
>
> [Rabbi Yehoshu'a] replied, "I would like to walk along with you and observe the wonders that you perform in this world."
>
> Elijah said to him, "You will not be able to endure my actions as you see them." . . .
>
> Elijah laid down the condition that once Rabbi Yehoshu'a asked him to explain the reasons for his actions, he would have to leave him.

As they travel along together, Elijah commits several strange acts. First, after a poor man hosts them graciously, Elijah kills the man's only valuable possession: a cow. Rabbi Yehoshu'a asks why Elijah repaid the man's generosity with such cruelty, but Elijah warns him to be silent or else he'll leave. After walking all day, they come to the house of a wealthy man who ignores them and offers them nothing to eat. Yet the next morning, Elijah miraculously rebuilds one of the rich man's walls, which had collapsed. After another day's journey, they reach a magnificent synagogue with chairs of gold and silver, but the congregants offer them only bread and salt and leave them to spend the night on the synagogue floor. In the morning, as they depart, Elijah says to the people, "May God make all of you chiefs!"

That night, they stay with some wretchedly poor people, who treat them as generously as they can, providing abundant food and comfortable beds. The next morning, when the two guests depart, Elijah says, "May God grant you only one chief!"

"At this, Rabbi Yehoshu'a could no longer hold himself back, so he said to Elijah, 'My lord, deliver me from these perplexities, even though I will then have to leave you. I can no longer bear patiently what I observe you doing.'"

As in the Qur'an, the mystifying master explains his bewildering actions. For example, Elijah rebuilt the miser's wall so that he wouldn't find the treasure buried in its foundation. To the stingy congregants, he expressed the wish "May God make all of you chiefs!" because "a place in which there are many chiefs is bound to be ruined." Fittingly, the generous poor people deserve to have only one chief, through whose singular wisdom they will surely prosper.

Most likely, Nissim did not borrow this tale directly from the Qur'an. As he writes in his introduction, he gathered numerous Jewish stories. This one may have evolved after a Jew heard the qur'anic tale from a neighbor or in the marketplace or during a religious debate. As the tale was retold in Jewish circles, Moses could not be presented as needing to learn the ways of God from another, so he was replaced by Rabbi Yehoshu'a son of Levi. In an Islamic culture where al-Khiḍr was associated (or even identified) with Elijah, it was easy for the Jewish reteller to substitute Elijah for the Verdant One.[29]

Both al-Khiḍr and Elijah convey esoteric knowledge. In Sufism, the mystical branch of Islam, al-Khiḍr is the supreme guide. Nearly every saint's hagiography describes a visit from the Verdant One, who transmits wisdom or a potent prayer.[30] If a seeker spontaneously realizes spiritual truth, al-Khiḍr is the one who taught him; for when the disciple is ready, the master appears. Like Elijah, he personifies the experience of revelation and validates what the seeker has discovered beyond or within.

According to Sufi tradition, the celebrated poet Ḥāfiẓ was inspired by al-Khiḍr.[31] The renowned philosopher, poet, and mystic Ibn 'Arabī never called himself a Sufi, but later Sufis claimed him as the Greatest Master. In his writings, Ibn 'Arabī describes meeting with the Verdant One and twice receiving al-Khiḍr's mantle of initiation. This scene recalls Elijah casting his prophetic mantle upon his disciple, Elisha. It also accords with a tradition about the early kabbalists dwelling in Provence—contemporaries of Ibn 'Arabī, who was then living not far away in Andalusia. These founders of Kabbalah, as mentioned above, are said to have experienced *gillui Eliyyahu* (a revelation of Elijah).[32]

In the culture of Islam, Al-Khiḍr and Elijah are sometimes identical and sometimes form a pair. Their equivalence is demonstrated by various shrines—in addition to Elijah's cave—dedicated to both of them. Some Islamic sources reflect a total fusion of the two personalities, which is also conveyed by certain Arabic-speaking Jews who refer to Elijah as al-Khiḍr.[33]

In one legend, the two are pictured as brothers.[34] According to another tradition, every year during the month of Ramadan, the two meet in Jerusalem and together perform the hajj, making pilgrimage to Mecca.[35] How do they interact during their annual reunion? An answer is offered by a medieval account of a discussion between Elijah and an anonymous man. At one point, the man asks Elijah, "Do you and al-Khiḍr meet?" Elijah replies, "Yes, every year at Arafat"—referring to a sacred hill near Mecca, visited as part of the hajj. When the man asks how the two of them spend their time there, Elijah replies, "He obtains from my knowledge, and I obtain from his."[36]

5

Rituals of Anticipation

We know nothing about Elijah's family, neither his parents' identity nor whether he ever married or had children. The biblical Elijah was a loner, declaring or complaining again and again, *I alone remain.*[1] Yet gradually, he was welcomed into Jewish ritual life, including some of the family's most meaningful moments. These moments he continues to enrich with his imagined presence.

He is anticipated at each Passover seder, the most familial event in the Jewish calendar. When a baby boy is circumcised, Elijah is invited to preside and witness, occupying a ceremonial chair. And every Saturday night, as the Sabbath departs, his name is invoked as part of Havdalah.

Each of these is a rite of passage. The seder celebrates liberation from slavery, meant to be experienced anew. Through circumcision, the infant enters the covenant of Abraham. Havdalah distinguishes between light and dark, marking the transition from Sabbath holiness to the mundane weekday world. All three rituals are liminal (threshold) moments, fittingly enhanced by Elijah, the liminal personality—part human, part angel—the mysterious stranger who spans heaven and earth, virtuoso of the in-between.[2]

ELIJAH AT THE SEDER

Most Jews are not familiar with the biblical Elijah nor with his talmudic transformation. They know of him because of childhood memories of the seder—when his goblet of wine (the Cup of Elijah) adorned the table, or when the front door was opened in expectation that he would appear. Neither custom has a precise beginning or a clear explanation. Rather, they evolved over centuries in various lands; only later did learned rabbis attempt to explain or validate them.[3]

Both customs are associated with the belief that Elijah will herald the Messiah, and that Israel's final redemption will take place on the anniversary of the original redemption from Egyptian slavery on the first night of Passover. That anniversary is instituted in the Torah: *It is a night of watch for YHVH, for bringing them out of the land of Egypt; this night is YHVH's, a watch for all the Israelites through their generations* (Exodus 12:42). Commenting on this verse, an early midrash predicts: "On that night they were redeemed, and on that night they are destined to be redeemed."[4] A later midrash elaborates: "On that very night, the Messiah and Elijah will appear. . . . The blessed Holy One said, '. . . On the day when I wrought salvation for you [on Passover in Egypt]—know that on that very night I will redeem you.'"[5]

The phrase in Exodus—*leil shimmurim*, "a night of watch [or, of vigil]"—reads literally *a night of watches* [or, *watchings*]. The word *shimmurim* reappears in the same verse: shimmurim, *a watch* [literally, *watches*], *for all the Israelites through their generations.* Various rabbis wondered about all this watching. One suggested that *a night of watchings* alludes to the final redemption, "a night that has been continually watched for since the six days of creation." His colleague applied the phrase *leil shimmurim* to the unique quality of every Passover eve: "a night under constant protection ['watching'] against the demons."[6]

On the basis of this talmudic guarantee of protection, it became customary to leave the door of one's home open or unlocked during the first night of Passover. In some places, opening the door was associated with the declaration near the beginning of the Haggadah: "Let all who are hungry come and eat; let all who are needy come and celebrate Passover." But the eleventh-century North African scholar Nissim Gaon associates the open door with Elijah: "I saw that . . . my father would not close the doors of our house . . . at all. And until now this is our custom, and [on the night of Passover] the doors of the house are open. When Elijah comes, we will go out to greet him quickly without any delay."[7]

If Elijah is expected to appear on the first night of Passover to announce the Messiah, wouldn't he need a cup of wine? So reasoned Zelikman Binga, a fifteenth-century Ashkenazic commentator on the Talmud, who is the earliest known author to mention the Cup of Elijah:

> I have seen some people on the night of Passover who pour a special cup and place it on the table, saying that this is the cup for Elijah the prophet—and I don't know the reason. But it seems that the reason derives from this: If Elijah the prophet comes on the night of Passover, as we hope and expect, he too will need a cup, for even a poor person among Israel must drink no less than four cups. And if the cup is not ready, we would have to prepare it for him, which might delay the Seder.[8]

Some linked Elijah's cup with the declaration near the beginning of the seder (mentioned above): "Let all who are hungry come and eat; let all who are needy come and celebrate Passover." As one author noted, "Since one calls for 'all who are needy' to 'come and eat,' he should prepare a cup for a guest who may come; and they call that cup 'the Cup of Elijah the prophet,' because we hope for this guest."[9]

A more utilitarian explanation was offered in the seventeenth century by the Sephardic authority Ḥayyim Benveniste, who reports what he saw:

> It seems this is the custom I saw among a few Ashkenazim: to leave on the table one empty cup . . . in which to pour all the wine left over in the cups of all those reclining there [after they have drunk at least the required minimum from their cups]. This cup is called the Cup of Elijah the prophet (gratefully remembered). This custom pleased me, and I follow it. From the remains of those cups, poured into this cup, I drink during the meal.[10]

Other Sephardic scholars also approved the Ashkenazic custom of preparing a special cup for Elijah, though one of them criticized pouring leftover wine into Elijah's empty cup, since this showed disrespect toward the venerable prophet.[11]

Among the various attempts to explain the Cup of Elijah, one relates to how many cups of wine a person is required to drink at the seder. The standard practice is to quaff four cups over the course of the evening (technically, at least 2.9 fluid ounces from each cup). But according to early manuscripts and citations of the Talmud, Rabbi Tarfon mentions a "fifth cup." Medieval commentators were troubled by this. Some (such as Rashi) concluded that the word "fifth" was a mistake and should be emended to "fourth." Others, including Maimonides, ruled that the fifth cup was optional rather than obligatory. A variant of this opinion (offered by Abraham ben David of Posquières) was that although the fifth cup was not obligatory, it was still praiseworthy and recommended.[12]

According to the Talmud, one day Elijah will come and resolve all halakhic disputes. Presumably, he will then determine the status of this additional cup, so the cup is appropriately named for him! This explanation was attributed to another famous Elijah—Elijah ben Solomon, the Gaon of Vilna:

> We have the custom of pouring a fifth cup and calling it the Cup of Elijah the prophet. The reason is that there is a dispute in the Gemara over whether one needs a fifth cup, and the halakhah is not determined. When Elijah comes, the doubt will be clarified. Therefore, based on this doubt, the cup is poured but not drunk, and it is called the Cup of Elijah, for when he comes, all doubts will be clarified, including this doubt.[13]

Eventually, Elijah will indicate whether drinking a fifth cup is required. For now, that cup is poured for him alone.

Originally, Elijah's cup was filled at the beginning of the seder. In some communities this changed as the ritual of opening the door was moved to a later stage of the evening, following the meal, right before the recitation of several biblical verses, beginning: Shefokh ḥamatekha, *Pour out Your wrath, upon the nations that do not know You. . . . For they have devoured Jacob and laid waste his habitation* (Psalms 79:6–7).

The custom of reciting these verses originated under the stress of persecution in the Middle Ages—likely in the wake of the Rhineland massacres of Jews, perpetrated by peasant crusaders in 1096 during the First Crusade. Later, the notorious, widespread blood libel accused Jews of kidnapping Christian children and using their blood as an essential ingredient in baking matzah. In some communities, "opening the door" may have been intended not—or not only—to welcome Elijah, but for a more earthly purpose: to rebut the blood libel by demonstrating the innocence of the Passover proceedings, or to catch anyone trying to "plant" the corpse of a Christian child in order to substantiate the false allegation.[14]

The intense yearning for deliverance and redemption is depicted in several Ashkenazic Haggadah manuscripts from the fifteenth century, where next to the word *shefokh* (pour out) appear images of the Messiah seated on a donkey with Elijah blowing a shofar to herald him. Such depictions may have been influenced by the Christian custom of processions on Palm Sunday, in which sculptured wooden figures of Christ and his messianic donkey were carried on carts and wheeled to the gates of a mock Jerusalem. Jewish leaders may have felt the need to emphasize that the Messiah was yet to come.[15]

In some communities it became customary to pour the Cup of Elijah at this late point in the seder, rather than at the beginning. An additional element was (and in some cases still is) to stand as the door is opened and greet the invisible guest with *Barukh ha-ba*, "Blessed is the one who comes!" In certain areas a dramatic enactment developed: as the door was opened, someone in disguise would enter quickly, "as if he were Elijah himself," proclaiming the arrival of the Messiah.[16]

On Passover, Elijah is literally liminal, expected to appear on the "threshold." Anticipated at the doorway, he mediates between home and community, between private space and the wider, uncertain world. He links the ancient liberation from Egyptian slavery with messianic deliverance, bridging the chasm between this unredeemed earth and the final redemption.

Memories of Elijah and the seder can be bittersweet, recalling the annual disappointment of not finding him at the door. Once, before Passover, according to a Hasidic tale, the disciples of Menaḥem Mendel (the Kotsker Rebbe) complained to him about this. He promised them that Elijah would be revealed to them at the upcoming seder. On the first night of the festival, the room was full, the atmosphere charged, with Elijah's cup waiting on the table. The seder proceeded, and finally the door was opened. What happened next left the disciples astonished. Nothing; no one appeared. Crushed, they turned to their Rebbe, whose face was beaming. Seeing their distress, he asked, "What's troubling you?" They told him. "Fools!" he thundered. "Do you think Elijah the prophet enters through the door? He enters through the heart."[17]

WITNESSING THE COVENANT OF CIRCUMCISION

In the Jewish imagination, Elijah attends every ritual circumcision, where he occupies a special seat, known as the Chair of Elijah. This custom is first mentioned in an eighth-century midrash, *Pirqei de-Rabbi Eli'ezer.* There we are told that after the death of King Solomon, when the Israelite tribes split into the Northern and Southern Kingdoms, the northerners rejected the practice of circumcision. This inflamed the prophet:

> Elijah (gratefully remembered) arose and became mightily zealous, and he adjured the heavens not to send down dew or rain upon the earth. Jezebel heard and sought to kill him. . . . Elijah arose and fled from the land of Israel [to Mount Horeb]. . . . The blessed Holy One appeared to him and said, "*What are you doing here, Elijah?*" (1 Kings 19:9).
>
> [Elijah] replied, "*I have been very zealous [for YHVH, God of Hosts, for the Israelites have forsaken Your covenant—Your altars they have destroyed, Your prophets they have killed by the sword, and I alone remain, and they have sought to take my life*]" (1 Kings 19:10).
>
> The blessed Holy One said to him, "You are always zealous! You were zealous at Shittim on account of fornication, as is said *Phinehas son of Eleazar [son of Aaron the priest turned away My wrath from the Israelites by zealously enacting My zeal in their midst, so I did not annihilate the Israelites by My zeal]* (Numbers 25:11). And here too you are zealous. By your

> life! Israel shall not enact *berit milah* (the covenant of circumcision) until you see it with your eyes."
>
> Because of this, the Sages ordained that a seat of honor be prepared [at every circumcision] for the Angel of the Covenant, as is said: *The angel of the covenant, whom you desire—look, he is coming!* (Malachi 3:1).[18]

When God tells Elijah, "You are always zealous!," this assumes a strange notion we have encountered: Elijah is identical with Phinehas, grandson of Aaron the high priest. In the first phase of his biblical life, Phinehas/Elijah zealously killed two fornicators indulging in idolatry at Abel Shittim (Brook of the Acacias), thereby alleviating God's wrath at Israel's betrayal of the covenant. Several hundred years later, in his new identity in the book of Kings, Elijah/Phinehas is still fighting zealously for the covenant abandoned by Israel.[19]

God swears that no circumcision will be performed until Elijah witnesses it. This divine decree could be a reward for Elijah's zeal, but it is generally interpreted as a rebuke and an educational punishment for his being *too* zealous. According to this latter sense, Elijah must appear at every circumcision in order to see his error and acknowledge his excessive harshness. As the *Zohar* paraphrases God's words: "By your life! At every site of circumcision you will appear, and the mouth that testified this [i.e., that *the Israelites have forsaken Your covenant*] will testify that Israel is fulfilling the covenant."[20] By his presence, Elijah refutes his own accusation, attesting to Israel's loyalty. The inflamed biblical accuser is transmuted into a covenantal witness.[21]

Elijah becomes the Angel of the Covenant, foretold by the prophet Malachi: *The angel of the covenant, whom you desire—look, he is coming!* The same biblical chapter concludes with the famous verses about Elijah: *Look, I am sending to you Elijah the prophet . . .* (Malachi 3:23–24). Although Malachi does not identify *the angel of the covenant* with Elijah, here *Pirqei de-Rabbi Eli'ezer* does, and subsequently he often bears this title. As Angel of the Covenant, Elijah is the unseen guest at every *berit milah* (covenant of circumcision), and "a seat of honor" is prepared for him.

Though this special chair is mentioned for the first time here, the custom is older, since *Pirqei de-Rabbi Eli'ezer* refers to it as "ordained" by the sages. On the basis of this midrashic passage, the custom spread more widely. If anyone wondered how Elijah could possibly appear at numerous far-flung circumcisions simultaneously, an answer emerged: "Elijah sends one spark [of himself] to every single circumcision."[22]

Traditionally, when the infant is brought into the room, the *mohel* (circumciser) or all those who are present declare *Barukh ha-ba*, "Blessed is the one who comes," referring to the baby but, according to some, alluding to Elijah.[23] The special chair is identified aloud by the *mohel*, based on a passage in the *Zohar*: "One must prepare a chair for him and declare: 'This is the Chair of Elijah!' Otherwise, he does not abide there."[24]

As one would expect with a folk custom, practices vary from one community to another. Some early sources mention two special chairs, one for Elijah and the other for the *sandaq* (godfather), who holds the baby during the circumcision. Many communities still follow this practice, with Elijah's chair being placed to the right of the *sandaq*'s. In the eighteenth and nineteenth centuries, some congregations acquired large double chairs, in which the *sandaq* would sit on one half, leaving the other half free for Elijah. In some places, the infant is placed briefly on Elijah's chair and then given to the *sandaq*. Elsewhere, the *sandaq* himself sits on the Chair of Elijah. In certain synagogues, Elijah's chair is a small symbolic chair installed on the wall.[25]

What was the original reason for inviting Elijah to the circumcision ceremony and arranging a chair for him? The explanation offered in *Pirqei de-Rabbi Eli'ezer*—that God decreed this practice as either a reward or a corrective for Elijah's zeal—is a post hoc justification for an already existing custom. The initial motivation was probably so that Elijah would protect the baby. Given the high mortality rate of newborns (and birthing mothers) before modern medicine, it is understandable that families would invoke the Angel of the Covenant as the baby's guardian angel.

It is likely that the Chair of Elijah derives ultimately from ancient pagan customs.[26] In biblical times it was common to set up in the home a table bedecked with food and drink, dedicated to the Canaanite deities Gad and Meni (Luck and Destiny). The prophet Isaiah denounces those who do so: *As for you who forsake YHVH, who forget My holy mountain, who set a table for Gad (Luck) and fill a jug of mixed wine for Meni (Destiny)—I will destine you for the sword, all of you will kneel down to be slaughtered* (Isaiah 65:11–12).

The phrase *arsa de-gadda* (the bed of Gad) appears several times in the Talmud, referring to a bed in the home upon which no one slept or sat, but which rather was intended and reserved for good luck.[27] Meanwhile, there was a custom of setting a table for good luck in front of a woman in childbirth, and an early rabbinic text condemns this: "One who sets a table in front of [a woman in, or immediately following, childbirth]—this is an Amorite [i.e., heathenish] practice."[28] This resembles the Roman custom of setting a meal in the courtyard of the house of a newborn child, dedicating it to the deity who was believed to protect children from sickness. Despite rabbinic opposition, the custom persisted in certain forms, specifically relating to circumcision. In the fourteenth century, the Spanish talmudist Jeroham ben Meshullam writes: "Regarding the practice in certain countries of setting a table, placing upon it various kinds of food on the night preceding a circumcision, and saying that this is done for good luck for the newborn infant—

I have seen my rabbis forbidding this and protesting against it, saying that this is in the category of *setting a table for Gad* (Isaiah 65:11)."[29] Two hundred years later, Joseph Caro was still battling the same practice: "Those who are accustomed to set a table with various kinds of food on the eve of a circumcision, saying that this is for good luck for the infant—it is forbidden."[30]

Some Jews referred to this table as "the table of Elijah," and in the eighteenth century, rabbinic authorities argued whether this was permitted or forbidden.[31] However, dedicating the table to Elijah was not widespread. Eventually, the custom of setting a meal on the table on the eve of a circumcision was integrated into *Vakhnakht*, the "night vigil" preceding a circumcision. This vigil was meant to protect the infant from any lurking demonic forces, while the meal could be seen as intended for those keeping the vigil. On that night, Kurdish Jews used to bring Elijah's chair from the synagogue and dance around it. Among the Jews of Morocco and the Caucasus Mountains, that night was called explicitly "the Night of Elijah the Prophet." The following day, in communities far and wide, Elijah was invited to occupy the seat of honor at the circumcision ceremony—to preside as Angel of the Covenant and protect the newborn. In certain communities, in order to extend the protection, the Chair of Elijah was left for three days afterward.

Apparently, Elijah superseded the pagan guardian deity. His biblical career prepared him for this role, since back then he revived a lifeless child.[32] Since according to later tradition he attained immortality, he was well equipped to save babies from the Angel of Death. By the Middle Ages, Elijah acquired the role of protector against demons, especially those attacking newborns and their mothers. In one legend, Elijah confronts the famous demoness Lilith:

> Elijah the prophet was walking on the road, and he encountered the wicked Lilith along with all her cohorts. He said to

> her, "Where are you going, Impure One, Impure Spirit, with all your accompanying impure cohorts?"
>
> She replied, "My master Elijah, I am going to the house of the woman who has just given birth . . . so-and-so daughter of so-and-so, to bring her the sleep of death and to take her newborn child, to suck his blood, to suck the marrow of his bones, and to snatch his flesh."

Immediately, Elijah paralyzes Lilith, forcing her to swear that she will abandon her plot to kill the mother and baby. She promises that from then on, whenever she hears or sees her numerous names (which she dutifully lists), she will be powerless to inflict any harm. Subsequently, this story along with Lilith's names was recorded on many amulets to ensure the safety of mothers and infants.[33]

Thanks to Elijah, Lilith can be thwarted and vulnerable babies protected. As for the circumcision ceremony, the demoness would not dare to intrude, since Elijah's chair is prominently displayed and his arrival anticipated. Beyond guaranteeing the infant's well-being, Elijah presides over the baby's rite of passage from being a nameless newborn to joining the covenantal community of Israel. At this crucial moment, the timeless loner without a family welcomes a new junior member into the global, intimate Jewish family.

ELIJAH AT HAVDALAH

Anticipated at the seder, provided with a special chair at each circumcision, Elijah is also invoked weekly. Every Saturday night, as Shabbat departs, Jews around the world sing the opening lines of a hymn: "*Eliyyahu ha-Navi* (Elijah the prophet), Elijah the Tishbite, Elijah the Gileadite! May he come to us speedily with the Messiah son of David!" This hymn has become linked with Havdalah (Differentiation), the service "separating" the Sabbath from the new week. Characteristically,

Elijah is the one in-between, signaling here the transition from holiness to secular time.

As with Elijah's roles at the seder and the circumcision, the origins of this custom are uncertain. A Gaonic tradition commends singing hymns to Elijah as a way of honoring and escorting the Sabbath as it departs.[34] Among the songs mentioned in medieval sources are various versions of *Eliyyahu ha-Navi* (quoted above) and a hymn whose title expresses yearning for redemption: "Elijah the prophet, how long will you delay?"[35]

In the twelfth or thirteenth century, an Ashkenazic poet, Jesse son of Mordechai, composed *Ish ḥasid hayah* (There was a devout man). This is a lyrical revision of a tale about a pious man who was so poor that he needed to borrow clothing in order to go and find food for his family. Trusting in God, he ventured out and met Elijah, who insisted that the man sell him as a slave and then use the money to provide for his wife and children. Elijah is sold to the king's vizier, but the king promises to set him free if he can quickly construct a royal palace. Miraculously, a palace is built overnight, and before the king can thank him, Elijah disappears.[36]

Why was this particular hymn chanted on Saturday night? Probably because the departure of Shabbat meant the end of leisure and the beginning of a new workweek. At this transitional moment, it was appropriate to recall Elijah, who represents the hope of overcoming material deprivation.

Regarding the other Elijah hymns, Shabbat provides a taste of eternal bliss, "resembling the world to come," and as the day fades away, it is natural to yearn and sing for the messianic herald, who will proclaim an eon "that is entirely Shabbat."[37]

Before long, learned rabbis sought to provide a halakhic basis for this widespread practice. In the first book of European Jewish customs (*Sefer ha-Manhig*, composed in the early thirteenth century), Abraham ben Nathan linked the expectation of Elijah on Saturday night with a tradition about when he will *not* arrive. According to the Talmud, "Israel has already been assured that Elijah will not come on the eve of Shabbat [i.e., on Friday] or on the eve of a Festival, due to the effort [required to prepare for the holy day]."[38] As Rashi explains, Elijah will not come then "because people would abandon the necessary preparations for Shabbat and go out to greet him." From the rabbinic perspective, preparations for the Sabbath take precedence even over welcoming the harbinger of the Messiah. Accordingly, Elijah will avoid every Friday.

If Elijah will not arrive on Friday, the Messiah will not arrive on Shabbat, since the talmudic assumption is that Elijah precedes the Messiah by one day. But could Elijah himself arrive on Shabbat, proclaiming imminent redemption fittingly on the holiest day of the week, which resembles the world to come? Well, that depends on the uncertain answer to a hypothetical question. According to halakhah, on Shabbat it is forbidden to travel more than two thousand cubits (about half a mile) beyond the city limits. Elijah himself (who, as we have seen, is involved in the halakhic process) follows the law. So this travel restriction would seem to prevent him from flying from heaven to Jerusalem on Shabbat to announce the next day's arrival of the Messiah.

The Talmud wonders, though, whether the restriction of traveling two thousand cubits applies if one is moving at least ten handbreadths (about 2½ feet) above the ground—for example, if one is on an ocean voyage and the bottom of the ship remains at least ten handbreadths above the seabed. If such travel is permitted, then the same would apply to Elijah, winging through the air. However, the question of whether "[Sabbath] limits apply above ten [handbreadths]" is left unresolved in the Talmud, so we don't know whether or not Elijah can fly on Shabbat.[39]

As soon as the Sabbath departs, any restrictions on Elijah's travel no longer apply, so he could appear at any moment. Consequently, Elijah's name is invoked right as Shabbat ends—as if to say, "Now that you can come and redeem us, please do!"[40]

Perhaps one Saturday night, Elijah will arrive, heralding the Messiah. Meanwhile, for those who celebrate Shabbat, singing songs about him as the Sabbath departs eases the transition from a day of holy rest to the pressures of the impending week. By conjuring Elijah, one can draw strength to contend with tomorrow's demands and risks. According to a custom, if on Saturday night one recites all the biblical verses mentioning Elijah, "his ways will be successful all week long."[41]

Following Havdalah, Elijah too has to get back to work. Yet, as one tradition describes, his regular Saturday night activity still pertains to the Sabbath. He "sits beneath the Tree of Life [in the Garden of Eden], recording the merits of those who have observed Shabbat."[42] The harsh prophet who could not stop accusing Israel now busies himself with inscribing their good deeds.

This loving act rewards and reinforces the observance of Shabbat, while demonstrating Elijah's transformation. His eternal zeal now impels him to care deeply for all of Israel—not only those who faithfully keep the Sabbath, but even those suffering in hell. The Talmud teaches that the tranquility of Shabbat extends throughout the world, including hell; so one day a week, all those condemned to be there are allowed to rest. As soon as the Sabbath departs, however, they return to their torments. Yet according to a medieval source, if someone has suffered enough in hell and been purged of sinfulness, Elijah comes on Saturday night to transport that person straight to paradise. And if someone led a basically virtuous life on earth but is still being purged on account of some minor sins, Elijah offers to accept that person's punishment upon himself, thereby liberating the person immediately from hell.[43]

Hebrew hymns to Elijah are still being written. When I was a boy, my father introduced one to our family, which we would sing together every week, sitting around the living room before Havdalah, sharing the last moments of the presence of the Sabbath Queen. The poem does not mention Elijah's messianic role or his power to help the needy, but rather his gift of mouthing Torah. I still find myself singing it in Hebrew, as I'm wafted back in time some sixty years. Here is a translation:

On the shores of the Sea of Galilee
A palace of vast splendor,
A divine garden planted there
In which no tree stirs.
Who lives there? Just a boy
Like a bird in forest silence.
There he is studying Torah
From the mouth of Elijah.
Hush! Not a wave rolls,
Every flying bird
Stands still, listening—
God's Torah he is imbibing.[44]

ON SPECIAL DAYS AND EVERY DAY

Earlier each Sabbath, long before Havdalah, Elijah is invoked in the synagogue, after the chanting of the weekly Torah portion. This is the moment of the haftarah, a passage from the Prophets relating to the Torah portion (or occasionally to a special Sabbath or a festival). Following the haftarah, this blessing is recited: "Gladden us, YHVH our God, with Elijah the prophet, Your servant, and with the kingdom of the House of David, Your anointed one. May he come speedily and delight our heart. . . ."[45] In this blessing, probably formulated in the first century, Elijah appears in partnership with the Messiah, announcing his arrival.[46]

As for the haftarah itself, twice a year the weekly prophetic passage focuses on Elijah, and a third time it mentions him. The two "Elijah *haftarot*" associate him with his two biblical models, Moses and Phinehas.

In the Torah portion *Ki Tissa* (Exodus 30:11–34:35), the Israelites worship the golden calf and Moses assuages God's wrath, persuading Him not to annihilate His fickle people. Then Moses rebukes the Israelites and instructs the Levites to kill many of the idol worshipers. Finally, he wins God's promise to lead the people to the promised land.

For the haftarah of *Ki Tissa*, the rabbis turned to Elijah, who in numerous ways resembles Moses. They selected Elijah's contest with the prophets of Baal on Mount Carmel. There, as we recall, Elijah rebuked the people for worshiping Baal and strove to restore them to YHVH. When he defeated the doomed prophets by calling down fire, *all the people saw and fell on their faces and said, "YHVH, He is God; YHVH, He is God!"*[47]

The Torah portion *Pinḥas* (Numbers 25:10–30:1) opens in the aftermath of a zealous deed performed by Aaron's grandson, Phinehas. Many Israelite men had gone *whoring with the daughters of Moab* (Numbers 25:1) and had worshiped their heathen god, Baal Peor. God was incensed and inflicted a plague upon the people. Seeing a tribal chieftain fornicating with a Midianite princess, Phinehas immediately killed the sinning couple, and the plague ceased. As a reward, Phinehas was granted *eternal priesthood . . . for him and his seed after him* (Numbers 25:13).[48]

The haftarah for the portion *Pinḥas* begins just seven verses after the end of the first "Elijah haftarah" (for the portion *Ki Tissa*). As it opens, Elijah has just defeated and killed the prophets of Baal and won back the hearts of the Israelites for YHVH. Empowered by the spirit, he sprints ahead of King Ahab's chariots: *The hand of YHVH came upon Elijah, and he girded his loins and ran before Ahab all the way to Jezreel* (1 Kings 18:46). But his moment of glory quickly fades. Seeking revenge for the prophets of Baal, Queen Jezebel threatens to kill Elijah. He flees to the desert, where he asks God to take his life. Restored by an angel, he treks on to Mount Horeb, where God demands to know, *What are you doing here, Elijah?* To which he replies, *I have been so zealous for YHVH, God of Hosts, for the Israelites have forsaken Your covenant* (1 Kings 19:9–10). Then he receives a revelation in *a sound of sheer stillness* (1 Kings 19:12).[49]

The combination of this Torah portion with its haftarah demonstrates that Phinehas and Elijah are the two great biblical zealots. Phinehas is praised by God for *zealously enacting My zeal* (Numbers 25:11), while Elijah declares *I have been so zealous.* As discussed earlier, many believed that beyond sharing this trait, the two biblical heroes were actually one and the same: "Phinehas is Elijah."[50]

The third haftarah involving Elijah is chanted on the Sabbath preceding Passover, known as *Shabbat ha-Gadol.* This designation may mean "the Great Sabbath" or it might refer to the word *ha-gadol* (the great), in the conclusion of the haftarah: *Look, I am sending to you Elijah the prophet before the coming of the day of YHVH,* ha-gadol, *great, and awesome* (Malachi 3:23). As we have mentioned, the exodus from Egypt (celebrated each Passover) is the model for the final redemption, to be heralded by Elijah.[51]

Malachi's promise that God is *sending . . . Elijah the prophet* is echoed in the grace after meals, which includes this request: "May the Compassionate One send us Elijah the prophet (gratefully remembered), who will bring us good tidings of salvation and comfort."

So an observant Jew recalls Elijah at every seder, every circumcision, every Shabbat (following the haftarah and again at Havdalah), and several times a day after each meal. Fittingly, at the climax of Yom Kippur, immediately before the day concludes with a long shofar blast, the entire congregation chants seven times: *YHVH, He is God!* On this holiest day of the year, the final words of prayer are the words exclaimed twice by the

Israelites on Mount Carmel, when they saw Elijah call down fire from heaven.

Elijah frequents the rituals of Jewish life. And when a Jew is about to leave this life, after reciting a personal *viddu'i* (confession), it is customary to declare, *YHVH, He is God; YHVH, He is God!* The axiom of faith inspired by Elijah is affirmed amid one's final spoken words.[52]

6

Becoming Elijah

SPANNING HEAVEN AND EARTH, Elijah seems nearly divine. In the words of the kabbalist Moses Cordovero, "The closest that divinity can possibly come to humanity is the mystery of Elijah." In the Midrash, God Himself affirms their similarity: "The blessed Holy One said, 'I revive the dead, and Elijah revived the dead. . . . I bring down rain, and Elijah brought down rain. I stop the rains, and so did Elijah. . . . I brought down fire and brimstone upon Sodom, and Elijah similarly brought down [fire]. . . . He lived and will go on living until the revival of the dead.'"[1]

Like other righteous heroes, he can alter the divine will, as when he called down fire to consume his offering: "Elijah ascended Mount Carmel and decreed upon the blessed Holy One, who fulfilled the decree."[2]

Of all the divine qualities, Elijah emulates one in particular: *qin'ah*, "zeal" blended with "jealousy." YHVH demands total loyalty and is jealous of any false, rival god. As He commands Moses and Israel on Mount Sinai, *You shall not bow down to another god, for YHVH—whose name is* Qanna, *Jealous*—El qanna, *a jealous God, is He* (Exodus 34:14). His prophet Elijah imitates Him, declaring, *Qanno qinneiti*, "I have been so zealous."[3]

Was he too zealous? Did he really need to inflict an extended drought upon Israel, slaughter hundreds of false prophets, and incinerate a hundred royal troops? Of course, the biblical Elijah can feel compassion—as when he saves the widow of Zarephath from starvation and implores God to revive her child. He also champions the innocent and fights injustice, as when he dooms King Ahab and his dynasty after the judicial murder of Naboth. But some of the rabbis were troubled by Elijah's zealotry, and they criticize him for condemning Israel harshly and failing to defend them. According to one early midrash, the prophet's lack of respect for Israel provoked God to terminate Elijah's career and tell him bluntly: "I do not want your prophesying."[4]

Later in the Bible, we again glimpse Elijah's tenderness. According to the closing lines of Malachi, Elijah will return on the eve of the day of YHVH and *bring fathers' hearts back to their children and children's hearts to their fathers* (Malachi 3:23–24). Here the zealot is destined to reappear as the ultimate reconciler, restoring harmony between the generations.

Having ascended to heaven in a fiery chariot, Elijah will eventually return at the end of days. But as we've seen, he does not wait until then. In his postbiblical life, he reappears often—to help, rescue, and inspire. Perhaps, as one medieval thinker reasoned, Elijah was taken to heaven while still alive so that he would be available whenever necessary.[5]

ELIJAH'S *TIQQUN*

When he reappears, Elijah's severe temperament has mellowed. The rabbis, it seems, could not bear the harsh, fanatical contours of his biblical personality. He was too extreme, too remote and exalted, unable to mediate between God and mere humans. As was well known, in the first century the Zealots of Judea—who venerated Phinehas and Elijah—instigated the revolt against Rome, leading to the destruction of the Temple. This painful memory was a likely factor in the rabbis' criticism of Elijah. Beyond criticizing him, they refashioned him, softening and refining his image, engendering Elijah the Compassionate. Thereby they effected his *tiqqun* (mending, rectification).

Elijah's *tiqqun* changes his perspective and his mission. In the words of the twentieth-century mystic Abraham Isaac Kook, "Originally, before he was sweetened, he perceived acutely the depth of ugliness and contamination in which this lowly world is immersed. Therefore he blazed with zeal to eradicate the spirit of impurity and those clinging to it. After being sweetened, he perceives every spark of holiness in this world and redeems it."[6]

From another angle, Elijah effects his own *tiqqun.* He becomes immortal because his task has not been completed; he needs to mend his ways. Frequently returning to earth, he harnesses his zeal to help the persecuted and wretched. Instead of castigating the people of Israel, he fervently defends them. His wrath is spent. Now, in helping others, he cultivates kindness; his heart opens, and he discovers how to love.[7]

On Mount Horeb, he experienced a divine revelation—not through wind, earthquake, or fire, but through *a sound of sheer stillness.* Centuries later, he finally grasps an implication of that theophany: to succeed in transforming others, fierce power is often less effective than patient gentleness.

Despite that revelation, on Horeb Elijah could not stop accusing Israel of faithlessness. Now, at every circumcision, he witnesses and confirms their loyalty. His ritual presence upon the Chair of Elijah links one generation to the next; his endless engagement with Israel guarantees their perennial fruitfulness.

The biblical Elijah was a loner without a family who compelled his disciple, Elisha, to abandon his own family. Now he is invited into the home each year for the seder. In the book of Kings, he prayed in solitude; in later folklore, he sustains communal worship by appearing suddenly as the tenth man for a minyan.[8] Atoning for his past harshness toward his people, he insists that their meritorious deeds be recorded.[9] His involvement and care extend beyond Israel: "When [the blessed Holy One] causes His world to quake, Elijah recalls the merit of the Patriarchs . . . , and the blessed Holy One is filled with compassion for His world."[10]

In the Bible, Elijah saw everything as black-and-white—most clearly on Mount Carmel, where he accused the people of wavering and demanded that they make a choice: *How long will you keep hopping between the two branches? If YHVH is God, follow Him; and if Baal, follow him!* (1 Kings 18:21). In his later phase of existence, he realizes that conflicting views can sometimes be equally true: "Both these and those are words of the Living God."[11] He reveals the unity within the contradictions of tradition. Eventually, paving the way for the Messiah, he will "harmonize disputes." The biblical zealot who slayed his opponents will come "to make peace in the world."[12]

Having mended himself, he can stimulate others to strive for personal and social *tiqqun*. His transformation from harsh battler to benevolent sage increases his potency, enabling him to extend his victory on Mount Carmel, when he temporarily brought Israel back to God. Now he is charged with readying Israel for redemption by inspiring them to engage in more lasting *teshuvah* ("turning back" to God): "Through him [on Mount Carmel], Israel accepted upon themselves the Kingdom of Heaven and acknowledged that *YHVH is God.* And so too, through him they are destined to enact complete *teshuvah*."[13]

As noted by one commentator, before becoming eternal, Elijah was born perishable.[14] Having been flawed, Elijah recognizes failure. Having sunk so deeply in despair that he begged God to take his life, he learns how to lift anyone's spirit. True to his name—*Eliyyahu* (YHVH is my God)—he struggled to purge Israel of idolatry, a goal he never fully attained. Yet he inspired his successor, Elisha, to go further, devastating the cult of Baal and performing more miracles than Elijah himself.[15]

BEḤINAT ELIYYAHU (AN ASPECT OF ELIJAH)

On Mount Carmel, surrounded by throngs of vacillating Israelites, Elijah demonstrated God's power and dominion. Today, three millennia later, the prophet's zeal persists. According to Hasidic teaching, there is "an aspect (or quality) of Elijah" (*beḥinat Eliyyahu*) hidden within us, which can arouse the desire for God and stimulate spiritual growth:

> *Look, I am sending to you Elijah the prophet before the coming* [*of the day of YHVH, great and awesome*] (Malachi 3:23). The wording *sholeaḥ*, "am sending," is in the present tense, implying "even now," since it is not written *eshlaḥ*, "I will send." . . . For the truth is that all the yearning of Israel . . . for their Father in heaven comes about through *beḥinat Eliyyahu* (the aspect of Elijah), who heralds all that is whole.

By exploiting the present tense of the verb *sending*, the Hasidic author transforms the messianic promise into an immediate reality. Elijah is being sent to earth right now, as evidenced by people's yearning for God, which is fueled by the aspect of Elijah within them. The figure of the Messiah is still central, but now in a more personal way: "The aspect of Elijah arouses desire initially, and then comes the aspect of the Messiah. . . . As was said by the Ba'al Shem Tov (his soul rests in the Garden of Eden), 'Every one of Israel must mend and prepare that part of the stature of the Messiah pertaining to his own soul.' . . . Until eventually the entire stature is mended and prepared."[16]

Aroused by the aspect of Elijah, spiritual seekers devote

themselves to solving their part of the messianic puzzle by actualizing their unique, vital potential. One day, Elijah will bring the good news of redemption and spread the awareness of God to all, but already now he offers a preview via his aspect within:

> *Look, I am sending to you Elijah the prophet before the coming of the day of YHVH,* [*great and awesome*]. *He will bring fathers' hearts back* [*to their children and children's hearts to their fathers*] (Malachi 3:23–24). Truly, before the coming of the Messiah (speedily in our days), Elijah will bring the good news; and thereby awareness will be expanded, as is written: *The earth will be filled with knowledge of YHVH as waters cover the sea* (Isaiah 11:9). Similarly, this aspect exists in every one of Israel and at all times. . . .
>
> If some good news comes to a person—also during learning, when one is having difficulty with a certain matter, before *da'at* (knowing) reaches him, a kind of good news enters him, for he feels a single point entering his mind. This is called *beḥinat Eliyyahu* (the aspect of Elijah), after which *the earth will be filled with knowledge*, for his awareness expands and is suffused with vitality. Then he can easily unite the various parts of himself, bringing even his lower parts toward the good.
>
> For truly, a spark of Elijah is enveloped within anyone bearing good news, since [Elijah] is the bearer of all good tidings in the world, and now he clothes himself in that messenger; for the aspect of Elijah has existed since the six days of Creation. . . .
>
> Therefore, whenever there is good news to be delivered, everyone runs out to tell it, because his soul feels the aspect of Elijah, and he wants to draw it into himself. . . . If he had awareness, he could begin to serve God with that aspect of Elijah infusing him then, thereby ascending from rung to rung.
>
> The recipient of the good news also receives the spark of Elijah within himself, and his awareness expands. He too

> can cleave easily to the Creator, may He be blessed, even with his lower parts. This is then called *the coming of the great day of YHVH*, for he has thereby drawn God into himself.
>
> This is the meaning of: *Look, I am sending to you [Elijah the prophet]*—for the word *sending* is in the present tense, because it is constantly so, in each person and at all times.[17]

This type of "good news" from Elijah arrives as a flash of insight, clarifying what seemed difficult or puzzling in a book being studied. The sudden breakthrough illuminates not only the text but one's inner being, reorienting the recipient, enabling one to overcome the fragmentation of self, integrate conflicting tendencies, and taste wholeness.[18]

One of Elijah's titles is *Mevasser tov* (Herald of Goodness), referring to his destined role of proclaiming the Messiah.[19] Until he delivers that ultimate good news, there is an aspect of Elijah within each of us, making us eager to convey positive news, whether spiritual or mundane. The thrill of spreading happy news is intrinsically holy and redemptive. In the words of the grandson of the Baal Shem Tov, "All good news is gathered within [Elijah], and anyone who delivers good news is infused with Elijah."[20]

Is Elijah an immortal being who appears to the fortunate few or an inner quality accessible to anyone? From a Hasidic perspective, "the aspect of Elijah" hidden within produces an epiphany of the prophet: "This aspect is present in every person. . . . Therefore, our rabbis (may their memory be a blessing) said, 'Elijah was revealed to so-and-so.' For whatever was considered hidden was revealed to that person through his virtue—because everyone includes this aspect, but it is in hiding."[21] Here a revelation from Elijah is understood as the uncovering and actualization of the Elijah quality, bubbling up from the depths of one's own being.

Elijah conveys inspiration—sparking an intuition, stimulating a rush of creativity. This may be experienced from within (as the aspect of Elijah), or as a gift from beyond—delivered by the external figure of Elijah, the messenger of spiritual awareness who personifies *ruaḥ ha-qodesh* (the Holy Spirit).[22]

Elijah provides a human face for the transcendent, inviting seekers to learn the unknown. Over the ages, what sages and mystics discovered, he authenticated for them and their circles by his very presence, by his stature as vigilant defender of the faith and guarantor of tradition. If what they absorbed through Elijah seemed startlingly new, he validated it as simultaneously ancient, thereby revitalizing Judaism. Especially in Kabbalah, *gillui Eliyyahu* (an epiphany of Elijah) signals a shift in religious understanding.

Spiritual questers feel a bond with this earthling who surpassed his mortal limitations, while those who suffer and have lost all hope regain it by yearning for him. Throughout Jewish folklore, Elijah tends to appear when people find themselves in apparently inescapable predicaments. Elijah represents the possibility of deliverance, either immediately or finally when he will escort the Messiah. Redemption seems distant, but for millennia the expectation of Elijah has sustained belief in it.

In the middle of the nineteenth century, a black American slave named Wallis Willis dreamed of a better life than the one he was suffering, and the image of Elijah's chariot ride to heaven provided him not immediate liberation but confidence in an eventual, ultimate release. Envisioning that biblical ride, Willis composed out of his pain a song that became famous: "Swing Low, Sweet Chariot." Following the opening refrain, its first stanza mentions the Jordan River, from near which Elijah was taken above. Willis conjured a similar journey awaiting him:

> Swing low, sweet chariot
> Coming for to carry me home.
> Swing low, sweet chariot

Coming for to carry me home.
I looked over Jordan and what did I see
Coming for to carry me home?
A band of angels coming after me
Coming for to carry me home.

Elijah fills a need for hope—and for justice. Ever since he confronted King Ahab, denouncing him for murdering an innocent man, Elijah has humbled the powerful and arrogant, teaching them human decency and compassion. Among the countless tales of Elijah, many convey his zeal for social justice. Residing in heaven does not detach him from those on earth; rather, he craves opportunities to fight worldly wrongs, to expose reality. In the words of a Saturday night hymn, he is *Ish ha-Emet* (the Man of Truth).[23]

Occasionally, Elijah enlightens the mystics, but he spends most of his time helping the downtrodden. Since he can disguise himself as anyone—from a royal minister to a slave—one of the lessons he imparts is that whomever we encounter might be Elijah and should be treated accordingly. His greatest miracle is transforming how people act toward one another.

The identity of Elijah is variable, but always shaped by an ethical imperative. He is an ethical extremist, teaching how to treat others according to his *mishnat ḥasidim* (instruction for the devout).[24]

According to a Hasidic tale, a pious Jew once asked his rabbi why Elijah never appeared on the night of the seder, even though the door was opened for him and his goblet of wine was waiting on the table. The rabbi told him: "There is a very poor family in your neighborhood. Go visit them and propose that next year you and your family will celebrate Passover with them in their house and that you'll provide everything they need for the whole holiday. Then on the night of the Seder, Elijah will certainly come." The man did as he was told, but after the following Passover he returned to the rabbi, complaining that once again Elijah had failed to appear. The rabbi responded, "Elijah came, but you couldn't see him." Holding a mirror to the man's face, he continued, "Look, this was Elijah's face that night."[25]

Here the possibility of meeting Elijah is surpassed, as one learns to enact the prophet's quality of compassion, thereby *becoming* Elijah.

Having already been a person, Elijah turns into an animating energy. A spark of that energy lies within each of us, ready to be fanned into a flame. In moments of intensity, it radiates as an insight or a creative urge, a striving, an eagerness to uplift others.

The first biblical hero to revive the dead, Elijah fittingly proceeds to live forever, rejuvenating tradition and vivifying those who perceive him or those who discover his spark within. Over the centuries, he has tamed his fanaticism but never lost his passion, which he channels into mending himself, his people, and the world.

The story of Elijah is not relegated to the past; it is a play in two acts. The first consists of the biblical narrative in the book of Kings; the second is its sequel, still unfolding, endless. In the global audience, each of us is a latent participant in the performance. Your own potential scene—your experience of Elijah—is unscripted, for he appears only by surprise.

NOTES

Abbreviations

BT	Babylonian Talmud
JT	Jerusalem Talmud
M	Mishnah
v.	verse

Epigraph

Cordovero, *Or Yaqar, Tiqqunei ha-Zohar,* Vol. 2, 4:6, 44a.

Introduction

1. *Pesiqta Rabbati* 4, 13a.
2. Wiener, *Prophet Elijah*, 29.
3. See White, *Elijah Legends and Jehu's Coup*, 77–78; Coote, *Elijah and Elisha in Socioliterary Perspective*, ix. On Jehu's coup and its aftermath, see 2 Kgs 9–10.
4. Ginzberg, *Legends of the Jews*, 4:229.

5. See BT *Berakhot* 4b (four strokes), 29b (*tefillat ha-derekh*).

6. See Fisch, "Elijah and the Wandering Jew"; Fisch, *Remembered Future*, 71–80. On Elijah's role of making the world fit for the Messiah, see Maimonides, *Commentary on the Mishnah*, *Eduyyot* 8:7.

7. See Cohen, *Ishim min ha-Miqra*, 250; Segal, *Elijah*, 1.

Chapter 1. *I Have Been So Zealous for YHVH*

1. See Cogan, *1 Kings*, 431; Alter, *Hebrew Bible* 2:503.

2. *Pilgrimage of Egeria*, 16:1, p. 131.

3. According to some scholars, because of the unreliable orthography of this inscription, the number "2,000 (chariots)" may be an error for "200."

4. White, *Elijah Legends and Jehu's Coup*, 58.

5. BT *Megillah* 11a. The other two kings mentioned are Ahasuerus (king of Persia; see Esth 1:1) and Nebuchadnezzar (king of Babylon; see Jer 27:6–8). The prooftext adduced for Ahab is 1 Kgs 18:10.

6. Morgenstern, *Amos Studies*, 276–83.

7. Josephus, *Against Apion* 1.18, relying on the historian Menander of Ephesus. Cf. Josephus, *Antiquities of the Jews* 8.13.2.

8. The element of dung recurs in the grotesque prophecy of Jezebel's demise in 2 Kgs 9:37: *Jezebel's carcass shall be* ke-domen, *like dung, upon the ground in the field of Jezreel.* The same chapter describes how she was trampled by horses, and all that was left of her was the skull, feet, and hands. Her characterization as dung in combination with her missing carcass may have yielded the distorted name *Izevel*, "Where is the dung?" See White, *Elijah Legends and Jehu's Coup*, 73–75.

9. The title *king of the Sidonians* reflects the expansion and supremacy of Tyre over its northern neighbor, Sidon.

10. The negative evaluation of Ahab continues in rabbinic literature. According to M *Sanhedrin* 10:2, he is one of only a few Israelites who have no portion in the world to come.

11. See Gray, *I and II Kings*, 377.

12. *Seder Eliyyahu Zuta*, 8, p. 185. Cf. BT *Sanhedrin* 113a.

13. *Yahu* is an abbreviation of YHVH.

14. See Exod 34:14; Deut 4:24, 6:15, 32:21; Ezek 16:38, 42; 39:25.

15. See Exod 16.

16. See Gen 38:14.

17. Recalling the request of Abraham's servant to Rebekah in Gen 24:17.

18. See Alter, *Hebrew Bible*, 2:505. For the view that the boy did not actually die, see Josephus, *Antiquities of the Jews* 8.13.3; *Targum Yonatan*, 1 Kgs 17:20; Maimonides, *Guide of the Perplexed* 1:42; David Kimḥi, on 1 Kgs 17:17, 20; Gray, *I and II Kings*, 382–83; Zevit, "First and Second Kings," 697. Cf. Dan 10:17, where the nearly identical wording—*no breath is left in me*—is purely hyperbolic, implying that Daniel is close to fainting.

19. See Gray, *I and II Kings*, 382; Alter, *Hebrew Bible*, 2:505. Cf. *Bereshit Rabbah* 50:11; Rashi, on this verse. According to one fanciful midrash, the widow is implying, "*You have come to me* (1 Kgs 17:18) for sexual intercourse." See *Pirqei de-Rabbi Eli'ezer*, 33; David Luria, ad loc., n. 17; *Pirqei de-Rabbi Eli'ezer*, ed. Higger, 32; *Yalqut Shim'oni*, 1 Kings 209.

20. Samet, *Pirqei Eliyyahu*, 83–84.

21. See David Kimḥi and Gersonides, on 1 Kgs 17:21, 2 Kgs 4:34; Cogan, *1 Kings*, 429; Alter, *Hebrew Bible*, 2:505.

22. See Cogan, *1 Kings*, 432.

23. In *Bereshit Rabbah* 33:5, Elijah is described as "a righteous one who will arise and parch the world." In rabbinic literature, years of severe drought and famine are called *shanim ki-shnei Eliyyahu*, "years like those of Elijah." See, e.g., *Vayiqra Rabbah* 35:9.

24. Zevit, "First and Second Kings," 697.

25. See Cogan, *1 Kings*, 438; Zevit, "First and Second Kings," 698. On the power of *the spirit of YHVH* to transport a prophet, see Ezek 37:1. Cf. Judg 13:25.

26. The plural *Baalim* may reflect the belief that the Canaanite god Baal had many manifestations. See Gray, *I and II Kings*, 393; Cogan, *1 Kings*, 438.

27. Cf. Isa 35:2, mentioning *the splendor of Carmel.*

28. See Cogan, *1 Kings*, 439.

29. See Simon, *Reading Prophetic Narratives*, 179; Zevit, "First

and Second Kings," 698. The clause *poseḥim al shetei ha-se'ippim*, "hopping between the two branches," can be rendered in other ways: *hopping between the two crevices, hobbling on two crutches, hopping between two thoughts*. See Gray, *I and II Kings*, 396; Cogan, *1 Kings*, 439.

30. Elijah's claim to be the only surviving *prophet of YHVH* is not technically correct, because Ahab's steward, Obadiah, had hidden a hundred such prophets. Elijah's claim could be prophetic hyperbole. (See Cogan, *1 Kings*, 440; cf. 1 Kgs 19:10, 14.) Alternatively, the other prophets are not mentioned here because they were driven underground and could not function. (See Simon, *Reading Prophetic Narratives*, 316, n. 71.) Other prophets of YHVH appear as well in the stories concerning Ahab's wars with Aram. See 1 Kgs 20:13; 22:1–28.

31. Elijah had instructed Ahab to gather *the four hundred fifty prophets of Baal and the four hundred prophets of Asherah* (1 Kgs 18:19), so why aren't *the prophets of Asherah* mentioned here when everyone gathers on the mountain? The Septuagint does in fact include them here. On the other hand, some commentators contend that there was originally no reference to *the prophets of Asherah* and that the mention of them (in v. 19) is a later intrusion. It seems more plausible, however, that the reference to the *prophets of Asherah* was accidentally deleted here (and in v. 40) rather than intentionally added to v. 19. See Simon, *Reading Prophetic Narratives*, 315, n. 65.

David Kimḥi (on v. 19) contends that Jezebel did not allow her *prophets of Asherah* to participate in the contest on Mount Carmel. Cf. Garsiel, *From Earth to Heaven*, 65–68.

David Noel Freedman speculates that *the prophets of Asherah* are not mentioned here because "when Yahweh defeated Baal in the contest at Mount Carmel, Asherah, who had been associated with the latter, now became the former's consort." In other words, "The winner gets the girl." See Freedman, "Yahweh of Samaria and his Asherah," 249; Zevit, *Religions of Ancient Israel*, 652; Friedman, *Exodus*, 191. Cf. Dever, *Did God Have a Wife?*, 211.

32. Does the subject "you" (*shall call on the name of your god*) refer to the Israelites or to the prophets of Baal? The literal con-

text—*Elijah said to the people* (1 Kgs 18:22)—implies the Israelites, but the full narrative favors the prophets of Baal, to whom Elijah immediately says, *Call on the name of your god* (1 Kgs 18:25). Simon (*Reading Prophetic Narratives*, 316, n. 72) feels compelled to alter the wording here to *Let them call on the name of their god*. Cogan (*1 Kings*, 440) contends that Elijah is identifying the wayward people as adherents of Baal.

33. Or, *that he gave them*. This seems to contradict v. 23 (*Let them choose for themselves one bull*) and v. 25 (*Choose one of the bulls for yourselves*); but perhaps this implies that he offered them two bulls, allowing them to choose. See Alter, *Hebrew Bible*, 2:508. A charming midrash (*Tanḥuma*, *Mas'ei* 8) solves this textual problem creatively:

> What did Elijah do? He said to them, "Select two bulls that are twins from the same mother and who have been raised on one feeding trough, and cast lots for them—one [to be offered] for the sake of Heaven and one for the sake of Baal." . . .
>
> The bull for Elijah immediately followed him. As for the bull designated for Baal, all those prophets of Baal and prophets of Asherah gathered together to move it, but they were unable to do so, until Elijah intervened and said to [that bull], "Go with them."
>
> The bull replied to Elijah in front of all the people, "My fellow and I issued from the same womb, and we were raised in the same pasture from the same feeding trough. Yet he has fallen to the lot of the Omnipresent, and the name of the blessed Holy One will be sanctified over him, whereas I have fallen to the lot of Baal, provoking my Creator!"
>
> Elijah said to it, "Go with them, and let them not find any excuse [for their failure]. For just as the name of the blessed Holy One will be sanctified by the [bull] that is with me, so it will be sanctified by you." [Elijah is implying that the impending failure of the prophets of Baal is inseparable from his own success. Despite, and because of, being sacrificed to Baal, the bull will soon sanctify God's name.]

> [The bull] replied, "Is this how you advise me? Then I swear I will not budge from here until you yourself hand me over to them." As is said: *They took the bull that he gave them* (1 Kgs 18:26). Who gave it to them? Elijah.

34. The prophets of Baal perform a ritual dance. The verb *vayphasseḥu*, "they hopped [or, they hobbled]," echoes Elijah's taunt of the Israelites in v. 21: *How long* attem poseḥim, *will you keep hopping, between the two branches?* See Uffenheimer, *Early Prophecy in Israel*, 361–63; Simon, *Reading Prophetic Narratives*, 180.

35. This is arguably the meaning of the Hebrew clause *ki si'aḥ ve-khi sig lo*. Alternatively, it could mean, *He may be in conversation or have wandered off.* For the scatological sense, see Rendsburg, "Mock of Baal in 1 Kings 18:27"; Rendsburg, "Hebrew *św/yḥ* and Arabic *šḫḫ*"; Gray, *I and II Kings*, 397–98. Cf. *Targum Yonatan* and Rashi, on the verse.

36. Elijah's taunt of Baal being on a journey may allude to the motif of Baal's journeys in Ugaritic myth. See Cogan, *1 Kings*, 441.

37. The taunt of Baal being asleep likely refers to the ritual of awakening Baal from his slumber. See Josephus, *Antiquities of the Jews* 8.5.3; Uffenheimer, *Early Prophecy in Israel*, 359–61, 365–67; Gray, *I and II Kings*, 398–99; Cogan, *1 Kings*, 441. According to rabbinic sources, when the gates of the Temple in Jerusalem were thrown open each morning, certain Levites or priests (known as the "Awakeners") would exclaim, *Awake, why do You sleep, O Lord?* (Ps 44:24). Eventually, this practice was abolished because of its resemblance to pagan rites of awakening the gods, practiced every morning in Hellenistic Egyptian temples. See M *Ma'aser Sheni* 5:15; *Sotah* 9:10; *Tosefta, Sotah* 13:9; JT *Sotah* 9:10, 24a; BT *Sotah* 48a; Lieberman, *Hellenism in Jewish Palestine*, 139–43; Fishbane, *Biblical Myth and Rabbinic Mythmaking*, 177–78.

38. The Hebrew verb *va-yitnabbe'u* can mean "they prophesied," but here the sense is "they raved, flung themselves into a state of ecstasy or frenzy." See Num 11:25–26; 1 Sam 10:5–6, 10; 18:10; 19:20–24; Jer 29:26.

39. Gen 35:10.

40. In the following chapter (1 Kgs 19:10), Elijah complains to

God: *Your altars they have destroyed, Your prophets they have killed by the sword.*

41. David Kimḥi, on 18:34; Cogan, *1 Kings*, 443; Alter, *Hebrew Bible*, 2:509. On the twelve stones, cf. Exod 24:4, Deut 27:1–8, Josh 4.

42. Gray, *I and II Kings*, 399; Uffenheimer, *Early Prophecy in Israel*, 339; Cogan, *1 Kings*, 442.

43. JT *Ta'anit* 2:4, 65d.

44. *Sifrei*, Deuteronomy 175. See *Sifrei*, Deuteronomy 70; BT *Yevamot* 90b; Ginzberg, *Legends of the Jews*, 6:319, n. 13; Samet, *Pirqei Eliyyahu*, 232–39.

45. The title reappears later in Mal 3:23 (*Eliyyah ha-Navi*) and 2 Chr 21:12, both discussed later in this chapter.

46. Simon, *Reading Prophetic Narratives*, 187–88. David Kimḥi (on the verse) brings several such interpretations, including that of Saadiah Gaon, *Emunot ve-De'ot*, chap. 4. Cf. *Targum Yonatan*, on the verse. For a fuller discussion of Elijah's statement, see Greenberg, "Ve-Attah Hasibbota et Libbam Aḥorannit"; Samet, *Pirqei Eliyyahu*, 188–93.

47. As evidenced by all the other occurrences of the word: Gen 9:23, 1 Sam 4:18, 2 Kgs 20:10, Isa 38:8.

48. Rashi, on 1 Kgs 18:37. Cf. Rashi, on BT *Berakhot* 32a, s.v. *di-khtiv*, recording God's admission: "I caused them [to sin], for I created the evil impulse."

49. Maimonides, *Mishneh Torah, Hilkhot Teshuvah* 6:3. Cf. Maimonides, *Shemonah Peraqim*, chap. 8.

50. BT *Berakhot* 31b.

51. *Bemidbar Rabbah* 18:12. See JT *Sanhedrin* 10:1, 28a; *Tanḥuma* (Buber), *Qoraḥ*, add. 3; Rashi and David Kimḥi, on the verse.

52. Greenberg, "Ve-Attah Hasibbota et Libbam Aḥorannit," 66. This notion is paralleled by one of Elijah's prophetic successors: *Why do You make us stray, YHVH, from Your ways, why harden our hearts until we cease revering You? . . . Look, You raged, and so we sinned; when You hid Yourself we transgressed* (Isa 63:17, 64:4). Earlier in the book of Isaiah, a divine command dovetails with this view: *Dull the heart of this people and block its ears and seal its eyes. Lest it see*

with its eyes and with its ears hear and its heart understand and it turn back and be healed (Isa 6:10). On God's hardening the heart (of Pharaoh), see, e.g., Exod 4:21, 7:3, 9:12. Cf. Deut 2:30.

53. A similar description appears in Leviticus, at the end of the consecration of the altar (and of Aaron and his sons) in Lev 9:24: *A fire came out from before YHVH and consumed on the altar the ascent offering and the fat, and all the people saw and shouted with joy and fell on their faces.* See the parallels in 1 Chr 21:26 (David's dedication of the altar at the site of the future Temple) and 2 Chr 7:1–3 (Solomon's dedication of the Temple). The formulation *YHVH, He is God* appears also in Deut 4:35, 39; 1 Kgs 8:60; Ps 100:3; 2 Chr 33:13. Cf. Josh 24:18.

54. *Yalqut Shim'oni*, Judges 47.

55. See Exod 32:26–29, Num 25:7–8, 1 Sam 15:32–33.

56. Isaac Arama, *Aqedat Yitsḥaq*, Numbers 83.

57. See BT *Berakhot* 34b; *Avodah Zarah* 17a; Elior, *Heikhalot Zutarti*, 36–37; *Zohar* 3:166b; Idel, *Kabbalah*, 78–79; Idel, *Ascensions on High in Jewish Mysticism*, 31–35; Idel, *Ben*, 151–53; Fenton, "Rosh bein ha-Birkayim"; Mach and Marks, "Head upon the Knees"; Wiener, *Prophet Elijah*, 82. On the fetal position, see *Vayiqra Rabbah* 14:8; BT *Niddah* 30b. Hai Gaon (tenth to eleventh centuries) recommends this posture as part of a technique for attaining mystical vision: "One who is worthy . . . when he seeks to gaze at the [Divine] Chariot and the palaces of the supernal angels, there are methods to follow: He should fast for a certain number of days and place his head between his knees, and softly chant many specific songs and praises toward the earth. Thereby he will gaze within—like one who sees seven palaces with his very eyes, as if he is entering from palace to palace, seeing what is inside each one." See Lewin, *Otsar ha-Ge'onim*, *Ḥagigah*, 14. Scholem (in *Major Trends in Jewish Mysticism*, 49) describes this posture as "an attitude of deep self-oblivion."

58. Ḥananel ben Shemuel, *Commentary on the Haftarot*. See Fenton, "Rosh bein ha-Birkayim," 26.

59. See Simon, *Reading Prophetic Narratives*, 196; 320–21, n. 113.

60. See Alter, *Hebrew Bible*, 2:510. Jezreel was located about

seventeen miles southeast of Mount Carmel. There, Ahab had a winter palace, while his main palace stood in the capital, Samaria. Some commentators interpret Elijah's racing before Ahab's chariot as a gesture of honor and respect for royalty. See *Mekhilta*, *Pisḥa* 13; David Kimḥi, on 1 Kgs 18:46; Kadari, "Did Elijah Show Respect to Royalty?" Cf. 1 Sam 8:11, 2 Sam 15:1, 1 Kgs 1:5.

61. According to the Septuagint, Jezebel opens her message by declaring, *If you are Elijah, I am Jezebel!*

62. *Midrash Shemu'el* 22:3.

63. Elijah's desperate plea resembles that of Moses: *Why have You done evil to Your servant, and why have I not found favor in Your eyes, to put the burden of all this people upon me? . . . I alone cannot carry this entire people, for they are too heavy for me. If this is how You treat me, kill me, please, if I have found favor in Your eyes—so that I no longer see my wretchedness* (Num 11:11, 14–15). When Moses learns of the Israelites' sin of the golden calf, he begs God to forgive them, pleading as follows: *Now, if You would bear their sin! And if not, please wipe me out of Your book that You have written* (Exod 32:32). Elijah's formulation—*Now, YHVH, take my life*—is nearly identical with that of the prophet Jonah, who declares, *Now, YHVH, please take my life from me, for better my death than my life* (Jonah 4:3).

64. See Zakovitch, "'Qol Demamah Daqqah,'" 332; Alter, *Hebrew Bible*, 2:511.

65. See above at n. 55, and n. 63; below, Chap. 2, at nn. 96–105; White, *Elijah Legends*, 3–11; Savran, *Encountering the Divine*, 204–29. On Moses's times on the mountain, see also Exod 24:18, 34:28; Deut 9:18, 10:10. On Moses and Horeb, see Exod 3:1, 33:6–7.

66. The Hebrew word *ha-me'arah* means literally "the cave," though it can also be rendered "a cave." See Simon, *Reading Prophetic Narratives*, 204; 322, n. 124. A midrashic tradition identifies the cave of Elijah with Moses's *cleft of the crag* (Exod 33:22). See *Mekhilta*, *Vayassa* 5; *Sifrei*, Deuteronomy 355; BT *Pesaḥim* 54a, *Megillah* 19b; Rashi, David Kimḥi, and Isaac Abravanel, on 1 Kgs 19:9. Cf. Onkelos on Exod 33:22.

67. See Malbim, on 1 Kgs 19:9; Garsiel, *From Earth to Heaven*, 95; Alter, *Hebrew Bible*, 2:511.

68. Shortly before, on Mount Carmel, he had declared, "*I alone remain a prophet of YHVH*" (1 Kgs 18:22). See above, n. 30.

69. Elijah is commanded, "*Go out and stand on the mountain*"—just as Moses was instructed: "*Take your stance on the crag*" (Exod 33:21) and "*Take your stance for Me there on the mountaintop*" (Exod 34:2). Elijah is told, "*Look, YHVH is passing by,*" paralleling the description in Exodus: *YHVH passed before him* (Exod 34:6).

According to many translators and commentators, God's words to Elijah include only "*Go out and stand on the mountain before YHVH,*" while the rest of this passage (*Look, YHVH is passing by . . . a sound of sheer stillness*) is a report of what occurred. Simon (*Reading Prophetic Narratives*, 324, n. 141) argues for construing the entire passage as divine speech.

70. Other biblical theophanies also involve wind, earthquake, and fire. See Judg 5:4–5; Ezek 1:4; Nah 1:3–6; Pss 50:3, 68:9, 97:3.

71. The word *demamah* means "stillness, silence, murmur." See Job 4:16: Demamah, *Stillness, and a sound did I hear.* See also Ps 107:29: *He turns the storm into* demamah, *stillness*—or the whistling of the wind as the storm dies down. See Simon, *Reading Prophetic Narratives*, 213. The phrase *qol demamah daqqah* consists of two nouns (*qol* and *demamah*, the second in genitive relationship to the first) followed by a single adjective (*daqqah*, modifying the second noun)—not a noun followed by two adjectives. So the famous, felicitous translation of the King James Version (*a still, small voice*) is technically incorrect.

Rashi (on this verse) comments: "I have heard [the interpretation]: A sound emerging from the silence [or, stillness]—'retentissement' [in medieval French, meaning "reverberation, echo"]—and no actual sound is heard." The German biblical translation of Buber-Rosenzweig renders the phrase as "eine Stimme verschwebenden Schweigens" (a voice of floating silence).

On the *sound of sheer stillness* as befitting both divine and earthly royalty, see BT *Berakhot* 58a. The medieval philosopher Joseph Albo interprets *qol demamah daqqah* as implying that God's essence is completely concealed, incomprehensible, and inexpressible; it can be described only by negation. See his *Sefer ha-Iqqarim*, 2:31.

72. See Cross, *Canaanite Myth and Hebrew Epic*, 148–94.

73. See Gersonides on 1 Kgs 19:12; Isaac Arama, *Aqedat Yitsḥaq*, Numbers 83; Malbim on 1 Kgs 19:11, 13; Uffenheimer, *Ancient Prophecy in Israel*, 233–34; Samet, *Pirqei Eliyyahu*, 293; Garsiel, *From Earth to Heaven*, 98–99.

74. See David Kimḥi, on 1 Kgs 19:11–13; Zakovitch, "'Qol Demamah Daqqah,'" 340; Simon, *Reading Prophetic Narratives*, 210–13.

75. Alter, *Hebrew Bible*, 2:512.

76. See Gersonides, on 1 Kgs 19:10; Moses Alsheikh, on 1 Kgs 19:9–10, 13–14; Samet, *Pirqei Eliyyahu*, 284, 287; Hellner-Eshed, "Ha-Meqanne la-Berit u-Va'al ha-Shigyonot," 161–62.

77. *Shir ha-Shirim Rabbah* on 1:6.

78. *Seder Eliyyahu Zuta*, 8, p. 186. See *Shir ha-Shirim Zuta* 8:6: "*Fierce as Sheol is jealousy* [or, *zeal, zealousness*] (Song 8:6). *Fierce* was the *zealousness* that Elijah unleashed upon Israel, as is said: *I have been so zealous for YHVH, God of Hosts, for the Israelites have forsaken Your covenant*. . . . Elijah should have gone to the place where his ancestors stood [i.e., Mount Horeb] and should have sought mercy for Israel; but he did not. So the blessed Holy One said to him, 'You sought your own needs. *Go, return to Damascus* [. . . *and Elisha son of Shaphat from Abel-meholah you shall anoint as prophet in your place*].'"

79. *Mekhilta, Pisḥa* 1. Cf. *Pesiqta Rabbati* 11, 42b. See Rashi, on 1 Kgs 19:16: "[*And Elisha son of Shaphat*] *you shall anoint as prophet in your place*—'I do not want your prophesying, since you are accusing My children!'"

80. David Kimḥi, on 1 Kgs 19:16. See Zakovitch, "'Qol Demamah Daqqah,'" 343–46.

81. See Chap. 4, at nn. 12–14. For various interpretations of Elijah's reply, see Rashi; David Kimḥi; Gersonides; Gray, *I and II Kings*, 413; Cogan, *1 Kings*, 455; Zevit, "First and Second Kings," 701; Alter, *Hebrew Bible*, 2:513.

82. Zakovitch, "Tale of Naboth's Vineyard," 387.

83. See Lev 25:8–17, 23–28; Num 27:1–11, 36:7; Ezek 46:18; Ruth 4:1–10; Uffenheimer, *Early Prophecy in Israel*, 386–87; Alter, *Hebrew Bible*, 2:519.

84. See Uffenheimer, *Early Prophecy in Israel*, 388; Alter, *Hebrew Bible*, 2:519.

85. Alter, *Hebrew Bible*, 2:520.

86. See Cogan, *1 Kings*, 480. On the requirement of two witnesses, see Deut 17:6, 19:15; cf. Numb 35:30. On stoning as the punishment for blaspheming God, see Lev 24:15–16. Cf. Exod 22:27: *You shall not blaspheme God, nor shall you curse a chief among your people.*

87. See Kiel, *Sefer Melakhim*, 1:419. Cf. Maimonides, *Mishneh Torah, Hilkhot Rotseaḥ* 4:9.

88. On the association of Jezebel with dung, see above, at n. 8, and n. 8.

89. See Gersonides; Alter, *Hebrew Bible*, 2:526. For further discussion of the clause *and the whores bathed*, see Gray, *I and II Kings*, 455–56; Kiel, *Sefer Melakhim*, 1:435–36; Cogan, *1 Kings*, 495.

90. Compare the corruption of Jezebel's name, mentioned above at n. 8. In the New Testament, Jesus is accused of expelling demons by the power of Beelzebul, a name for the "prince of demons," that is, Satan. See Matt 12:24–27 (and parallels).

91. See Alter, *Hebrew Bible*, 2:530; Zevit, "First and Second Kings," 711.

92. The miracle here also echoes the miraculous crossing of the Jordan by Joshua and the Israelites, as described in Josh 3:9–17.

93. See Deut 21:17; David Kimḥi (quoting his father) and Gersonides, on 2 Kgs 2:9; Gray, *I and II Kings*, 475; Cogan and Tadmor, *II Kings*, 32; Samet, *Pirqei Eliyyahu*, 515–24; Zevit, "First and Second Kings," 713–14. Cf. Zech 13:8, where the phrase means "two-thirds." According to a rabbinic tradition, the wording *a double share* implies that whereas Elijah performed eight miracles, Elisha succeeded in performing sixteen. See *Mishnat Rabbi Eli'ezer* 1, p. 13; *Yalqut Shim'oni*, Genesis 92. Cf. BT *Sanhedrin* 47a.

94. See Num 11:16–17, 24–26.

95. See Cogan and Tadmor, *II Kings*, 32; Zevit, "First and Second Kings," 714; Alter, *Hebrew Bible*, 2:533. The identical exclamation—*My father, my father! Israel's chariots and horsemen!*—is uttered over Elisha himself as he is about to die, by King Joash of

Israel. See 2 Kgs 13:14. Cf. 2 Kgs 6:17. On Elisha's role as defender of Israel, see 2 Kgs 6:8–23, 13:15–19. It should be noted that the term *rekhev*, which appears twice in 2 Kgs 2:11–12, can be rendered as either singular or plural: *chariot* or *chariots*. The plural is more likely and fitting in v. 12 and is definitely the sense in 2 Kgs 6:17.

96. On rending one's clothes as a sign of grief and mourning, see Gen 37:34; 2 Sam 1:11, 13:31; Job 1:20. According to Rabbi Yoḥanan (in BT *Mo'ed Qatan* 26a), Elisha was mistaken in thinking that his master had died, because actually Elijah evaded death, becoming immortal. Explaining Elisha's point of view, Rabbi Yoḥanan says, "Since it is written *And he saw him no more* (2 Kgs 2:12), from [Elisha's] perspective, he seemed to be dead."

97. See above, at n. 25.

98. *Vayiqra Rabbah* 27:4, in the name of Rabbi Yehudah; *Bereshit Rabbah* 21:5, in the name of Rabbi Ḥanina. Cf. BT *Mo'ed Qatan* 26a, in the name of Resh Lakish: "Elijah is [still] alive!" See *Seder Olam*, 1, 17; *Avot de-Rabbi Natan* B, 38; BT *Bava Batra* 121b; *Qohelet Rabbah* 3:15; *Tanḥuma*, *Bereshit* 7; Ginzberg, *Legends of the Jews*, 6:322–23, n. 32; Heschel, *Torah min ha-Shamayim*, 2:53–56.

99. Gersonides, on 2 Kgs 2:1. See Yisraeli, *Pitḥei Heikhal*, 87.

100. BT *Sukkah* 5a. Cf. *Mekhilta*, *Baḥodesh* 4.

101. Josephus, *Antiquities of the Jews*, 9.2.2.

102. David Kimḥi, on 2 Kgs 2:11. Cf. his comment on Mal 3:23.

103. Kimḥi, on 2 Kgs 2:1. Cf. Levi ben Abraham, *Livyat Ḥen*, 331, cited by Yisraeli, *Pitḥei Heikhal*, 88. See also Moses Sofer, *She'elot u-Tshuvot Ḥatam Sofer*, 6:98.

104. Kimḥi, on 2 Kgs 2:1.

105. Naḥmanides, *Sha'ar ha-Gemul*, in *Kitvei Ramban*, 2:304. See Yisraeli, *Pitḥei Heikhal*, 89–91.

106. Naḥmanides, on Lev 18:4–5. Cf. *Seder Eliyyahu Rabbah*, 4, p. 18: "Every disciple of the wise who engages in Torah from childhood to old age and then dies, does not really die; rather, he remains alive forever and ever."

107. 2 Kgs 2:3, 5, 9–10. See Elijah's plea to God (in 1 Kgs 19:4; above, at n. 63): *Enough! Now, YHVH, take my life, for I am no better than my ancestors.*

108. The wording *va-yiqbor oto*, "and He buried him," can also be rendered "and he was buried." See Alter, *Hebrew Bible*, 1:743.

109. *Sifrei*, Deuteronomy 357. See BT *Sotah* 13b; Ginzberg, *Legends of the Jews*, 6:161–62, n. 951. On Moses and Elijah, see above, at n. 65, and n. 65.

110. 2 Chr 21:12–15.

111. See Rothstein, "First and Second Chronicles," 1799; Alter, *Hebrew Bible*, 3:960.

112. Rothstein, "First and Second Chronicles," 1799. Cf. Japhet, *I & II Chronicles*, 812; Myers, *II Chronicles*, 121.

113. *Seder Olam*, 17. The biblical chronology of this period is extremely perplexing. See 2 Kgs 1:17, 3:11; Gray, *I and II Kings*, 66–67; Milikowsky, *Seder Olam*, 2:278–80.

114. Cogan and Tadmor, *II Kings*, 34, n. 2.

115. See Rashi, Gersonides, Malbim on 2 Chr 21:12; Ibn Ezra, on Mal 3:24; Gersonides, on Judg 5 (end), 1 Kgs 17:1; Isaac Abravanel, on 2 Kgs 8:19. According to David Kimḥi, on 2 Chr 21:12, Elijah appeared from heaven to one of the prophets and dictated the letter to him. See Wiener, *Prophet Elijah*, 32; Samet, *Pirqei Eliyyahu*, 545–48.

116. The concluding phrase, *with sacred destruction*, renders the term *ḥerem*, which connotes "consecration through destruction." See Milgrom, *Leviticus*, 3:2391–93, 2417–21. Malachi is the final book in the Christian Old Testament, which thus concludes by predicting Elijah's return. The Christian canon then proceeds with the Gospels, in which (as we will see) Elijah figures prominently.

117. BT *Shabbat* 118a, in the name of Bar Kappara.

118. Ben Sira 48:1, 4, 9–11. The concluding exclamation may mean, "Happy is one who endures to witness Elijah's return!"

Chapter 2. The Compassionate Super-Rabbi

1. *Yalqut Shim'oni*, Genesis 133, quoting *Midrash Avkir*, in turn quoting Isa 63:1: *Who is this coming from Edom*, [*in ensanguined garments from Bosra?*]. Throughout rabbinic and medieval Jewish literature, the figure of Esau (and Edom) symbolizes the oppressors of Israel (Rome or its successor, Christendom). In *Bereshit*

Rabbah 71:9, Elijah is described as "the one destined to cut down the foundations of the heathen nations." Oded Yisraeli emphasizes the continuity between the biblical and rabbinic portrayals of Elijah. See his *Pitḥei Heikhal*, 300, and n. 51.

2. On Elijah as a kind of bodhisattva, see Wiener, *Prophet Elijah*, 179.

3. *Bereshit Rabbah* 71:9.

4. *Seder Eliyyahu Rabbah*, 18, p. 97. Cf. *Bereshit Rabbah* 71:9. The verse in Chronicles reads (according to the Masoretic Text), *Jaareshiah, Elijah, and Zikhri were the sons of Jeroham.*

5. *Midrash Mishlei* 9:2. Cf. *Targum Yerushalmi*, Deut 30:4, 33:11; *Targum Qohelet* 10:20.

6. BT *Bava Metsi'a* 114a–b.

7. *Midrash ha-Gadol*, Gen 5:24. On Enoch, see above, Chap. 1, at n. 107.

8. On Sandalphon, see BT *Ḥagigah* 13b; *Pesiqta Rabbati* 20, 97a. On Elijah as Sandalphon, see Cordovero, *Pardes Rimmonim*, 24:14; Margaliot, *Mal'akhei Elyon*, 154–55, n. 26; Wiener, *Prophet Elijah*, 99–100; below, Chap. 3, at n. 30, and n. 30. In his mystical diary, Joseph Caro identifies Elijah as Metatron. See his *Maggid Meisharim*, 15c (*parashat miqets*).

9. *Targum Qohelet* 10:20; *Midrash Tehillim* 8:7. In *Targum*, Eccl 10:20, and *Ma'yan Ḥokhmah* (Jellinek, *Beit ha-Midrash*, 1:60), Elijah is identified as "Master of Wings."

10. BT *Berakhot* 4b. The passage concludes: "During a plague, however, [the Angel of Death reaches his destination] in one." See Maharsha, *Ḥiddushei Aggadot*, *Berakhot* 4b; *Zohar* 1:13a, 46b, 93a; Yisraeli, *Pitḥei Heikhal*, 84–85.

11. Others appearing on such lists include Enoch, Eliezer (servant of Abraham), the Messiah, King Hiram of Tyre, Bityah (daughter of Pharaoh), and Rabbi Yehoshu'a son of Levi. See *Derekh Erets* 1:18; *Kallah Rabbati* 3:23; *Yalqut Shim'oni*, Genesis, 42.

12. *Avot de-Rabbi Natan* B, 38. See *Seder Olam*, 1; BT *Bava Batra* 121b. According to JT *Eruvin* 5:1, 22b, Ahijah the prophet (who lived in the days of Jeroboam) was Elijah's teacher.

13. BT *Bava Metsi'a* 85b.

14. For example, BT *Ketubbot* 77b.

15. BT *Sanhedrin* 97b.

16. See Lindbeck, *Elijah and the Rabbis*, 54.

17. BT *Ta'anit* 22a.

18. JT *Kil'ayim* 9:4, 32b (and parallels). For another example of Elijah's healing powers, see BT *Shabbat* 109b.

19. See Esth 7:9; *Ester Rabbah* 10:9; *Pirqei de-Rabbi Eli'ezer*, 50 (and David Luria, ad loc., n. 131). Cf. JT *Megillah* 3:6, 74b; *Soferim* 14:3; Ginzberg, *Legends of the Jews*, 6:325, n. 45.

20. BT *Ta'anit* 21a. See BT *Sanhedrin* 108b–9a; Lindbeck, *Elijah and the Rabbis*, 107. On Abraham's magic dust, see *Bereshit Rabbah* 42:3.

21. BT *Avodah Zarah* 18a–b.

22. See Lindbeck, *Elijah and the Rabbis*, xix, 109.

23. In rabbinic literature, the formula *zakhur la-tov*, "gratefully remembered," is reserved almost exclusively for Elijah—so much so that even without his name attached, the bare formula can still refer to him. See JT *Demai* 2:1, 22c; Ginzberg, *Legends of the Jews*, 6:325, n. 45; Lieberman, *Greek in Jewish Palestine*, 70, n. 23.

24. Since ancient times throughout the world, incantations are often accompanied by ceremonial spitting. See BT *Sanhedrin* 101a. Saliva's medicinal properties are described by the first-century Roman polymath Pliny the Elder (*Natural History*, 28.7). According to the New Testament (Mark 8:22–26, John 9:1–7), with saliva Jesus restored the sight of a blind man.

25. *Devarim Rabbah* 5:15. Earlier Aramaic versions of the story appear in JT *Sotah* 1:4, 16d; *Vayiqra Rabbah* 9:9; *Bemidbar Rabbah* 9:20.

26. *Seder Olam*, 17. See Milikowsky, *Seder Olam*, 2:277–78; Milikowsky, "Trajectories of Return, Restoration and Redemption," 275. According to Milikowsky, the editor(s) of *Seder Olam* knew of the tradition that Elijah's return was connected to the Messiah and also, of course, of the biblical tradition (in Mal 3) that Elijah's return was connected with the apocalyptic battles of *the day of YHVH* (signified here by the mythological figure Gog, representing the eschatological enemy). The editor(s) combined the two, thereby creating a new tradition that Elijah will return twice. On Elijah as

the heavenly scribe recording human deeds, see *Vayiqra Rabbah* 34:8; BT *Qiddushin* 70a; *Rut Rabbah* 5:6; Wertheimer, *Battei Midrashot*, 1:296; *Zohar Ḥadash* 23b (*Midrash ha-Ne'lam*); *Zohar: Pritzker Edition*, 10:264–65; Milikowsky, *Seder Olam*, 2:290–92.

27. Elijah is encountered by rabbis far more frequently in the Babylonian Talmud than in the Jerusalem Talmud. In the Tannaitic midrash *Sifra* (*Beḥuqqotai* 6:4, 112a), Elijah appears (at the time of the destruction of Jerusalem) to a languishing victim of famine who happens to be an avid idol worshiper. The prophet assures the suffering sinner that he can survive if he simply recites the opening words of the *Shema*, but he stubbornly refuses and meets a grisly end. See BT *Sanhedrin* 63b–64a.

28. See Ginzberg, *Legends of the Jews*, 6:333, n. 93; Lindbeck, *Elijah and the Rabbis*, 49.

29. BT *Bava Batra* 7b.

30. BT *Ketubbot* 61a.

31. *Bereshit Rabbah* 35:2.

32. *Pesiqta de-Rav Kahana* 18:5.

33. *Massekhet Geihinnom*, in Jellinek, *Beit ha-Midrash*, 1:148.

34. BT *Ketubbot* 77b. See above, n. 11.

35. BT *Makkot* 11a.

36. *Bereshit Rabbah* 94:9. Cf. JT *Terumot* 8:11, 46b. See Daube, *Collaboration with Tyranny in Rabbinic Law*.

37. See Lindbeck, *Elijah and the Rabbis*, xviii, 99.

38. BT *Sanhedrin* 98a.

39. BT *Ketubbot* 105b–6a.

40. See Braude and Kapstein, *Tanna dĕbe Eliyyahu*, 10. Some scholars date the book earlier.

41. See Elbaum, "Bein Midrash le-Sefer Musar," 146–53; Scholem, *Shedim, Ruḥot u-Nshamot*, 251–52.

42. *Seder Eliyyahu Rabbah*, 10, p. 48. Cf. Gal 3:28.

43. BT *Ḥagigah* 15b. For Rabbi Me'ir's teaching quoted here, see M *Sanhedrin* 6:5.

44. See Peli, "Eliyyahu ha-Navi be-Veit Midrasham shel Ḥazal," 156–57.

45. See Lindbeck, *Elijah and the Rabbis*, 122–23.

46. Judg 19.

47. BT *Gittin* 6b. The statement "Both these and those are words of the Living God" appears in one other talmudic account. See BT *Eruvin* 13b, in the name of Samuel: "For three years the House of Shammai and the House of Hillel disputed. These said, 'The halakhah is in accordance with our view,' and those said, 'The halakhah is in accordance with our view.' Then a heavenly echo issued, proclaiming, 'Both these and those are words of the Living God. However, the halakhah is in accordance with the view of the House of Hillel.'"

48. See Lindbeck, *Elijah and the Rabbis*, x, 120–21.

49. BT *Megillah* 15b.

50. On the "seventy faces (or facets) of Torah," see *Bemidbar Rabbah* 13:16, where Torah is compared to wine: "Just as *yayin* (wine) is numerically equivalent to seventy, so Torah assumes seventy faces." On Elijah's hermeneutic pluralism, see Peli, "Eliyyahu ha-Navi be-Veit Midrasham shel Ḥazal," 144.

51. BT *Bava Metsi'a* 59b (per Munich MS 95). See Elon, *Ha-Mishpat ha-Ivri*, 1:227; Peli, "Eliyyahu ha-Navi be-Veit Midrasham shel Ḥazal," 155–56; Rubenstein, *Talmudic Stories*, 34–63. On God's delight in being defeated, see BT *Pesaḥim* 119a.

52. BT *Berakhot* 3a (per Munich MS 95). See Lindbeck, *Elijah and the Rabbis*, 64–65.

53. BT *Bava Metsi'a* 114a–b. See Lindbeck, *Elijah and the Rabbis*, 65.

54. BT *Yevamot* 63a. See *Seder Eliyyahu Rabbah*, 10, p. 51.

55. *Rut Rabbah* 4:1.

56. BT *Qiddushin* 40a.

57. *Kallah Rabbati* 4:31. Cf. BT *Berakhot* 29b.

58. BT *Sanhedrin* 113a–b. See Lindbeck, *Elijah and the Rabbis*, 103–4.

59. See Tosafot, *Bava Metsi'a* 114a, s.v. *mahu; Sefer ha-Ḥinnukh*, *mitsvah* 350 ("We have no doubt concerning the words of Elijah"); Joseph Ḥabiba, *Nimmuqei Yosef*, *Bava Metsi'a* 69b; Urbach, *Me-Olamam shel Ḥakhamim*, 32, n. 96.

60. *Sifra*, *Beḥuqqotai* 13:7, 115d. See JT *Megillah* 1:4, 70d; BT

Shabbat 104a, *Yoma* 80a, *Megillah* 2b, *Avodah Zarah* 36a, *Temurah* 16a; *Rut Rabbah* 4:5; Maimonides, *Mishneh Torah, Hilkhot Yesodei ha-Torah* 9:1.

61. See BT *Yevamot* 102a, *Menaḥot* 32a.

62. *Midrash Mishlei* 9:2. See BT *Bava Metsi'a* 114a–b (above, at n. 6); Peli, "Eliyyahu ha-Navi be-Veit Midrasham shel Ḥazal," 159–60.

63. See above, at n. 51.

64. BT *Bava Metsi'a* 114a.

65. M *Eduyyot* 8:7. See *Tosefta, Eduyyot* 3:4; BT *Qiddushin* 71a. On Elijah's concern with family and ethnic purity, see also BT *Qiddushin* 70a, 72b; *Seder Eliyyahu Zuta,* 1, p. 169. On Elijah's future legal role, see Ginzberg, *Unknown Jewish Sect,* 256; Urbach, *Me-Olamam shel Ḥakhamim,* 29–30.

66. Rashi, on BT *Shabbat* 108a, s.v. *mai im yavo Eliyyahu.* See Rashi, on BT *Bekhorot* 24a, s.v. *ad yavo;* and Chajes, "Beirur Eliyyahu," 20a–b.

67. See Chajes, "Beirur Eliyyahu," 17–23 (especially 18b–19b). Cf. 1 Macc 4:44–46.

68. BT *Pesaḥim* 13a. Cf. BT *Pesaḥim* 34a.

69. M *Bava Metsi'a* 3:4.

70. M *Bava Metsi'a* 2:8. Cf. M *Bava Metsi'a* 1:8. For another example of Elijah's ability to determine an uncertain identity, see BT *Gittin* 42b.

71. BT *Berakhot* 35b.

72. For other examples of Elijah's eventually revealing what is now unknown, see BT *Shabbat* 108a, *Pesaḥim* 13a.

73. BT *Menaḥot* 45a.

74. The acronym is mentioned (and dismissed) by Elijah Levita in his Hebrew lexicon, *Sefer ha-Tishbi* (1541), s.v. *teiq* (recording the form ובעיות [*u-v'ayot*], "and questions"). Among others who mention it are Joseph ben Issachar, *Yosef Da'at,* intro, 2; Yom Tov Lipmann Heller, *Tosefot Yom Tov, Eduyyot* 8:7; and Isaiah Horowitz, *Shenei Luḥot ha-Berit, torah she-be-al peh,* s.v. *teiqu.* See Samet, *Pirqei Eliyyahu,* 544, n. 11. In his first biblical appearance (1 Kgs 17:1), Elijah is called Elijah the Tishbite.

75. See above, at n. 60.

76. Maimonides, *Commentary on the Mishnah*, *Eduyyot* 8:7.

77. *Otiyyot de-Rabbi Aqiva A*, in Wertheimer, *Battei Midrashot*, 2:367. On the Torah of the Messiah, cf. *Qohelet Rabbah*, 11:8: "The Torah that a person learns in this world is *hevel*, 'futility [literally, mere breath],' compared with the Torah of the Messiah." See *Qohelet Rabbah* 2:1; *Tanḥuma*, *Ki Tavo* 4.

78. *Shir ha-Shirim Zuta* 5:2; *Aggadat Shir ha-Shirim*, ed. Schechter, 38. In the latter, see the manuscript variant on p. 85: "of which this entire Torah is but one line." See Urbach, *Ḥazal*, 274, n. 65.

79. See Wiener, *Prophet Elijah*, 66. The two biblical quotations from *Sefer ha-Yashar* appear in Josh 10:12–14 and 2 Sam 1:18–27.

80. See above, at nn. 46–50; Peli, "Eliyyahu ha-Navi be-Veit Midrasham shel Ḥazal," 143.

81. *Seder Olam*, 17. See above, at n. 26; Milikowsky, "Eliyyahu ve-ha-Mashiaḥ"; Milikowsky, "Trajectories of Return, Restoration and Redemption," 273–74. Some scholars claim that the motif of Elijah heralding the Messiah originated in Christianity and developed later in Judaism, but Milikowsky rebuts this persuasively; see "Trajectories of Return," 276–77.

82. Justin Martyr, *Dialogue with Trypho*, chap. 49.

83. See *Mekhilta*, *Vayassa* 5, p. 172, which describes "three things that Elijah will eventually restore to Israel: the vessel of manna [which was preserved, according to Exod 16:32–34], the vessel of purifying water [for one who has been contaminated by touching a human corpse, according to Num 19], and the vessel of anointing oil." According to *Seder Eliyyahu Zuta*, 21 (appendix, p. 34), when Elijah and the Messiah finally arrive, they will together be carrying "the vessel of anointing oil." In his *Vikkuaḥ ha-Ramban* (*Kitvei Ramban*, 1:306), Naḥmanides mentions Elijah anointing the Messiah. See Ginzberg, *Unknown Jewish Sect*, 245–46; Ginzberg, *Legends of the Jews*, 6:340, n. 112.

84. BT *Eruvin* 43b. Cf. *Sifrei*, Deuteronomy 342.

85. *Pesiqta Rabbati* 35, 161a.

86. *Tefillat Rabbi Shim'on ben Yoḥai*, in Jellinek, *Beit ha-Midrash*, 4:125.

87. *Ma'aseh Daniyyel*, in Jellinek, *Beit ha-Midrash*, 5:128. See Ginzberg, *Legends of the Jews*, 4:234.

88. *Bemidbar Rabbah* 14:1, in the name of Rabbi Shim'on son of Lakish. Cf. *Tanḥuma, Naso* 28. According to *Pirqei de-Rabbi Eli'ezer*, 33, Elijah's plea to God to revive the widow's son includes the statement, "Now the generations will learn that there is revival of the dead." This particular role of Elijah is recorded in M *Sotah* 9:15 (part of a later addition to the Mishnah): "The resurrection of the dead will come through Elijah (gratefully remembered)."

89. *Shir ha-Shirim Zuta* 7:14.

90. *Shemot Rabbah* 18:12. See David Luria, ad loc.; *Mekhilta, Pisḥa* 14; *Mekhilta de-Rashbi*, Exod 12:42; BT *Rosh Hashanah* 11a–b; *Tanḥuma, Bo* 9.

91. BT *Eruvin* 43b.

92. *Leqaḥ Tov*, Song 2:8. The verse in Isaiah describes the messenger announcing redemption, whom the Midrash identifies as Elijah. See *Pesiqta Rabbati* 35, 161a.

93. *Midrash Mishlei* 19:21. See Margaliyot, *Eliyyahu ha-Navi*, 177; Wiener, *Prophet Elijah*, 69–70.

94. *Tanḥuma* (Buber), *Mishpatim* 12.

95. *Pirqei de-Rabbi Eli'ezer*, 43. See David Luria, ad loc.; Ibn Ezra on Mal 3:24. Cf. BT *Sanhedrin* 97b; JT *Ta'anit* 1:1, 63d.

96. *Pesiqta Rabbati* 4, 13a.

97. *Devarim Rabbah* 3:17.

98. *Pesiqta Rabbati* 4, 13a. This midrash records some thirty parallels, including many of those listed here. See above, Chap. 1, at n. 65, and n. 65.

99. Deut 33:1; 1 Kgs 17:18.

100. See above, Chap. 1, at n. 66, and n. 66.

101. See above, Chap. 1, at n. 65, and n. 65.

102. See above, Chap. 1, at n. 63, and n. 63.

103. See above, Chap. 1, at n. 78, and n. 78.

104. *Pesiqta Rabbati*, 4, 13b.

105. See above, Chap. 1, at nn. 67, 78–79.

106. See above, Chap. 1, at n. 63. Jonah's situation, however, is radically different from Elijah's. Whereas for Elijah, the failure of

his mission generates his death wish, for Jonah the very success of his mission (stimulating the inhabitants of Nineveh to repent and be saved) is unbearable. He is intensely disappointed that God has not fulfilled his prophecy: *Forty days more, and Nineveh shall be overthrown!* (Jonah 3:4).

107. See 1 Kgs 17:17–24 (above, Chap. 1, at nn. 18–20); JT *Sukkah* 5:1, 55a; *Bereshit Rabbah* 98:11, pp. 1261–62; *Midrash Tehillim* 26:7; *Pirqei de-Rabbi Eli'ezer*, 33; *Midrash Ḥaserot vi-Yterot* (Wertheimer, *Battei Midrashot*, 2:299–300). Cf. *Seder Eliyyahu Rabbah*, 18, pp. 97–98. On the relation between Elisha and Jonah, see *Seder Olam*, 18; *Mishnat Rabbi Eli'ezer* 8, p. 153; *Sifrei Zuta*, Num 14:34, p. 279.

108. *Zohar* 2:197a (*Zohar: Pritzker Edition*, 6:122). No extant rabbinic source connects the name of Jonah's father, Amittai, with the word *emet* in the verse from Kings; but the church father Jerome quotes this midrashic interpretation in the introduction to his commentary on Jonah. See Ginzberg, *Legends of the Jews*, 6:318, n. 9; Liebes, "Yonah ben Amittai ke-Mashiaḥ ben Yosef," 304–5.

109. See *Seder Eliyyahu Rabbah*, 18, pp. 97–98; Ginzberg, *Legends of the Jews*, 6:318, n. 9; 6:351, n. 38; Liebes, "Yonah ben Amittai ke-Mashiaḥ ben Yosef."

110. See Matt 12:38–41; Luke 11:30.

111. 2 Kgs 1. See above, Chap. 1, at n. 91.

112. See JT *Sanhedrin* 9:6, 27b (in the name of Rabbi Yehudah son of Pazzi); Milgrom, *JPS Torah Commentary: Numbers*, 215.

113. Literally, "Phinehas—he is Elijah." An alternative formulation, appearing frequently, is *Pinḥas zeh Eliyyahu*, literally, "Phinehas—this is Elijah." On various theories concerning the origin of this identification, see Aptowitzer, *Die Parteipolitik der Hasmonäerzeit*, 95–104; Hayward, "*Phinehas—The Same Is Elijah*"; Hengel, *Zealots*, 162–77; Ayali, "Eliyyahu me-Heikhan Ba?," 55–58; Yisraeli, *Pitḥei Heikhal*, 295–96.

114. *Zohar* 3:214a (*Zohar: Pritzker Edition*, 9:511).

115. See Milikowsky, *Seder Olam*, 2:316, n. 33; cf. his "Chronology of the Period of the Judges," on p. 219.

116. See David Kimḥi, on Judg 20:28; Mal 2:5; 1 Chr 9:20; Abravanel, on Judg 20:27–28. According to Baḥya ben Asher, on

Num 25:7, Phinehas lived more than four hundred years, a life span that would make him contemporaneous (and possibly identical) with Elijah. Baḥya accepted that "Phinehas is Elijah," as is clear from the continuation of his commentary (on Num 25:11–12). On Phinehas's longevity, see also *Seder Olam*, 20; *Bereshit Rabbah* 60:3; *Vayiqra Rabbah* 1:1; Rashi and David Kimḥi, on Judg 2:1, 6:8; 1 Kgs 19:4; Gersonides, on Judg 6:8; Sforno, on Num 25:12.

117. The Septuagint, though, does record the death of Phinehas in the concluding verse of the book of Joshua (24:33).

118. See Kugel, *Traditions of the Bible*, 811–14.

119. On Phinehas, see *Targum Yerushalmi*, Num 25:12 (quoted below); *Tanḥuma*, *Pinḥas* 1; *Bemidbar Rabbah* 21:3. On Elijah, see above, Chap. 1, at n. 98.

120. Pseudo-Philo, *Biblical Antiquities*, 48.1–2. See Harrington, "Pseudo-Philo," 362.

121. Origen, *Commentary on the Gospel of John* 6.7.

122. *Targum Yerushalmi*, Exod 6:18. Cf. *Targum Yerushalmi*, Exod 4:13; and Num 25:12: "I will make him [i.e., Phinehas] Angel of the Covenant, and he will live forever to proclaim the news of redemption at the end of days."

123. See above, at nn. 5–6; Rashi, on BT *Bava Mets'ia* 114b, s.v. *lav kohen mar.*

124. *Sifrei*, *Numbers* 131.

125. Wertheimer, *Battei Midrashot*, 1:296, in the name of Rabbi Shim'on son of Lakish (Resh Lakish). On angelic sacrifices in heaven, see BT *Ḥagigah* 12b; *Menaḥot* 110a, and Tosafot, on that passage, s.v. *u-Mikhael.* On Elijah's power of atonement, see *Seder Eliyyahu Rabbah*, 26, p. 141. On Elijah as the heavenly scribe, see above, n. 26. Cf. the tradition in the name of Resh Lakish in *Midrash Aggadah*, Num 25:13: "Phinehas is none other than Elijah. The blessed Holy One said to [Phinehas], 'You made peace between Me and the Israelites. So, too, in the time to come you are destined to make peace between Me and them, as is said: *Behold, I am sending to you Elijah the prophet* [*before the coming of the great and awesome day of YHVH. And he will bring fathers' hearts back to their children and children's hearts to their fathers*]' (Mal 3:23–24)."

126. *Pirqei de-Rabbi Eli'ezer*, 47 (according to the first edition). See *Yalqut Shim'oni*, Numbers 771.

127. *Pirqei de-Rabbi Eli'ezer*, 29.

128. Abraham Ibn Ezra, on Num 25:13; Moses Ha-Darshan, on 1 Chr 9:20; see Epstein, *Kitvei R. Avraham Epshtain*, 1:232.

Chapter 3. Inspiring the Mystics

1. See *Tosefta, Sotah* 4:7; *Eduyyot* 3:4; *Mekhilta, Beshallaḥ, Petiḥta;* BT *Sotah* 13a.

2. On Ahijah, see 1 Kgs 11:29–39. On his being Elijah's teacher, see JT *Eruvin* 5:1, 22b; Milikowsky, *Seder Olam*, 2:21. Cf. above, Chap. 2, at n. 12. According to Hasidic tradition, Ahijah was also the teacher of the Ba'al Shem Tov, which could imply the claim that the latter attained the level of Elijah. See Jacob Joseph of Polonnoye, *Toledot Ya'aqov Yosef*, 156a (*parashat balaq*).

3. Maimonides, *Mishneh Torah*, introduction.

4. On Ahijah's esoteric knowledge, see BT *Sanhedrin* 102a; *Midrash Tehillim* 5:8.

5. JT *Berakhot* 5:1, 8d. See *Pesiqta de-Rav Kahana* 12:22.

6. See Scholem, *Origins of the Kabbalah*, 35–38; Scholem, *Ha-Qabbalah be-Provans*, 57–64, 73–74, 83; Heschel, "Al Ruaḥ ha-Qodesh bi-Ymei ha-Beinayim," 190–93; Huss, *Ke-Zohar ha-Raqia'*, 78–82; Wolfson, "Beyond the Spoken Word," 190–92; Yisraeli, "Jewish Medieval Traditions," 23–31; Yisraeli, "Le-Mi Hitgallah Eliyyahu?" Cf. *Zohar* 2:216b; Tishby, *Wisdom of the Zohar*, 3:1006, n. 260. On *gillui Eliyyahu*, see also Ginzberg, *Legends of the Jews*, 6:333–34, n. 93; Heschel, "Al Ruaḥ ha-Qodesh bi-Ymei ha-Beinayim," 198–208; Margaliot's introduction to Jacob of Marvège, *She'elot u-Tshuvot min ha-Shamayim*, 36–41. Isaac the Blind is called *avi ha-Qabbalah* (father of the Kabbalah) by Baḥya ben Asher in his Commentary on Gen 32:10.

7. See *Tosefta, Sotah* 13:3, 12:5. On the number of prophets in the days of Elijah, see *Shir ha-Shirim Rabbah* on 4:11. On Elijah and the Holy Spirit, see above, Chap. 2, at n. 25.

8. *Midrash Tehillim* 3:7.

9. *Seder Olam*, 17. See above, Chap. 2, at n. 26.

10. Scholem, *On the Kabbalah and Its Symbolism*, 20; Scholem, *Origins of the Kabbalah*, 35–36.

11. Scholem, *Origins of the Kabbalah*, 245–46.

12. See above, Chap. 1, at n. 57, and n. 57. In the Talmud, Elijah offers Rabbi Yose some practical advice on prayer. See above, Chap. 2, at n. 52.

13. Cordovero, "Derishot be-Inyenei ha-Mal'akhim," 5:7, p. 64. See *Zohar Ḥadash* 103a (*Tiqqunim*); Wiener, *Prophet Elijah*, 85.

14. Judah Loew ben Bezalel, *Netsaḥ Yisra'el*, chap. 28. See Wiener, *Prophet Elijah*, 85–86. On the relationship between individual creativity and divine revelation, see the remark by the thirteenth-century kabbalist Jacob ben Sheshet, who after recording a certain innovation writes ("Ha-Emunah ve-ha-Bittaḥon," 370): "Do not think that this is far-fetched. If I hadn't invented it in my mind, I would say that it was transmitted to Moses at Sinai."

15. Heschel, "Al Ruaḥ ha-Qodesh bi-Ymei ha-Beinayim," 178.

16. *Sefer ha-Peli'ah*, introduction.

17. BT *Shabbat* 33b. For another encounter between Rabbi Shim'on and Elijah in rabbinic literature, see *Bereshit Rabbah* 35:2.

18. *Zohar Ḥadash* 59c (*parashat ki tavo*); *Zohar: Pritzker Edition*, 12:688.

19. See Huss, *Ke-Zohar ha-Raqia'*, 69. On the earlier midrashic identification of Elijah's cave with Moses's *cleft of the crag* (Exodus 33:22), see above, Chap. 1, n. 66.

20. See Huss, *Ke-Zohar ha-Raqia'*, 64–70.

21. *Zohar* 1:1b–2a (*Zohar: Pritzker Edition*, 1:7–8).

22. *Zohar* 1:100b (*Midrash ha-Ne'lam*); *Zohar: Pritzker Edition*, 10:327. For similar encounters with Elijah, see, e.g., *Zohar* 1:151a, 217a; 3:221a, 231a, 241b–42a; *Zohar Ḥadash* 25b–c (*Midrash ha-Ne'lam*).

23. *Zohar* 2:210b (*Zohar: Pritzker Edition*, 6:199).

24. See above, Chap. 2, at nn. 43, 46.

25. *Zohar* 3:241b–42a (*Zohar: Pritzker Edition*, 9:614–17). At the conclusion of the *Zohar*'s *Idra Rabba*, Elijah appears and explains to Rabbi Shim'on that he had begged God to be invited to this gathering to hear the secrets revealed by Rabbi Shim'on and the Companions, but he was instead sent on a rescue mission. See

Zohar 3:144b (*Zohar: Pritzker Edition*, 8:456–57); Hellner-Eshed, *Mevaqqeshei ha-Panim*, 371–74; Benarroch, *Sava ve-Yanuqa*, 368–72.

26. On the verse in Proverbs, see *Pesiqta de-Rav Kahana* 1:4; *Pesiqta Rabbati* 5, 15a–b. On Moses and the cloud, see BT *Yoma* 4a: "Moses ascended in the cloud, was covered by the cloud, and made holy within the cloud, to receive Torah for Israel in holiness." See BT *Shabbat* 88b.

27. *Zohar* 2:197a (*Zohar: Pritzker Edition*, 6:121). On the Book of Adam, which contains the genealogy of the entire human race, see BT *Bava Metsi'a* 85b–86a.

28. *Zohar* 1:46b (*Zohar: Pritzker Edition*, 1:250).

29. *Zohar Ḥadash* 84c (*Midrash ha-Ne'lam, Rut*); *Zohar: Pritzker Edition*, 11:183–84.

30. This likely alludes to the angel Sandalphon, with whom Elijah is identified. See Tishby, *Ḥiqrei Qabbalah u-Shluḥoteha*, 61, n. 218; above, Chap. 2, n. 8.

31. Moses ben Shem Tov de León, "She'elot u-Tshuvot be-Inyenei Qabbalah," 61–62, 69–70. On the angels' opposition to creating a human being, see *Bereshit Rabbah* 8:5–6; BT *Sanhedrin* 38b; *Midrash Konen*, in Jellinek, *Beit ha-Midrash*, 2:26–27; Azriel ben Menaḥem of Gerona, *Peirush ha-Aggadot*, 66–67.

32. Cordovero, *Pardes Rimmonim*, 24:14. See Margaliot, *Mal'akhei Elyon*, 16, n. 25; Heschel, *Torah min ha-Shamayim ba-Aspaqlaryah shel ha-Dorot*, 2:55–56.

33. *Zohar* 1:209a (*Zohar: Pritzker Edition*, 3:282–83). "Dust" alludes here to *Shekhinah*. On the various divine qualities (*sefirot*), which include *Tif'eret* and *Shekhinah* (or *Malkhut*), see later in this chapter; Matt, *Essential Kabbalah*, 7–11. In the book of Kings, the phrase *separating the two of them* refers to the separation of Elijah from his disciple, Elisha. Here the *Zohar* interprets the phrase as alluding to the separation of Elijah's spirit from his body.

34. *Zohar* 1:209a–b (*Zohar: Pritzker Edition*, 3:284–85). The *Zohar* is drawing here on several midrashic motifs. The idiom of "locking the door" derives from BT *Sanhedrin* 113a, where it pertains to Elijah in a different context. On Elijah subduing the Angel

of Death, see *Zohar Ḥadash* 76a (*Midrash ha-Ne'lam, Rut*); *Zohar: Pritzker Edition*, 11:38–39.

35. See *Mekhilta, Pisḥa* 1 (quoted above, Chap. 1, at n. 79); Hellner-Eshed, "Nefesh ha-Qanna be-Sefer ha-Zohar," 109–12; Hellner-Eshed, *River Flows from Eden*, 347–48; Hellner-Eshed, "Ha-Meqanne la-Berit u-Va'al ha-Shigyonot," 159–63; Yisraeli, *Pitḥei Heikhal*, 303–7. For the *Zohar*'s critical attitude toward Elijah's condemnation of Israel, see *Zohar* 1:93a, 2:190a; *Zohar Ḥadash* 23b (*Midrash ha-Ne'lam*).

See David ben Solomon ibn Abi Zimra, *She'elot u-Tshuvot*, 6:2, §2294. "When the blessed Holy One saw that Elijah was constantly a zealot and did not plead Israel's cause . . . and that he saw Israel's distress, how they were dying from famine, and did not pray [for them] . . . He said, 'This one is not fit to endure in the world.' So He said, '*And Elisha . . . you shall anoint as prophet in your place* (1 Kgs 19:16). To take his life is impossible, since I already gave him [namely, Phinehas, who is identical with Elijah] *My covenant of peace* (Num 25:12). To leave him in the world is impossible, since he will always be a zealot and will fail to defend Israel. Consequently, he will be taken away to the celestial heights.'"

36. *Zohar Ḥadash* 23b (*Midrash ha-Ne'lam*); *Zohar: Pritzker Edition*, 10:264–65. See above, Chap. 2, at nn. 103–5.

37. *Zohar Ḥadash* 62c (*Shir ha-Shirim*); *Zohar: Pritzker Edition*, 11:360. See *Zohar Ḥadash* 63d (*Shir ha-Shirim*); *Zohar: Pritzker Edition*, 11:379; Huss, *Ke-Zohar ha-Raqia'*, 56; Asulin, "Ha-Parshanut ha-Mistit le-Shir ha-Shirim," 281–86. On the divine title "the Ancient of Days," see Dan 7:9. On words appearing above before the Ancient of Days, see *Zohar* 1:4b–5a.

38. The first of these appears in *Zohar Ḥadash* 62b (*Shir ha-Shirim*); *Zohar: Pritzker Edition*, 11:356. See Hecker's n. 22 there; Asulin, "Ha-Parshanut ha-Mistit le-Shir ha-Shirim," 233–36.

39. *Zohar Ḥadash* 73c (*Shir ha-Shirim*); *Zohar: Pritzker Edition*, 11:512. Cf. BT *Berakhot* 22a.

40. *Zohar Ḥadash* 71c (*Shir ha-Shirim*); *Zohar: Pritzker Edition*, 11:483.

41. See *Zohar Ḥadash* 62c–d, 69c, 70b–c (*Shir ha-Shirim*); *Zohar: Pritzker Edition*, 11:362, 458, 469; Asulin, "Ha-Parshanut ha-Mistit le-Shir ha-Shirim," 295–302.

42. *Zohar* 3:276b–277a (*Ra'aya Meheimna*). Cf. *Zohar* 3:124a (*Ra'aya Meheimna*).

43. *Zohar* 3:27b–28a, 124a–26a (both *Ra'aya Meheimna*). On Moses as Elijah's teacher, see above, at n. 1.

44. *Tiqqunei ha-Zohar*, introduction, 17a–b. For a commentary on this passage, see Matt, *Essential Kabbalah*, 171–73.

45. *Tiqqunei ha-Zohar* 70, 134a. See Asulin, "Ha-Parshanut ha-Mistit le-Shir ha-Shirim," 150–61; Roi, *Ahavat ha-Shekhinah*, 309–400.

46. *Tiqqunei ha-Zohar*, add. 6, 144b–46a. See Roi, *Ahavat ha-Shekhinah*, 327–60.

47. *Zohar Ḥadash* 103b (*Tiqqunim*).

48. See Shelomoh Shlumil ben Ḥayyim, *Shivḥei ha-Ari*, 10a–b; Benayahu, *Sefer Toledot ha-Ari*, 29, 154; Vital, *Ets Ḥayyim*, introduction, 1:18d–19a; Hallamish, *Ha-Qabbalah bi-Tfillah ba-Halakhah uv-Minhag*, 183–84.

49. Scholem, *On the Kabbalah and Its Symbolism*, 21.

50. Vital, *Sha'arei ha-Qedushah*, 3:7, p. 41. On fasting as contributing or leading to a revelation of Elijah, see *Bereshit Rabbah* 94:9; JT *Terumot* 8:11, 46b; BT *Ketubbot* 105b–6a; *Pirqei de-Rabbi Eli'ezer*, 1; Lowy, "Motivation of Fasting in Talmudic Literature," 36–38.

51. Caro, *Maggid Meisharim*, 3d, 6b (*parashat bereshit*).

52. Caro, *Maggid Meisharim*, 26a (*parashat vayaqhel*). See Werblowsky, *Joseph Karo*, 21–22, 269–70.

53. See above, at nn. 13–15; Werblowsky, *Joseph Karo*, 81, n. 1; Scholem, *Sabbatai Ṣevi*, 82.

54. Scholem, *Sabbatai Ṣevi*, 138–39.

55. Scholem, *Sabbatai Ṣevi*, 140–41.

56. Elqayam, "Ha-Zohar ha-Qadosh shel Shabbetai Tsevi," 366. Shabbetai's personal manuscript of the *Zohar* is likely preserved in the Friedberg Collection of Rare Hebraica at the University of Toronto Library. See ibid., 347.

57. Elqayam, "Ha-Zohar ha-Qadosh shel Shabbetai Tsevi," 384–85. On the Chair of Elijah, see below, Chap. 5, at nn. 18–33. According to one source, in the tenth century Nissim Gaon's father sat on the Chair of Elijah at Nissim's circumcision, holding his infant son and seeking Elijah's blessing for him. See Aaron ben Jacob ha-Kohen of Lunel, *Orḥot Ḥayyim, hilkhot milah* 9.

58. BT *Pesaḥim* 50a, in the name of Rabbi Naḥman son of Yitsḥaq.

59. Scholem, *Sabbatai Ṣevi,* 159.

60. Scholem, *Sabbatai Ṣevi,* 258, 417–18.

61. Scholem, *Sabbatai Ṣevi,* 446.

62. Scholem, *Sabbatai Ṣevi,* 457.

63. Scholem, *Sabbatai Ṣevi,* 535.

64. Scholem, *Sabbatai Ṣevi,* 614. See Drower, "Evergreen Elijah," 21, n. 26.

65. Elqayam, "Ha-Zohar ha-Qadosh shel Shabbetai Tsevi," 375–78. On Shabbetai's last letter, see Scholem, *Sabbatai Sevi,* 917.

Chapter 4. Elijah and the Daughters of Judaism

1. Matt 3:11, Mark 1:7–8, John 1:26–27. See Meier, *Marginal Jew,* 2:1041.

2. On the hairy mantle of a prophet, see Zech 13:4.

3. Cf. Luke 1:17.

4. See John 1:21; Robinson, "Elijah, John and Jesus"; Meier, *Marginal Jew,* 2:90, n. 138. On Elijah and the Messiah, see above, Chap. 2, at nn. 81–95.

5. Matt 16:13–16, Mark 8:27–29, Luke 9:18–20. Cf. Mark 6:14–15, Luke 9:7–8.

6. Luke 4:24–27. Cf. Matt 13:57, Mark 6:4.

7. See 1 Kgs 17:17–24, Luke 7:11–17. Cf. 2 Kgs 4:17–37 (concerning Elisha); Matt 9:18–19, 23–26 (and parallels); John 11:1–44.

8. See 2 Kgs 4:42–44, Matt 14:15–21 (and parallels), 2 Kgs 5:1–14, Matt 8:1–4 (and parallels).

9. See Luke 24:51, Acts 1:9–11, 2 Kgs 2:11.

10. See Vermes, *Jesus the Jew,* 95; Meier, *Marginal Jew,* 2:699, 1043–45.

11. Matt 17:1–8, Mark 9:2–8, Luke 9:28–36.

12. See above, Chap. 1, at n. 81, and n. 81.

13. See Mark 1:16–20, Luke 5:4–11. Cf. Mark 2:14 (and parallels). See also Meier, *Marginal Jew*, 3:48–50.

14. See Luke 9:59–60; Matt 8:21–22, 10:37; Luke 14:25–26. A similar story is told about another Galilean Jewish mystic, Isaac Luria. One late Friday afternoon, as Shabbat was about to begin, Luria and his disciples went to the outskirts of Safed, as was their custom, to greet the Sabbath Bride close to sunset. Luria was dressed completely in white. As they were chanting prayers and hymns to welcome Shabbat, Luria said, "Companions, is it your wish that we should go to Jerusalem before Shabbat begins and celebrate Shabbat there?" (Jerusalem, of course, was a long distance away.) Some of his disciples agreed to follow their master right away, while others said, "Let us first go and tell our wives." Upon hearing this, Luria trembled, clapped his hands in despair, and said, "Woe to us, for we did not have the merit to be redeemed! If you had all responded unanimously that you wished to go joyously, all of Israel would have immediately been redeemed, for now the moment was ripe. But since you refused, exile has resumed its persistent flow." The story appears in Bacharach, *Emeq ha-Melekh*, third introduction, chap. 5, 11d–12a. See Samet, *Pirqei Eliyyahu*, 339.

15. See Matt 27:46–49, Mark 15:34–36.

16. See Meier, *Marginal Jew*, 4:652. As Christianity developed, Elijah was invested with a mission to the Jews. According to the church fathers, on the eve of the Second Coming Elijah will return to earth and expound for the Jews the true meaning of Scripture, thereby inspiring them to finally believe in Christ. See St. Augustine, *City of God*, 20:29; Shacham-Rosby, "Koso, Kis'o ve-Kha'aso," 63–65.

17. 1 Kgs 17:2–7. See above, Chap. 1, at n. 15.

18. *Commentary on Isaiah*, attributed to the Cappadocian church father Basil of Caesarea; quoted by Bardy, "Le souvenir d'Élie chez les Pères grecs," 142.

19. On Elijah's title the Man of Truth, see below, Chap. 6, n. 23.

20. The story is contained in early Aramaic fragments of *Toledot Yeshu,* which likely date from before the sixth century. See Ilan, *Lexicon of Jewish Names in Late Antiquity,* 517–18.

21. See above, Chap. 1, at n. 92. According to 2 Kgs 4:25, Elisha resided at least for a time on Mount Carmel; other passages place his home in the capital, Samaria (2 Kgs 5:3; cf. 2:25, 5:9, 6:32). As for Elijah, King Ahaziah's soldiers find him *sitting on a hilltop* (2 Kgs 1:9). In JT *Pesaḥim* 3:6, 30b, Elijah is imagined as spending Shabbat on Mount Carmel when he returns from heaven on the eve of redemption.

22. See Benjamin of Tudela, *Itinerary,* 19; Yaari, "Me'arat Eliyyahu be-Har ha-Karmel," 138. On Elijah's altar, see 1 Kgs 18:30–35; above, Chap. 1, at nn. 39–44.

23. Ackerman, *Elijah, Prophet of Carmel,* 119–31, 140–43.

24. Muḥammad ibn Ismāʿīl al-Bukhārī, *Ṣaḥīḥ al-Bukhārī,* 4:406, cited in Halman, *Where the Two Seas Meet,* 75. The earliest form of the name is *al-Khaḍir.* Later traditions and popular usage employ the secondary form *al-Khiḍr* or sometimes simply *Khiḍr.*

25. Halman, *Where the Two Seas Meet,* 2, 9–11.

26. The passage appears in Qur'an 18:60–82. Of the thirty equal sections of the Qur'an, the sixteenth begins at 18:75, in the middle of this narrative. See Halman, *Where the Two Seas Meet,* 12; 60, n. 10.

27. See Halman, *Where the Two Seas Meet,* 72.

28. For Nissim's tale, see Nissim ben Jacob Gaon, *Elegant Composition,* 13–16. On Rabbi Yehoshu'a and Elijah, see above, Chap. 2, at nn. 31–38. On Nissim and Elijah, see Chap. 5, at n. 7; Chap. 3, n. 57; Chap. 5, n. 36.

29. See Schwarzbaum, *Mi-Meqor Yisra'el ve-Yishma'el,* 170, 176; Wheeler, "Jewish Origins of Qur'ān 18:65–82?"; Yassif, *Hebrew Folktale,* 266–68.

30. Halman, *Where the Two Seas Meet,* 244.

31. Halman, *Where the Two Seas Meet,* 237–38.

32. See Halman, *Where the Two Seas Meet*, 212–13; Scholem, *Origins of the Kabbalah*, 246; above, Chap. 3, at nn. 6–16.

33. See Drower, "Evergreen Elijah," 32, 58–62; Meri, "Re-Appropriating Sacred Space," 251–52.

34. Lakhnavi and Bilgrami, *Adventures of Amir Hamza*, 650, 914, 916.

35. Cited by the fourteenth-century historian Ibn Kathīr. See Noegel and Wheeler, *Historical Dictionary of Prophets in Islam and Judaism*, 101.

36. Ibn Ḥajar al-'Asqalānī, *al-Iṣābah fī tamyīz al-Ṣaḥābah*, 1:439, cited by Wheeler, "Jewish Origins of Qur'an 18:65–82?," 165.

Chapter 5. Rituals of Anticipation

1. 1 Kgs 18:22; 19:10, 14.

2. See Hoffman, *Beyond the Text*, 44; Lindbeck, *Elijah and the Rabbis*, 153.

3. See Avida, *Koso shel Eliyyahu;* Lindbeck, *Elijah and the Rabbis*, 158–68.

4. *Mekhilta*, *Pisḥa* 14, in the name of Rabbi Yehoshu'a.

5. *Shemot Rabbah* 18:12. See above, Chap. 2, at n. 90.

6. BT *Rosh ha-Shanah* 11b, in the names of Rabbi Yehoshu'a and Rabbi Eli'ezer, respectively.

7. Lewin, *Otsar ha-Ge'onim*, *Pesaḥim*, 112.

8. Binga, *Massekhet Pesaḥim*, 195. On the requirement to drink four cups of wine at the seder, see M *Pesaḥim* 10:1. Cf. JT *Pesaḥim* 10:1, 37b–c; *Bereshit Rabbah* 88:5; *Shemot Rabbah* 6:4. On the image of Elijah among Jews in medieval Ashkenaz (Franco-Germany), see Shacham-Rosby, "Koso, Kis'o ve-Kha'aso."

9. Shammash, *Minhagim di-Qhillat Qodesh Vermaisha*, 1:85 (annotations).

10. Benveniste, *Pesaḥ Me'ubbin*, §182.

11. Ḥagiz, *Shetei ha-Leḥem*, 48b.

12. See BT *Pesaḥim* 118a, and Rashi, ad loc., s.v. *hakhi garsinan revi'i;* Maimonides, *Mishneh Torah*, *Hilkhot Ḥamets u-Matsah* 8:10; Abraham ben David, *Hassagot al Ba'al ha-Ma'or*, *Pesaḥim* 26b (on *Pesaḥim* 118a); Kasher, *Haggadah Shelemah*, 94–95 (English pagina-

tion), 161–78 (Hebrew pagination). On the requirement of four cups, see above, n. 8.

13. Elijah ben Solomon of Vilna, *Divrei Eliyyahu*, 17b (*parashat va'era*). On Elijah as the one who will clarify all halakhic doubts, see above, Chap. 2, at nn. 59–80. The attribution of this explanation to the Gaon of Vilna has been challenged by Yehuda Avida, in his *Koso shel Eliyyahu*, 53–57. On the relationship between Elijah the Gaon of Vilna and Elijah the Prophet, see Liebes, "Talmidei ha-Gr'a," 286–89; Liebes, "Ho'il Moshe Be'er," 11–16; Liebes, "Toda'ato ha-Atsmit shel ha-Ga'on mi-Vilna," 620; Roi, "'Hayu Mashqim la-Torah,'" 35–43.

14. See Levinsohn, *Efes Damim*, 39–40; Hirshovitz, *Otsar Kol Minhagei Yeshurun*, 139; Levine, *Misunderstood Jew*, 207; Gaster, *Passover*, 66.

15. Gutmann, "Messiah at the Seder," 29–38; Goitein, "Mezigat Kos le-Eliyyahu ha-Navi." The image of the redeemer riding on a donkey derives from Zech 9:9.

16. Margaritha, *Der gantze jüdische Glaube*, 47–48. See Hahn, *Yosif Omets*, §788; Avida, *Koso shel Eliyyahu*, 20–23.

17. See Lindbeck, *Elijah and the Rabbis*, 168.

18. *Pirqei de-Rabbi Eli'ezer*, 29.

19. On Elijah's being identical with Phinehas (and on the incident at Abel Shittim), see above, Chap. 2, at nn. 111–28.

20. *Zohar* 1:93a (*Zohar: Pritzker Edition*, 2:88–89). Cf. *Zohar* 1:209a–b (*Zohar: Pritzker Edition*, 3:284); *Zohar* 2:190a (*Zohar: Pritzker Edition*, 6:72–73). For the view that Elijah's appearance at every circumcision is a reward, see Joshua Falk, *Perishah*, *yoreh de'ah* 265:25; Ginzberg, *Legends of the Jews*, 6:338, n. 103. This view is also reflected in versions of the passage from *Pirqei de-Rabbi Eli'ezer* quoted in various medieval sources, including Lewin, ed., *Otsar ha-Ge'onim*, *Shabbat*, 139 (in a responsum attributed to Sherira Gaon); Simḥah ben Samuel, *Maḥazor Vitri*, 505; Isaac ben Moses, *Or Zaru'a*, 2, 107:2; Zedekiah ben Abraham Anav, *Shibbolei ha-Leqet*, *hilkhot milah* 6; and Yeḥiel ben Yekutiel, *Tanya*, 96.

21. See David Luria's annotation in *Pirqei de-Rabbi Eli'ezer*, 29, n. 64; Hellner-Eshed, "Nefesh ha-Qanna," 109, 112; Hellner-

Eshed, "Ha-Meqanne la-Berit u-Va'al ha-Shigyonot," 163; Samet, *Pirqei Eliyyahu*, 565.

22. Glasberg, *Zikhron Berit la-Rishonim (ḥeleq ha-millu'im)*, §9. Among the halakhic authorities who mention the Chair of Elijah are Abraham ben Nathan ha-Yarḥi, *Sefer ha-Manhig*, 2:583; Isaac ben Moses, *Or Zaru'a*, 2, 107:2; Jacob ben Asher, *Tur, yoreh de'ah* 265; Joseph Caro, *Shulḥan Arukh, yoreh de'ah* 265:11. The question of Elijah's simultaneous appearances played a part in medieval Jewish-Christian polemical literature. When Jewish authorities claimed that the Christian doctrine of transubstantiation was impossible, since one being (Jesus) could not appear on many altars at the same time, some Christians responded that Jews held a similar belief concerning Elijah's simultaneous appearances at many circumcisions. See Lasker, "Transubstantiation, Elijah's Chair, Plato, and the Jewish-Christian Debate."

23. Simḥah ben Samuel, *Maḥazor Vitri*, 505; Abraham ben Nathan ha-Yarḥi, *Sefer ha-Manhig*, 2:583; Yeḥiel Michal Halevi Epstein, *Arukh ha-Shulḥan, yoreh de'ah* 265:14. On the custom of welcoming Elijah on the first night of Passover with the greeting *Barukh ha-ba*, see above, at n. 16.

24. *Zohar* 1:13a (*Zohar: Pritzker Edition*, 1:90). See *Zohar* 2:169a (*Zohar: Pritzker Edition*, 5:484); Joseph Caro, *Sḥhulhan Arukh, yoreh de'ah* 265:11; Hallamish, *Ha-Qabbalah bi-Tfillah ba-Halakhah uv-Minhag*, 45–47, 299–300.

25. See Klein, *Time to Be Born*, 185; Jacoby, "Small Elijah Chair."

26. See Schauss, *Lifetime of a Jew*, 34–37; Gaster, *Holy and the Profane*, 63–65; Klein, *Time to Be Born*, 185; Lindbeck, *Elijah and the Rabbis*, 159.

27. See BT *Mo'ed Qatan* 27a, *Nedarim* 56a–b, *Sanhedrin* 20a; Rashi, on all of these passages, s.v. *arsa de-gadda*.

28. *Tosefta*, *Shabbat* 6:4. See Lieberman, *Tosefta ki-Fshutah*, 3:84.

29. Jeroham ben Meshullam, *Toledot Adam ve-Ḥavah*, 17:5.

30. Joseph Caro, *Shulḥan Arukh, yoreh de'ah* 179:17. Cf. Caro, *Beit Yosef*, loc. cit.

31. Ḥayyim Joseph David Azulai, *Birkei Yosef*, on *Shulḥan Arukh, yoreh de'ah* 179:17.

32. 1 Kgs 17:17–24. See above, Chap. 1, at nn. 18–22.

33. See Montgomery, *Aramaic Incantation Texts from Nippur*, 258–64; Yassif, *Sippurei Ben Sira*, 68–69; Scholem, *Shedim, Ruḥot u-Nshamot*, 60–79; Gaster, *Holy and the Profane*, 18–28; Klein, *Time to Be Born*, 147–48; Sabar, "Childbirth and Magic," 707; Lindbeck, *Elijah and the Rabbis*, 154–55.

34. Isaac ben Moses, *Or Zaru'a*, 2:95, mentioning a Gaonic responsum.

35. See Simḥah ben Samuel, *Maḥazor Vitri*, 203; *Sefer Abudarham, seder motsa'ei shabbat;* Bar-Tikva, "Eliyyahu ha-Navi be-Fiyyutei ha-Havdalah," 248.

36. See Simḥah ben Samuel, *Maḥazor Vitri*, 203; Bar-Tikva, "Eliyyahu ha-Navi be-Fiyyutei ha-Havdalah," 269–74. The story first appears in Nissim ben Jacob Gaon's eleventh-century Judeo-Arabic work *An Elegant Composition concerning Relief after Adversity*, 99–102.

37. The phrase *me-ein olam ha-ba*, "resembling the world to come," appears in the Sabbath hymn *Mah yedidut menuḥatekh*. The idea derives from BT *Berakhot* 57b, where Shabbat is described as being "one-sixtieth of the world to come." In M *Tamid* 7:4, the world to come is described as "a day that is entirely Shabbat."

38. BT *Eruvin* 43b. Cf. *Pesaḥim* 13a.

39. See BT *Eruvin* 43a–b. According to a tradition reported in the name of the House of Hillel in JT *Pesaḥim* 3:6, 30b, "We have been assured that Elijah will come neither on *Shabbat* nor on a Festival." See Tosafot, *Eruvin* 43b, s.v. *hai tanna.*

40. See Abraham ben Nathan ha-Yarḥi, *Sefer ha-Manhig, hilkhot shabbat* 71. Among later authors who include this explanation of the custom are Jacob ben Asher, *Tur, oraḥ ḥayyim* 295; Mordechai Jaffe, *Levush, oraḥ ḥayyim* 295:1; Abraham Gombiner, *Magen Avraham, oraḥ ḥayyim* 295:1.

41. Jacob ben Asher, *Tur, oraḥ ḥayyim* 299. This practice, Jacob adds, reportedly strengthens the memory.

42. Shalom ben Isaac of Neustadt, *Hilkhot u-Minhagei Rabbeinu Shalom mi-Noishtat*, 94. See Jacob ben Moses Moellin, *Sefer Maharil, hilkhot shabbat* 40. On Elijah as scribe, see above, Chap. 2, n. 26.

43. The tradition about Elijah helping those in hell appears in Bonn, *Shikhehat Leqet, eliyyahu ve-elisha*, §7. On Elijah's power of atonement, see *Seder Eliyyahu Rabbah*, 26, p. 141; above, Chap. 2, at n. 125. On the tranquility of Shabbat even in hell, see *Bereshit Rabbah* 11:5; BT *Sanhedrin* 65b.

44. This Hebrew poem by Jacob Fichman was originally published in 1922 under the title "Aggadah" (Legend), though the song is widely known by its opening line: *Al sefat yam kinneret* (On the shores of the Sea of Galilee).

45. *Soferim* 13:12.

46. See Ginzberg, *Unknown Jewish Sect*, 251–52; Milikowsky, "Trajectories of Return, Restoration and Redemption," 276, n. 35.

47. This is the concluding verse of the haftarah, which consists of 1 Kgs 18:1–39. In the Sephardic ritual, the haftarah begins later in the chapter, at v. 20. See above, Chap. 1, at nn. 23–54. On Elijah and Moses, see above, Chap. 2, at nn. 96–105.

48. See above, Chap. 2, at n. 112.

49. The haftarah consists of 1 Kgs 18:46–19:21. See above, Chap. 1, at nn. 60–81. If the Torah portion *Pinhas* is read after the seventeenth of *Tammuz*, in most communities a different haftarah is chanted.

50. See above, Chap. 2, at nn. 111–28.

51. See above, Chap. 2, at n. 90; Chap. 5, at nn. 4–5. This haftarah consists of Mal 3:4–24. Traditionally, when the haftarah is chanted, v. 23 is repeated after v. 24, so as not to conclude with the threatening words *lest I come and strike the land with sacred destruction.* On these verses in Malachi, see above, Chap. 1, at nn. 116–18.

52. See Aaron Berechiah of Modena, *Ma'avar Yabboq* 1:19.

Chapter 6. Becoming Elijah

1. *Tanhuma, Bereshit* 7. See *Bereshit Rabbah* 77:1; *Devarim Rabbah* 10:3. For the context (and source) of Cordovero's remark, see the Epigraph (and its unnumbered note).

2. *Shir ha-Shirim Zuta* 7:6. See *Zohar* 1:209a (*Zohar: Pritzker Edition*, 3:281): "Whatever Elijah decreed, the blessed Holy One fulfilled."

3. See above, Chap. 1, at n. 14.

4. See above, Chap. 1, at n. 79.

5. Isaac Abravanel, on 2 Kgs 2:12.

6. Kook, *Orot ha-Qodesh*, 3:365.

7. On the *tiqqun* of Elijah, see David Luria, on *Pirqei de-Rabbi Eli'ezer*, 29, n. 64; Cohen, *Ishim min ha-Miqra*, 252–55; Wiener, *Prophet Elijah*, 76–77; Samet, *Pirqei Eliyyahu*, 522, 562–65; Asulin, "Ha-Parshanut ha-Mistit le-Shir ha-Shirim," 303–5.

8. Elijah enacts this role in various tales. According to legend, one year in a certain synagogue in Jerusalem, as Yom Kippur was about to begin, Elijah miraculously completed the minyan. Subsequently this synagogue (one of Jerusalem's oldest functioning ones) was renamed the Synagogue of Elijah the Prophet. See Angel-Malachi, "Tenth for the Minyan."

9. See David Luria, on *Pirqei de-Rabbi Eli'ezer*, 15, n. 6; above, Chap. 3, at n. 36; Chap. 5, at n. 42.

10. *Bereshit Rabbah* 71:9. See 1 Kgs 18:36; *Vayiqra Rabbah* 36:6; *Pesiqta Rabbati* 4, 13b; *Ester Rabbah* 7:13.

11. See BT *Gittin* 6b; above, Chap. 2, at nn. 47–48.

12. See M *Eduyyot* 8:7; above, Chap. 2, at n. 65.

13. David Luria, on *Pirqei de-Rabbi Eli'ezer*, 15, n. 6. Later in his commentary (chap. 43, n. 85), Luria interprets Elijah's title *ha-Tishbi* (the Tishbite) as alluding to *teshuvah*. See above, Chap. 2, at n. 95; *Pirqei de-Rabbi Eli'ezer*, 47, and Luria's nn. 38–39.

14. Isaac Abravanel, on 2 Kgs 2:12.

15. See above, Chap. 1, at n. 78; Chap. 1, n. 93.

16. Menaḥem Naḥum of Chernobyl, *Me'or Einayim*, 54d–55a (*parashat pinḥas*), and *Light of the Eyes*, 633–34.

17. Menaḥem Naḥum of Chernobyl, *Me'or Einayim*, 23b (*parashat vayetse*), and *Light of the Eyes*, 316–17. See Wiener, *Prophet Elijah*, 122–23.

18. See Fishbane, *JPS Bible Commentary: Haftarot*, 366; Menaḥem Naḥum of Chernobyl, *Light of the Eyes*, 317, n. 104.

19. See above, Chap. 2, at n. 92.

20. Moses Ḥayyim Ephraim of Sudylkow, *Degel Maḥaneh Ephrayim, shemot, derush le-Purim*. The Baal Shem Tov's great-

grandson, Naḥman of Bratslav, concurs (in his *Sefer ha-Middot, besorah* 1): "Whoever regularly delivers good news is imbued with the aspect of Elijah."

21. Menaḥem Naḥum of Chernobyl, *Me'or Einayim*, 44c (*parashat aḥarei mot*), and *Light of the Eyes*, 533. See above, Chap. 3, at nn. 6–16.

22. See above, Chap. 2, at n. 25; Chap. 3, at nn. 7–8.

23. This title of Elijah appears at the end of the hymn *Ish ḥasid hayah*, on which see above, Chap. 5, at n. 36. The designation is based on the response by the widow of Zarephath after Elijah revived her child: *Now I know that you are a man of God, and the word of YHVH in your mouth is truth* (1 Kgs 17:24). See above, Chap. 1, at n. 20; Chap. 2, at n. 108, and n. 108. Cf. Rashi, on Ps 43:3; Baḥya ben Asher, "Kad ha-Qemaḥ," 123.

24. On *mishnat ḥasidim*, see above, Chap. 2, at nn. 36–37.

25. This Hasidic tale is recorded by Wiener, *Prophet Elijah*, 139. Cf. above, Chap. 5, at n. 17.

BIBLIOGRAPHY

This bibliography includes works cited and used by the author, except for standard rabbinic and medieval texts.

Aaron Berechiah of Modena. *Ma'avar Yabboq*. Vilna: Romm, 1896.

Ackerman, Jane. *Elijah, Prophet of Carmel.* Washington, D.C.: ICS Publications, 2003.

Aggadat Shir ha-Shirim (*Aggadath Shir Hashirim*). Edited by Solomon Schechter. Cambridge: Deighton Bell, 1896.

Alter, Robert. *The Hebrew Bible: A Translation with Commentary.* 3 vols. New York: Norton, 2019.

Angel-Malachi, Shaul. "The Tenth for the Minyan." In Ben-Amos, *Folktales of the Jews*, 1:2–6.

Aptowitzer, Victor. *Die Parteipolitik der Hasmonäerzeit im rabbinischen und pseudoepigraphischen Schrifttum.* Vienna: Verlag der Kohut-Foundation, 1927.

Asulin, Shifra. "Ha-Parshanut ha-Mistit le-Shir ha-Shirim be-Sefer ha-Zohar ve-Riq'ah." PhD diss., Hebrew University, 2007.

Augustinović, Augustin. *"El-Khadr" and the Prophet Elijah*. Translated by Eugene Hoade. Jerusalem: Franciscan Printing Press, 1972.

Avida, Yehuda. *Koso shel Eliyyahu ha-Navi: Naftulei Minhag be-Hitraqqemuto*. Edited by Eliezer Yehudah Brodt. 2nd ed. Betar Illit: Brodt, 2013.

Ayali, Meir. "Eliyyahu me-Heikhan Ba?: Yiḥuso u-Motsa'o shel Eliyyahu ha-Navi bi-Drashot Ḥazal." *Tura* 3 (1994): 43–66.

Azriel ben Menaḥem of Gerona. *Peirush ha-Aggadot le-Rabbi Azri'el*. Edited by Isaiah Tishby. 2nd ed. Jerusalem: Magnes, 1982.

Bacharach, Naftali. *Emeq ha-Melekh*. Amsterdam: Immanuel Benveniste, 1648.

Baḥya ben Asher. "Kad ha-Qemaḥ." In *Kitvei Rabbeinu Baḥya*, edited by Chaim D. Chavel, 9–451. Jerusalem: Mossad Harav Kook, 1970.

Bardy, Gustave. "Le souvenir d'Élie chez les Pères grecs." In Bardy et al., *Élie le prophète*, 1:131–58.

Bardy, Gustave, et al., eds. *Élie le prophète*. 2 vols. Paris: Desclée de Brouwer, 1956.

Bar-Tikva, Binyamin. "Eliyyahu ha-Navi be-Fiyyutei ha-Havdalah." In *Le-Ot Zikkaron: Meḥqarim ba-Shirah ha-Ivrit uv-Moreshet Yisra'el, Sefer Zikkaron le-Aharon Mirsky*, edited by Ephraim Ḥazan and Yosef Yahalom, 239–79. Ramat Gan: Bar-Ilan University Press, 2007.

Ben-Amos, Dan, ed. *Folktales of the Jews*. 3 vols. Philadelphia: Jewish Publication Society, 2006–2011.

Benarroch, Jonatan M. *Sava ve-Yanuqa: Ha-El, ha-Ben ve-ha-Mashiaḥ be-Sippurei ha-Zohar*. Jerusalem: Magnes, 2018.

Benayahu, Meir. *Sefer Toledot ha-Ari*. Jerusalem: Ben-Zvi Institute, 1967.

Benjamin of Tudela. *The Itinerary of Benjamin of Tudela*. Edited and translated by Marcus N. Adler. New York: Feldheim, 1964.

Benveniste, Ḥayyim. *Pesaḥ Me'ubbin*. Venice: Bragadini, 1692.

Berdichevsky, Micah Joseph. *Mi-Meqor Yisra'el: Ma'asiyyot ve-Sippurei-am*. Tel Aviv: Devir, 1965.

Binga, Zelikman. *Massekhet Pesaḥim: Ḥiddushm, Bei'urim u-Fsaqim*.

Edited by Binyamin Z. Noizats, Mosheh Ḥ. Naiman, and Yisra'el M. Peles. Jerusalem: Mekhon Yerushalayim, 1985.
Bonn, Nathan ben Isaac Jacob. *Shikheḥat Leqet*. Frankfurt, 1660.
Braude, William G., and Israel J. Kapstein, trans. *Tanna dĕbe Eliyyahu: The Lore of the School of Elijah*. Philadelphia: Jewish Publication Society, 1981.
Bronner, Leah. *The Stories of Elijah and Elisha as Polemics against Baal Worship*. Leiden: E. J. Brill, 1968.
Carlson, Rolf A. "Élie à l'Horeb." *Vetus Testamentum* 19 (1969): 416–39.
Caro, Joseph. *Maggid Meisharim*. Vilna: Yehudah Leib Lipman, 1875.
Chajes, Ẓevi Hirsch. "Beirur Eliyyahu." In *Kol Sifrei Maharats Chajes*, 1:17–23. 2 vols. Jerusalem: Divrei Ḥakhamim, 1958.
Cogan, Mordecai. *1 Kings: A New Translation with Introduction and Commentary*. New York: Doubleday, 2001.
Cogan, Mordecai, and Hayim Tadmor. *II Kings: A New Translation with Introduction and Commentary*. New York: Doubleday, 1988.
Cohen, Israel. *Ishim min ha-Miqra*. Tel Aviv: Maḥbarot le-Sifrut, 1964.
Coote, Robert B., ed. *Elijah and Elisha in Socioliterary Perspective*. Atlanta: Scholars Press, 1992.
Cordovero, Moses. "Derishot be-Inyenei ha-Mal'akhim." In Margaliot, *Mal'akhei Elyon*, Appendix.
———. *Or Yaqar*. 21 vols. Jerusalem: Achuzat Israel, 1962–1995.
———. *Pardes Rimmonim*. Munkacs: Kahana and Fried, 1906. Reprint, Jerusalem: Mordechai Etyah, 1962.
Cross, Frank Moore. *Canaanite Myth and Hebrew Epic: Essays in the History of the Religion of Israel*. Cambridge, Mass.: Harvard University Press, 1973.
Daube, David. *Collaboration with Tyranny in Rabbinic Law*. London: Oxford University Press, 1965.
David ben Solomon ibn Abi Zimra. *She'elot u-Tshuvot ha-Radbaz*. New York: Otzar Hasefarim, 1966.
Dever, William G. *Did God Have a Wife? Archaeology and Folk Religion in Ancient Israel*. Grand Rapids, Mich.: William B. Eerdmans, 2005.

Drower, Ethel S. "Evergreen Elijah: Ritual Scenes from Jewish Life in the Middle East." In *Approaches to Ancient Judaism, Volume VI: Studies in the Ethnography and Literature of Judaism*, edited by Jacob Neusner and Ernest S. Frerichs, 3–63. Atlanta: Scholars Press, 1989.

Efrati, Barukh. "Eliyyahu Zeh Pinḥas." *Shema'tin* 156 (2004): 38–44.

Egeria. *The Pilgrimage of Egeria: A New Translation of the Itinerarium Egeriae with Introduction and Commentary*. Translated and edited by Anne McGowan and Paul F. Bradshaw. Collegeville, Minn.: Liturgical Press, 2018.

Elbaum, Yaakov. "Bein Midrash le-Sefer Musar: Iyyun bi-Fraqim 1–6 be-'Tanna de-Vei Eliyyahu.'" *Meḥqerei Yerushalayim be-Sifrut Ivrit* 1 (1981): 144–54.

Elijah ben Solomon of Vilna. *Divrei Eliyyahu*. Edited by Y. L. Farfel and Abraham David Bloch. Jerusalem: Tel-Talpiyot, 1948.

Elior, Rachel, ed. *Heikhalot Zutarti: Mahadurah Madda'it. Meḥqerei Yerushalyim be-Maḥashevet Yisrae'l, Musaf Alef.* Jerusalem: Magnes, 1982.

Elon, Menachem. *Ha-Mishpat ha-Ivri: Toledotav, Meqorotav, Eqronotav*. 3 vols. Jerusalem: Magnes, 1973.

Elqayam, Avraham. "Ha-Zohar ha-Qadosh shel Shabbetai Tsevi." *Kabbalah* 3 (1998): 345–87.

Epstein, Abraham. *Kitvei R. Avraham Epshtain*. Edited by A. M. Haberman. 2 vols. Jerusalem: Mossad Harav Kook, 1950–1957.

Faierstein, Morris M. "Why Do the Scribes Say That Elijah Must Come First?" *Journal of Biblical Literature* 100 (1981): 75–86.

Feldman, Louis H. "Josephus' Portrait of Elijah." *Scandinavian Journal of the Old Testament* 8 (1994): 61–86.

Fenton, Paul B. "Rosh bein ha-Birkayim: Terumah la-Meḥqar al Tenuḥat Meditatsyah ba-Mistiqah ha-Yehudit ve-ha-Islamit." *Da'at* 32–33 (1994): 19–29.

———. "La 'tête entre les genoux': contribution à l'étude d'une posture méditative dans la mystique juive et islamique." *Revue d'histoire et de philosophie religieuses* 72 (1992): 413–26.

Fichman, Jacob. "Aggadah." *Shibbolim* 2 (1922): 25.

Fisch, Harold. "Elijah and the Wandering Jew." In *Rabbi Joseph H. Lookstein Memorial Volume*, edited by Leo Landman, 125–35. New York: Ktav, 1980.

———. *A Remembered Future: A Study in Literary Mythology*. Bloomington: Indiana University Press, 1984.

Fishbane, Michael. *Biblical Myth and Rabbinic Mythmaking*. New York: Oxford University Press, 2003.

———. *The JPS Bible Commentary: Haftarot*. Philadelphia: Jewish Publication Society, 2002.

Frankel, Ellen. *The Classic Tales: 4,000 Years of Jewish Lore*. Northvale, N.J.: Jason Aronson, 1989, 575–607 and passim.

Freedman, David Noel. "Yahweh of Samaria and his Asherah." *Biblical Archaeologist* (December 1987): 241–49.

Friedman, Richard Elliott. *The Exodus*. New York: HarperCollins, 2017.

Friedmann, Meir, ed. *Seder Eliyyahu Rabbah ve-Seder Eliyyahu Zuta*. Vienna: Carl Fremme, 1902–1904.

Garsiel, Moshe. *From Earth to Heaven: A Literary Study of Elijah Stories in the Book of Kings*. Bethesda, Md.: CDL, 2014.

Gaster, Theodor H. *The Holy and the Profane: Evolution of Jewish Folkways*. New York: William Sloane Associates, 1955.

———. *Passover: Its History and Traditions*. Boston: Beacon, 1962.

Ginzberg, Louis. *Legends of the Jews*. 7 vols. Translated by Henrietta Szold and Paul Radin. Philadelphia: Jewish Publication Society, 1909–1938.

———. *An Unknown Jewish Sect*. New York: Jewish Theological Seminary, 1976.

Glasberg, Jacob. *Zikhron Berit la-Rishonim*. Cracow: Yosef Fisher, 1892.

Goitein, Tal. "Mezigat Kos le-Eliyyahu ha-Navi: Tei'ur lo Mukkar shel ha-Minhag me-ha-Me'ah ha-Ḥamesh-esreh be-Haggadat Erna Mikha'el." *Meḥqerei Yerushalyim be-Folqlor Yehudi* 29 (2015): 79–102.

Goldin, Barbara Diamond. *Journeys with Elijah: Eight Tales of the Prophet*. New York: Gulliver, 1999.

Gray, John. *I and II Kings: A Commentary*. 2nd ed. Philadelphia: Westminster, 1970.

Greenberg, Moshe. "Ve-Attah Hasibbota et Libbam Aḥorannit (1 Kings 18:37)." In *Meḥqarim be-Aggadah, Targumim u-Tfillot Yisra'el le-Zekher Yosef Heinemann*, edited by Ezra Fleischer and Jakob J. Petuchowski, 53–66. Jerusalem: Magnes, 1981.

Gregory, Russell. "Irony and the Unmasking of Elijah." In Hauser and Gregory, *From Carmel to Horeb*, 91–169.

Gutmann, Joseph. "The Messiah at the Seder: A Fifteenth-Century Motif in Jewish Art." In *Sefer Rephael Mahler*, edited by Shemuel Yeivin, 29–38. Merhavia: Sifriat Poalim, 1974.

Guttmann, Yehiel Michael. "Eliyyahu ha-Navi be-Aggadot Yisra'el." *He-Atid* 5 (1923): 14–46.

Ḥagiz, Moses. *Shetei ha-Leḥem*. Peremyshlyany: Zupnik, Knoller, and Wolf, 1898.

Hahn, Joseph Yuspa. *Yosif Omets*. Frankfurt: Johann Koellner, 1723.

Hallamish, Moshe. *Ha-Qabbalah bi-Tfillah ba-Halakhah uv-Minhag*. Ramat Gan: Bar-Ilan University, 2000.

Halman, Hugh Talat. *Where the Two Seas Meet: The Qur'ānic Story of al-Khiḍr and Moses in Sufi Commentaries as a Model of Spiritual Guidance*. Louisville: Fons Vitae, 2013.

Harrington, Daniel J., trans. "Pseudo-Philo." In *The Old Testament Pseudepigrapha*, edited by James H. Charlesworth, 2:297–377. Garden City, N.Y.: Doubleday, 1983–1985.

Hauser, Alan J. "Yahweh versus Death: The Real Struggle in 1 Kings 17–19." In Hauser and Gregory, *From Carmel to Horeb*, 9–89.

Hauser, Alan J., and Russell Gregory, eds. *From Carmel to Horeb: Elijah in Crisis*. Sheffield: Almond Press, 1990.

Hayward, Robert. "*Phinehas—The Same Is Elijah:* The Origins of a Rabbinic Tradition." *Journal of Jewish Studies* 29 (1978): 22–34.

Hellner-Eshed, Melila. "Ha-Meqanne la-Berit u-Va'al ha-Shigyonot: Eliyyahu va-Ḥavaqquq ba-Zohar—Al ha-Zekhari ve-ha-Neqevi be-Nefesh ha-Adam." *Kabbalah* 22 (2010): 149–92.

———. *Mevaqqeshei ha-Panim: Mi-Sodot ha-Idra Rabba she-be-Sefer ha-Zohar*. Rishon LeZion: Yedioth Ahronoth, 2017.

———. "Nefesh ha-Qanna be-Sefer ha-Zohar." *Ellu va-Ellu* 4 (1997): 98–116.

———. *A River Flows from Eden: The Language of Mystical Experience in the Zohar.* Translated by Nathan Wolski. Stanford, Calif.: Stanford University Press, 2009.

Hengel, Martin. *The Zealots: Investigations into the Jewish Freedom Movement from Herod I until 70 A.D.* Translated by David Smith. Edinburgh: T&T Clark, 1989.

Heschel, Abraham Joshua. "Al Ruaḥ ha-Qodesh bi-Ymei ha-Beinayim." In *Sefer ha-Yovel li-Khvod Alexander Marx li-Ml'ot Lo Shiv'im Shanah*, edited by Saul Lieberman, 175–208. New York: Jewish Theological Seminary, 1950.

———. *Torah min ha-Shamayim ba-Aspaqlaryah shel ha-Dorot.* 3 vols. London: Soncino, 1962–1965; Jerusalem: Jewish Theological Seminary of America, 1990.

Hirshovitz, Abraham Eliezer. *Otsar Kol Minhagei Yeshurun.* St. Louis: Moinester, 1917.

Hoffman, Lawrence A. *Beyond the Text: A Holistic Approach to Liturgy.* Bloomington: Indiana University Press, 1987.

Huss, Boaz. *Ke-Zohar ha-Raqia': Peraqim be-Hitqabbelut ha-Zohar uv-Havnayat Erko ha-Simli.* Jerusalem: Ben-Zvi Institute, 2008.

Idel, Moshe. *Ascensions on High in Jewish Mysticism: Pillars, Lines, Ladders.* Budapest: Central European University Press, 2005.

———. *Ben: Sonship and Jewish Mysticism.* New York: Continuum, 2007.

———. *Enchanted Chains: Techniques and Rituals in Jewish Mysticism.* Los Angeles: Cherub, 2005.

———. *Kabbalah: New Perspectives.* New Haven: Yale University Press, 1988.

Ilan, Tal. *Lexicon of Jewish Names in Late Antiquity: Part II, Palestine 200–650.* Tübingen: Mohr Siebeck, 2012.

Jacob ben Sheshet. "Ha-Emunah ve-ha-Bittaḥon." In *Kitvei Ramban*, edited by Chaim D. Chavel, 2:339–448. 2 vols. Jerusalem: Mossad Harav Kook, 1964.

Jacob Joseph ben Ẓevi Hirsh ha-Kohen Katz of Polonnoye. *Toledot*

Ya'aqov Yosef. Koretz: Ẓevi Hirsh ben Aryeh Lev, Shemu'el ben Yisachar Ber, 1780.

Jacob of Marvège. *She'elot u-Tshuvot min ha-Shamayim.* Edited by Reuven Margaliot. Jerusalem: Mossad Harav Kook, 1957.

Jacoby, Ruth. "The Small Elijah Chair." *Journal of Jewish Art* 18 (1992): 70–77.

Japhet, Sara. *I & II Chronicles: A Commentary.* Louisville: Westminster John Knox, 1993.

Jellinek, Adolph, ed. *Beit ha-Midrash.* 3rd ed. 2 vols. Jerusalem: Wahrmann Books, 1967.

Jeroham ben Meshullam. *Toledot Adam ve-Ḥavah.* Venice: Bragadini, 1553.

Joseph ben Issachar. *Yosef Da'at.* Prague: Gerhsom Katz, 1609.

Kadari, Adiel. *Ad she-Yavo Eliyyahu: Demuto shel Eliyyahu ha-Navi be-Sifrut ha-Tanna'im.* Jerusalem: Magnes, 2021.

———. "Did Elijah Show Respect to Royalty?" *Journal for the Study of Judaism* 46 (2015): 403–29.

———. "Hilkhat Eliyyahu: Yeda Shemeimi, Ḥasidut ve-Sakkanah." *Madda'ei ha-Yahadut* 54 (2019): 105–20.

Kaminka, Aharon. "Eliyyahu ha-Navi va-Miqra u-va-Aggadah." In his *Kitvei Viqqoret Historit: Ma'amarim Nivḥarim,* 1–16. New York: Shulsinger, 1944.

Kasher, Menaḥem M. *Haggadah Shelemah.* Jerusalem: Mekhon Torah Shelemah, 1967.

Kiel, Yehuda, ed. *Sefer Melakhim: Meforash bi-Ydei Yehudah Qil.* 2 vols. Jerusalem: Mossad Harav Kook, 1989.

Klapholz, Israel Jacob. *Sippurei Eliyyahu ha-Navi.* 2 vols. Tel Aviv: Aravah, 1967.

Klein, Michelle. *A Time to Be Born: Customs and Folklore of Jewish Birth.* Philadelphia: Jewish Publication Society, 1998.

Kook, Abraham Isaac. *Orot ha-Qodesh.* 4 vols. Jerusalem: Mossad ha-Rav Kook, 1953–1964.

Kugel, James L. *Traditions of the Bible: A Guide to the Bible as It Was at the Start of the Common Era.* Cambridge, Mass.: Harvard University Press, 1998.

Lakhnavi, Ghalib, and Abdullah Bilgrami (compilers of original

Urdu text). *The Adventures of Amir Hamza: Lord of the Auspicious Planetary Conjunction.* Translated by Masharraf Ali Farooqi. New York: Modern Library, 2007.

Lasker, Daniel J. "Transubstantiation, Elijah's Chair, Plato, and the Jewish-Christian Debate." *Revue des études juives* 143 (1984): 31–58.

Levi ben Abraham. *Livyat Ḥen.* Edited by Ḥayyim Kreisel. Jerusalem: Ha-Iggud ha-Olami le-Madda'ei ha-Yahadut, 2004.

Levine, Amy-Jill. *The Misunderstood Jew: The Church and the Scandal of the Jewish Jesus.* San Francisco: HarperSanFrancisco, 2006.

Levinsohn, Isaac Ber. *Efes Damim.* Vilna: Menachem Ben and Simḥah Zimmel, 1837.

Lewin, Benjamin M., ed. *Otsar ha-Ge'onim.* 12 vols. Jerusalem: Ḥ. Vagshal, 1962.

Lieberman, Saul. *Greek in Jewish Palestine: Studies in the Life and Manners of Jewish Palestine in the II–IV Centuries C.E.* New York: Jewish Theological Seminary of America, 1942.

———. *Hellenism in Jewish Palestine: Studies in the Literary Transmission, Beliefs and Manners of Palestine in the I Century B.C.E.–IV Century C.E.* 2nd ed. New York: Jewish Theological Seminary of America, 1962.

———. *Tosefta ki-Fshutah: A Comprehensive Commentary on the Tosefta.* 10 vols. New York: Jewish Theological Seminary of America, 1955–1988.

Liebes, Yehuda. "Ho'il Moshe Be'er." https://liebes.huji.ac.il/files/hoil.pdf.

———. "Talmidei ha-Gr'a, ha-Shabbeta'ut ve-ha-Nequdah ha-Yehudit." *Da'at* 50–52 (2003): 255–90.

———. "Toda'ato ha-Atsmit shel ha-Ga'on mi-Vilna ve-Yaḥaso el ha-Shabbeta'ut." In *Ḥallamish le-Ma'yeno Mayim: Meḥqarim be-Qabbalah, Halakhah, Minhag ve-Hagut Mugashim le-Prof. Moshe Ḥallamish*, edited by Avraham Elqayam and Haviva Pedaya, 603–22. Jerusalem: Carmel, 2016.

———. "Yonah ben Amittai ke-Mashiaḥ ben Yosef." *Meḥqerei Yerushalayim be-Maḥashevet Yisra'el* 3:1–2 (1983–1984): 269–311.

Lindbeck, Kristen H. *Elijah and the Rabbis: Story and Theology*. New York: Columbia University Press, 2010.

Lowy, Simeon. "The Motivation of Fasting in Talmudic Literature." *Journal of Jewish Studies* 9 (1958): 19–38.

Mach, Rudolf, and John H. Marks. "The Head upon the Knees: A Note to 1 Kings 18:42." In *The World of Islam: Studies in Honour of Philip K. Hitti*, edited by James Kritzeck and R. Bayly Winder, 68–73. London: Macmillian, 1959.

Margaliot, Reuven. *Mal'akhei Elyon*. Jerusalem: Mossad Harav Kook, 1945.

Margaliyot, Eliezer. *Eliyyahu ha-Navi be-Sifrut Yisra'el, be-Emunato, uv-Ḥayyei Ruḥo*. Jerusalem: Kiryat Sefer, 1960.

Margaritha, Antonius. *Der gantze jüdische Glaube*. Leipzig: F. Lanckisch, 1705.

Matt, Daniel C. *The Essential Kabbalah: The Heart of Jewish Mysticism*. San Francisco: HarperSanFrancisco, 1995.

Meier, John P. *A Marginal Jew: Rethinking the Historical Jesus*. 5 vols. New York: Doubleday, 1991.

Menaḥem Naḥum of Chernobyl. *The Light of the Eyes: Homilies on the Torah*. Translation and commentary by Arthur Green. Stanford: Stanford University Press, 2021.

———. *Me'or Einayim*. New York: Twersky Brothers, 1952.

Meri, Josef W. "Re-Appropriating Sacred Space: Medieval Jews and Muslims Seeking Elijah and al-Khaḍir." *Medieval Encounters* 5 (1999): 237–64.

Milgrom, Jacob. *The JPS Torah Commentary: Numbers*. Philadelphia: Jewish Publication Society, 1990.

———. *Leviticus: A New Translation with Introduction and Commentary*. 3 vols. New York: Doubleday, 1991–2000.

Milikowsky, Chaim. "Eliyyahu ve-ha-Mashiaḥ." *Meḥqerei Yerushalyim be-Maḥashevet Yisra'el* 2 (1982–1983): 491–96.

———, ed. *Seder Olam: Mahadurah Madda'it, Peirush u-Mavo*. 2 vols. Jerusalem: Yad Ben-Zvi Press, 2013.

———. "Trajectories of Return, Restoration and Redemption in Rabbinic Judaism: Elijah, the Messiah, the War of Gog and the World to Come." In *Restoration: Old Testament, Jewish, and*

Christian Perspectives, edited by James M. Scott, 265–77. Leiden: Brill, 2001.

Montgomery, James A. *Aramaic Incantation Texts from Nippur.* Philadelphia: University Museum, 1913.

Morgenstern, Julian. *Amos Studies.* Vol. 1. Cincinnati: Hebrew Union College Press, 1941.

Moses ben Shem Tov de León. "She'elot u-Tshuvot be-Inyenei Qabbalah." In *Ḥiqrei Qabbalah u-Shluḥoteha*, edited by Isaiah Tishby, 1:36–75. Jerusalem: Magnes, 1982.

Myers, Jacob M. *II Chronicles: Translation and Notes.* Garden City, N.Y.: Doubleday, 1965.

Naḥmanides, Moses. *Kitvei Ramban.* Edited by Chaim D. Chavel. 2 vols. Jerusalem: Mossad Harav Kook, 1964.

Nissim ben Jacob Gaon. *An Elegant Composition concerning Relief after Adversity.* Translated and edited by William Z. Brinner. New Haven: Yale University Press, 1977.

Noegel, Scott B., and Brannon M. Wheeler. *Historical Dictionary of Prophets in Islam and Judaism.* Lanham, Md.: Scarecrow, 2002.

Noy, Dov. "Eliyyahu ha-Navi be-Leil ha-Seder." *Maḥanayim* 44 (March 1960): 110–17.

Peli, Pinchas. "Eliyyahu ha-Navi be-Veit Midrasham shel Ḥazal." In *Be-Oraḥ Madda: Meḥqarim be-Tarbut Yisra'el Muggashim le-Aharon Mirsky bi-Ml'ot Lo Shiv'im Shanah*, edited by Zvi Malachi, 141–68. Lod: Mekhon Haberman le-Meḥqerei Sifrut, 1986.

Rendsburg, Gary A. "Hebrew *św/yḥ* and Arabic *šḫḫ*." In *Fucus: A Semitic/Afrasian Gathering in Remembrance of Albert Ehrman*, edited by Yoël L. Arbeitman, 419–30. Amsterdam: John Benjamins, 1988.

———. "The Mock of Baal in 1 Kings 18:27." *Catholic Biblical Quarterly* 50 (1988): 414–17.

Robinson, J. A. T. "Elijah, John and Jesus: An Essay in Detection." *New Testament Studies* 4 (1957–1958): 263–81.

Rofé, Alexander. *The Prophetical Stories: The Narratives about the Prophets in the Hebrew Bible; Their Literary Types and History.* Jerusalem: Magnes, 1988.

Roi, Biti. *Ahavat ha-Shekhinah: Mistiqah u-Pho'etiqah be-Tiqqunei ha-Zohar*. Ramat Gan: Bar-Ilan University, 2017.

———. "'Hayu Mashqim la-Torah': Ziqqat Ha-Ga'on mi-Vilna le-Sifrut Tiqqunei ha-Zohar." *Da'at* 79 (2015): 11–54.

Rosenberg, Yehuda Yudel. *Sefer Eliyyahu ha-Navi*. Piotrkow: Mordechai Tsederbaum, 1910.

Rothstein, David. "First and Second Chronicles: Introduction and Annotations." In *The Jewish Study Bible*, edited by Adele Berlin and Marc Zvi Brettler, 1703–1831. 2nd ed. New York: Oxford University Press, 2014.

Rubenstein, Jeffrey L. *Talmudic Stories: Narrative Art, Composition, and Culture*. Baltimore: Johns Hopkins University Press, 1999.

Sabar, Shalom. "Childbirth and Magic: Jewish Folklore and Material Culture." In *Cultures of the Jews: A New History*, edited by David Biale, 670–722. New York: Schocken, 2002.

Samet, Elhanan. *Pirqei Eliyyahu*. Jerusalem: Ma'aliyot, 2003.

Savran, George W. *Encountering the Divine: Theophany in Biblical Narrative*. London: T&T Clark International, 2005.

Schauss, Hayyim. *The Lifetime of a Jew throughout the Ages of Jewish History*. Cincinnati: Union of American Hebrew Congregations, 1950.

Scholem, Gershom G. *Major Trends in Jewish Mysticism*. 3rd ed. New York: Schocken, 1967.

———. *On the Kabbalah and Its Symbolism*. Translated by Ralph Manheim. New York: Schocken, 1969.

———. *Origins of the Kabbalah*. Edited by R. J. Zwi Werblowsky, translated by Allan Arkush. Philadelphia: Jewish Publication Society; Princeton: Princeton University Press, 1987.

———. *Ha-Qabbalah be-Provans*, edited by Rivka Schatz. Jerusalem: Academon, 1970.

———. *Sabbatai Ṣevi: The Mystical Messiah, 1626–1676*. Translated by R. J. Zwi Werblowsky. Princeton: Princeton University Press, 1973.

———. *Shedim, Ruḥot u-Nshamot: Meḥqarim be-Demonologyah me'et Gershom Shalom*. Edited by Esther Liebes. Jerusalem: Ben-Zvi Institute, 2004.

Schram, Peninnah. *Tales of Elijah the Prophet.* Northvale, N.J.: Jason Aronson, 1991.

Schwartz, Howard. *Tree of Souls: The Mythology of Judaism.* New York: Oxford University Press, 2004.

Schwarzbaum, Haim. *Mi-Meqor Yisra'el ve-Yishma'el: Yahadut ve-Islam be-Aspaqlaryat ha-Folqlor.* Tel Aviv: Don, 1975.

Sefer ha-Peli'ah. Peremyshlyany: Zupnik, Knoller and Hammerschmidt, 1883.

Segal, Samuel M. *Elijah: A Study in Jewish Folklore.* New York: Behrman's Jewish Book House, 1935.

Shacham-Rosby, Chana. "Koso, Kis'o ve-Kha'aso: Demuto shel Eliyyahu ha-Navi be-Olamam shel Yehudei Ashkenaz bi-Ymei ha-Beinayim." PhD diss., Ben Gurion University of the Negev, 2018.

Shalom ben Isaac of Neustadt. *Hilkhot u-Minhagei Rabbeinu Shalom mi-Noishtat.* Edited by Shelomoh Y. Spitzer. 2nd ed. Jerusalem: Mekhon Yerushalayim, 1997.

Shammash, Yuzpa. *Minhagim di-Qhillat Qodesh Vermaisha.* 2 vols. Jerusalem: Mekhon Yerushalayim, 1988–1992.

Shelomoh Shlumil ben Ḥayyim. *Shivḥei ha-Ari.* Premyshla: B. Luria, 1869.

Simon, Uriel. *Reading Prophetic Narratives.* Translated by Lenn J. Schramm. Bloomington: Indiana University Press, 1997.

Tishby, Isaiah. *Ḥiqrei Qabbalah u-Shluḥoteha.* Vol. 1. Jerusalem: Magnes, 1982.

———. *The Wisdom of the Zohar: An Anthology of Texts.* Vol. 3. Translated by David Goldstein. London: Littman Library of Jewish Civilization, 1989.

Uffenheimer, Benjamin. *Early Prophecy in Israel.* Translated by David Louvish. Jerusalem: Magnes, 1999.

Urbach, Ephraim E. *Ḥazal: Pirqei Emunot ve-De'ot.* Jerusalem: Magnes, 1971.

———. *Me-Olamam shel Ḥakhamim: Qovets Meḥqarim.* Jerusalem: Magnes, 1988.

Vermes, Geza. *Jesus the Jew: A Historian's Reading of the Gospels.* Philadelphia: Fortress, 1973.

Vital, Ḥayyim. *Ets Ḥayyim.* 3 vols. Jerusalem, 1988.
———. *Sha'arei ha-Qedushah.* Warsaw: Levensohn, 1873.
Weissfish, Eliezer. *Ramot Gil'ad.* 2 vols. Jerusalem: Ḥemed, 2005.
Werblowsky, R. J. Zwi. *Joseph Karo: Lawyer and Mystic.* Philadelphia: Jewish Publication Society, 1977.
Wertheimer, Shlomo Aharon, ed. *Battei Midrashot.* 2nd ed., revised by Abraham J. Wertheimer. 2 vols. Jerusalem: Ketav Vasepher, 1980.
Wheeler, Brannon M. "The Jewish Origins of Qur'ān 18:65–82? Reexamining Arent Jan Wensinck's Theory." *Journal of the American Oriental Society* 118 (1998): 153–71.
White, Marsha C. *The Elijah Legends and Jehu's Coup.* Atlanta: Scholars Press, 1997.
Wiener, Aharon. *The Prophet Elijah in the Development of Judaism: A Depth-Psychological Study.* London: Routledge & Kegan Paul, 1978.
Wolfson, Elliot. "Beyond the Spoken Word: Oral Tradition and Written Transmission in Medieval Jewish Mysticism." In *Transmitting Jewish Traditions: Orality, Textuality, and Cultural Diffusion,* edited by Yaakov Elman and Israel Gershoni, 166–224. New Haven: Yale University Press, 2000.
Yaari, Abraham. "Me'arat Eliyyahu be-Har ha-Karmel." *Karmelit* 3 (1956): 138–49.
Yassif, Eli. *The Hebrew Folktale: History, Genre, Meaning.* Translated by Jacqueline S. Teitelbaum. Bloomington: Indiana University Press, 1999.
———. *Sippurei Ben Sira bi-Ymei ha-Beinayim.* Jerusalem: Magnes, 1984.
Yisraeli, Oded. "Jewish Medieval Traditions concerning the Origins of the Kabbalah." *Jewish Quarterly Review* 106 (2016): 21–41.
———. "Le-Mi Hitgallah Eliyyahu? Le-Gilguleha shel Masoret Qabbalit mi-Kitvei Yad el ha-Defusim." In *Derekh Sefer: Shai li-Ze'ev Gries,* 117–31. Jerusalem: Carmel, 2018.
———. *Pitḥei Heikhal: Iyyunei Aggadah u-Midrash be-Sefer ha-Zohar.* Jerusalem: Magnes, 2013.

Zakovitch, Yair. "'Qol Demamah Daqqah': Tsurah ve-Tokhen bi-Mlakhim Alef, Yod-tet." *Tarbiẓ* 51 (1981–1982): 329–46.

———. "The Tale of Naboth's Vineyard: 1 Kings 21." In *The Bible from Within: The Method of Total Interpretation*, by Meir Weiss, 379–405 (Addendum). Jerusalem: Magnes, 1984.

Zevit, Ziony. "First and Second Kings: Introduction and Annotations." In *The Jewish Study Bible*, edited by Adele Berlin and Marc Zvi Brettler, 653–761. 2nd ed. New York: Oxford University Press, 2014.

———. *The Religions of Ancient Israel: A Synthesis of Parallactic Approaches*. New York: Continuum, 2001.

The Zohar: Pritzker Edition. Vols. 1–9. Translation and Commentary by Daniel C. Matt. Stanford: Stanford University Press, 2004–2016.

The Zohar: Pritzker Edition. Vols. 10–12. Translation and Commentary by Nathan Wolski and Joel Hecker. Stanford: Stanford University Press, 2016–2017.

GENERAL INDEX

Abel Shittim (Brook of the Acacias), 84, 88, 134, 135, 144
Abraham ben David of Posquières (Rabad), 92, 93, 131
Abraham ben Isaac of Narbonne, 92
Abraham ben Nathan, 140–41
Ahab, King: Ahaziah son of, 9, 38–40, 58, 75, 76, 84; competition between YHVH and Baal on Mount Carmel, 19–24, 40, 160n31, 160n32; condemnation of, 11–12, 13, 158n10; death of, 36–38; drought associated with, 13–14; Elijah raced before the royal chariot, 26, 144, 164n60; Elijah's confrontations with, 1, 13–14, 25, 26, 36–38, 155, 164n60; God's promise of rain, 25–26; idolatry of, 11–13, 36–38; Jehoram and, 37, 103; Obadiah, 17–19; reign of, 9–10, 13, 17–18, 38–39, 158n5; as repentant, 36. *See also* Jezebel, Queen
Ahasuerus, King, 158n5
Ahava, Rabbi, 92
Ahaziah, King, 9, 38–40, 58, 75, 76, 84
Aḥer (Elisha son of Avuyah), 63
Ahijah of Shiloh, 90–91, 92, 171n12, 180n2
aḥorannit, 23, 163n47
Akiva, Rabbi, 71–72
al-Khiḍr, 187n24; cave of, 123–24; Elijah as, 6, 123–24, 125–26, 127; as the Green One, 123–24, 126; Ḥāfiz (poet) and, 127; Ibn Arabī and, 127; mantle of initiation, 127; as servant of Allah, 125; as teacher, 126–27
Al sefat yam kinneret (Fichman), 143, 192n44
altars, 21–22, 81, 121, 162n40, 163n41, 164n53
Amittai (Jonah's father), 83, 178n108
Anan, Rabbi, 61–62
angel, Elijah as, 46, 52–54, 88, 99–102, 103, 134–36, 138, 171n8

fornication at Shittim, 84, 88, 134, 135, 144
Freedman, David Noel, 160n31

Gabriel (archangel), 52, 53
Gad (Canaanite deity), 137, 138
Garden of Eden, 45, 53, 69, 75, 107, 151, 171n11
garment, theme of the, 98–99
generosity, Elijah's rewards for, 58–59
Gersonides, 44, 169n99
Gilead, 8, 51
gillui Eliyyahu (revelation of Elijah), 92, 94, 109, 110, 125, 127, 154
God: challenged by Elijah, 16, 23–24, 163n52; delight in being defeated, 67, 72, 174n51; Elijah as advocate for Israel, 23–24, 103–4, 142, 149, 167n78, 183n35; on Elijah's flight, 28; on Elijah's zeal, 30–32, 88, 103, 183n35; as *El qanna*, 14, 147–48; on exile, 67–68; in the Heavenly Academy, 63–64; on Phinehas's zealousness, 85, 86, 88; promise of water, 25; *qol demamah daqqah* (a sound of sheer stillness), 28–29, 145, 149, 166n71; rabbis' influence on, 63–64; revelation of divine presence, 28–30, 166n69; *Shekhinah*, 1, 45, 63, 102, 104, 105, 108, 182n33; study habits of, 63–65, 67; upholding contrary views, 64–65
Gog, 58, 172n26
golden calf, 24, 80, 81, 103, 144, 165n63
good news, Elijah as bearer of, 152–53, 193n20
Gospels, 116–17
grace after meals, 7, 74, 145
gratefully remembered (reference to Elijah), 57, 67, 80, 87, 108, 109, 134, 172n23, 177n88
the Green One (al-Khiḍr), 123–24, 126
guild of prophets, 17, 41–42, 43–44, 121

Ḥāfiẓ (poet), 127
haftarot of Elijah, 143–45, 192n47
Haggadah manuscripts, messianic redemption in, 133
Hai Gaon, 164n57
hairy man imagery, 2, 18, 39, 116, 120, 185n2
halakhah, 66–67, 71–75, 109, 132, 138, 174n47, 175n74
Haman, 65–66
Harbonah, Elijah's impersonation of, 55
Hasidism, 133–34, 151–53, 155–56, 180n2, 193n20
Havdalah (concluding the Sabbath), 2, 7, 128, 139–40, 141–42
head between the knees position, 25, 94, 164n57
healing powers of Elijah, 54–55, 172n18
heaven, Elijah's ascent to, 2, 42, 44–47, 58, 183n35
Heavenly Academy, 63–64, 96
heavenly scribe, Elijah as, 58, 87, 172n26, 179n125
herald, Elijah as, 4, 49, 76–79, 129, 133, 139–43, 145, 153, 176n81
Heschel, Abraham Joshua, 95, 169n98
Hillel, House of, 174n47
Hiram (king of Tyre), 9
Ḥiyya, Rabbi, 54–55
Holy Spirit *(ruaḥ ha-qodesh)*, 5, 57, 93–94, 154
hopping, 20, 21, 24, 150, 159n29, 162n34
Horeb, Mount: divine revelation on, 28–29, 145, 149, 166n71; Elijah on, 97, 103, 120, 149, 167n78; sound of stillness, 28–29, 145, 166n71; Torah given on, 103
Ḥoza'ah, Beroka, Rabbi, 54
humor, 54
hymns, Shabbat, 139–43, 191n37, 194n23

Ibn Arabī, 127
Ibn Ezra, Abraham, 88, 180n128

Ra'aya Meheimna (The Faithful Shepherd), 105–6
Rabad (Abraham ben David of Posquières), 92, 93, 131
Rabbah son of Avuha, 52, 65, 69
Rabbah son of Sheila, 63–64
rabbinic encounters with Elijah, 58–62, 125–26; ethical behavior as condition of, 58–62; Evyatar, Rabbi, 64–65; halakhah discussed, 69; as inner experience, 69; Meir, Rabbi, 56–57, 63–64; as respectful, 69; Shim'on son of Yoḥai, 96–97, 98, 104–5, 181n25; Yehoshu'a son of Levi, 59–61, 95, 125–26; Yose, Rabbi, 67–70
rain, 1, 15, 17, 25–26, 94, 97, 159n23
Ramadan, 127
Rashi (Rabbi Shelomoh Yitsḥaqi), 23, 73, 131, 141, 159n19, 163n48, 166n71, 167n79, 178n116
Rava, 74
ravens, 14, 97, 110
Red Sea, 42, 80
Resh Lakish, 179n125
resurrection of the dead, 15–17, 23, 25, 77–78, 111, 177n88
return of Elijah, 2, 46, 48–51, 76, 78–79, 93, 151, 170n116, 172n26, 186n16
revealing what is now unknown, 73–74, 175n72
revival of son of widow of Zarephath, 15–17, 23, 25, 77, 120, 138, 148, 177n88
Rhineland massacres of Jews, 132
river crossings, 42, 168n92
Roman empire, 54–56, 60, 78, 96, 137, 149, 170n1
ruaḥ ha-qodesh (Holy Spirit), 5, 57, 93–94, 154

sacrifice: on Mount Carmel, 20, 21, 161n33; outside Jerusalem, 21–22
saliva: medicinal properties of, 57, 172n24
Samaria (capital of the Northern Kingdom), 9, 11, 33, 38
Sandalphon, 52, 171n8, 182n30
San Elias, 121
Scholem, Gershom, 164n57
Sea of Reeds, splitting of, 42, 80
Second Coming, 186n16
Seder Eliyyahu (The Arrangement of Elijah), 13, 61–62
Seder Olam, 48, 58, 68, 76, 86, 172n26
Sefer ha-Manhig (Abraham ben Nathan), 140–41
Sefer ha-Peli'ah, 95
Sefer ha-Yashar, 75, 176n79
sefirot, 106–7, 182n33
separating the two of them, 102, 182n33
set tables, 137–38
seventy facets of Torah, 66, 174n50
Shabbat: blessings after haftarah, 143; Elijah and, 2, 7, 128, 139–40, 187n21, 194n23; greeting the Sabbath Bride, 186n14; Havdalah (concluding the Sabbath), 2, 7, 128, 139–43; hymns for, 139–43, 191n37, 194n23; *Ish ḥasid hayah* (Jesse son of Mordechai), 140; travel restrictions on, 140–42, 191n40; as the world to come, 140, 191n37
Shabbat ha-Gadol, 145
Shabbetai Tsevi, 6, 110–14
Shammai, House of, 174n47
shanim ki-shnei Eliyyahu (years like those of Elijah). *See* drought
Shefokh ḥamatekha (Pour out Your wrath), recitation of, 132, 133
Shekhinah, 1, 45, 63, 102, 104, 105, 108, 182n33
Shema (prayer), 92, 173n27
Shim'on son of Yoḥai, Rabbi: on access to the *Shekhinah*, 105; cave of Elijah identified with cave of, 96–97; on the coming of Elijah, 72–73; Elijah and, 96–97, 98, 104–5, 181n25; encounter with Moses, 105–6; garment, theme of, 98–99; *The Prayer of Rabbi Shim'on son of Yoḥai*, 76–77; Rabbi El'azar son of, 96, 97, 100;

whirlwind: Elijah ascent in, 41, 44–45, 49, 80–81, 91, 98–100, 102
widow of Zarephath, 14–17, 23, 25, 83, 94, 120, 138, 148, 159n19, 177n88, 194n23
Willis, Wallis, 154–55
wind imagery, 4, 5, 28, 57–58, 93–94, 154, 166n71
wine at Passover seder, 130–32, 133
wing imagery, 5, 53, 59, 77, 154–55, 171n9
Wisdom of Ben Sira, 49

Yehoshu'a son of Levi, Rabbi, 59–61, 95, 125–26
Yehudah son of Pazi, Rabbi, 92
Yehudah the Prince, Rabbi, 54–55, 79–80
YHVH: Ahab's relations with, 12–13, 36–37, 158n10; angel of, 27, 38, 40; Asherah as consort of, 160n31; Baal and dominance of, 16–17; challenged by Elijah, 16, 23–24, 163n52; competition between YHVH and Baal on Mount Carmel, 19–24, 40, 160n31, 160n32; day of, 48–49, 75–76, 79–80, 153, 172n26; death of Elijah, 41–44; Elijah's prayer to revive widow's son, 16; Elijah's request for death, 26–27, 32, 81, 82–83, 144–45, 150–51, 165n63, 169n107; on Elijah's zeal, 14, 28, 29–32, 101, 103, 134, 145, 167n78; as *El qanna*, 14, 147–48; on execution of Naboth, 36–37, 148; final redemption of Israel, 129–30; Israelites, relationship with, 23–24, 144; *Keter Elyon* associated with, 107; on Mount Sinai, 99; omnipotence of, 16–17; Phinehas's zeal for, 85, 88
YHVH, He is God, 1, 24, 81, 101, 145–46, 150, 164n53
Yirmeyah, Rabbi, 67
Yisraeli, Oded, 170n1
Yoḥanan son of Zakkai, Rabban, 72
Yom Kippur, 113, 145–46, 193n8
Yose, Rabbi, 45, 67–68, 70
Yose son of Rabbi Ḥanina, Rabbi, 100
Yudan, Rabbi, 92

zakhur la-tov (gratefully remembered; reference to Elijah), 57, 67, 80, 87, 108, 109, 134, 172n23, 177n88
Zarephath, 14–15, 23, 83
zeal of Elijah: advocacy for Israel, 103–4, 142, 149; *Eliyyahu* reflecting, 1, 14; as extreme, 148–49; Hasidic teachings on, 151–52; incompatible with human society, 103, 183n35; for justice, 2, 33–37, 155; masculinity in, 102; *qin'ah*, 147–48; slaughter of prophets of Baal, 24–25, 26, 70, 80, 84, 144, 148; transgression of *mitsvah* of altar-building outside Jerusalem, 22; upholding the covenant, 134–35; for YHVH, 14, 28, 29–32, 101, 103, 134, 145, 167n78
Zealots of Judea, 149
Zohar: Elijah in, 98, 100–102, 104–6; Elijah's angelic origins, 100–102; God's criticism of Elijah, 103–4; on Jonah, 83; on Phinehas, 86; *Ra'aya Meheimna* (The Faithful Shepherd), 105–6; *shi'ur qomah*, 108; on Song of Songs, 104–5; *Tiqqunei ha-Zohar* (Embellishments on the *Zohar*), 105–8

INDEX OF SOURCES

Biblical Literature

TANAKH (HEBREW BIBLE)

Torah

BABYLONIAN TALMUD

JERUSALEM TALMUD

Rabbinic Literature: Midrash

Classical Antiquity

Medieval Sources

Early Modern and Modern Sources

Jewish Lives is a prizewinning series of interpretative biography designed to explore the many facets of Jewish identity. Individual volumes illuminate the imprint of Jewish figures upon literature, religion, philosophy, politics, cultural and economic life, and the arts and sciences. Subjects are paired with authors to elicit lively, deeply informed books that explore the range and depth of the Jewish experience from antiquity to the present.

Jewish Lives is a partnership of Yale University Press and the Leon D. Black Foundation. Ileene Smith is editorial director. Anita Shapira and Steven J. Zipperstein are series editors.

PUBLISHED TITLES INCLUDE:

Rabbi Akiva: Sage of the Talmud, by Barry W. Holtz
Ben-Gurion: Father of Modern Israel, by Anita Shapira
Judah Benjamin: The Brains of the Confederacy, by James Traub
Bernard Berenson: A Life in the Picture Trade, by Rachel Cohen
Irving Berlin: New York Genius, by James Kaplan
Sarah: The Life of Sarah Bernhardt, by Robert Gottlieb
Leonard Bernstein: An American Musician, by Allen Shawn
Hayim Nahman Bialik: Poet of Hebrew, by Avner Holtzman
Léon Blum: Prime Minister, Socialist, Zionist, by Pierre Birnbaum
Louis D. Brandeis: American Prophet, by Jeffrey Rosen
Martin Buber: A Life of Faith and Dissent, by Paul Mendes-Flohr
David: The Divided Heart, by David Wolpe
Moshe Dayan: Israel's Controversial Hero, by Mordechai Bar-On
Disraeli: The Novel Politician, by David Cesarani
Einstein: His Space and Times, by Steven Gimbel
Becoming Elijah: Prophet of Transformation, by Daniel C. Matt
Becoming Freud: The Making of a Psychoanalyst, by Adam Phillips
Emma Goldman: Revolution as a Way of Life, by Vivian Gornick
Hank Greenberg: The Hero Who Didn't Want to Be One, by Mark Kurlansky
Peggy Guggenheim: The Shock of the Modern, by Francine Prose
Ben Hecht: Fighting Words, Moving Pictures, by Adina Hoffman
Heinrich Heine: Writing the Revolution, by George Prochnik
Lillian Hellman: An Imperious Life, by Dorothy Gallagher

Theodor Herzl: The Charismatic Leader, by Derek Penslar
Houdini: The Elusive American, by Adam Begley
Jabotinsky: A Life, by Hillel Halkin
Jacob: Unexpected Patriarch, by Yair Zakovitch
Franz Kafka: The Poet of Shame and Guilt, by Saul Friedländer
Rav Kook: Mystic in a Time of Revolution, by Yehudah Mirsky
Stanley Kubrick: American Filmmaker, by David Mikics
Stan Lee: A Life in Comics, by Liel Leibovitz
Primo Levi: The Matter of a Life, by Berel Lang
Groucho Marx: The Comedy of Existence, by Lee Siegel
Karl Marx: Philosophy and Revolution, by Shlomo Avineri
Menasseh ben Israel: Rabbi of Amsterdam, by Steven Nadler
Moses Mendelssohn: Sage of Modernity, by Shmuel Feiner
Harvey Milk: His Lives and Death, by Lillian Faderman
Moses: A Human Life, by Avivah Gottlieb Zornberg
Proust: The Search, by Benjamin Taylor
Yitzhak Rabin: Soldier, Leader, Statesman, by Itamar Rabinovich
Walther Rathenau: Weimar's Fallen Statesman,
by Shulamit Volkov
Man Ray: The Artist and His Shadows, by Arthur Lubow
Admiral Hyman Rickover: Engineer of Power, by Marc Wortman
Jerome Robbins: A Life in Dance, by Wendy Lesser
Julius Rosenwald: Repairing the World, by Hasia R. Diner
Mark Rothko: Toward the Light in the Chapel,
by Annie Cohen-Solal
Gershom Scholem: Master of the Kabbalah, by David Biale
Bugsy Siegel: The Dark Side of the American Dream,
by Michael Shnayerson
Solomon: The Lure of Wisdom, by Steven Weitzman
Steven Spielberg: A Life in Films, by Molly Haskell
Alfred Stieglitz: Taking Pictures, Making Painters, by Phyllis Rose

Barbra Streisand: Redefining Beauty, Femininity, and Power, by Neal Gabler
Leon Trotsky: A Revolutionary's Life, by Joshua Rubenstein
Warner Bros: The Making of an American Movie Studio, by David Thomson

FORTHCOMING TITLES INCLUDE:

Franz Boas, by Noga Arikha
Mel Brooks, by Jeremy Dauber
Alfred Dreyfus, by Maurice Samuels
Anne Frank, by Ruth Franklin
Betty Friedan, by Rachel Shteir
George Gershwin, by Gary Giddins
Allen Ginsberg, by Ed Hirsch
Herod, by Martin Goodman
Abraham Joshua Heschel, by Julian Zelizer
Jesus, by Jack Miles
Josephus, by Daniel Boyarin
Louis Kahn, by Gini Alhadeff
Maimonides, by Alberto Manguel
Louis B. Mayer and Irving Thalberg, by Kenneth Turan
Golda Meir, by Deborah E. Lipstadt
Arthur Miller, by John Lahr
Robert Oppenheimer, by David Rieff
Ayn Rand, by Alexandra Popoff
Sidney Reilly, by Benny Morris
Philip Roth, by Steven J. Zipperstein
Edmond de Rothschild, by James McAuley
Ruth, by Ilana Pardes
Jonas Salk, by David Margolick
Rebbe Schneerson, by Ezra Glinter

Baruch Spinoza, by Ian Buruma
Henrietta Szold, by Francine Klagsbrun
Elie Wiesel, by Joseph Berger
Billy Wilder, by Noah Isenberg
Ludwig Wittgenstein, by Anthony Gottlieb